LINA KHATIB is the head of the Program on Arab Reform and Democracy at Stanford University's Center on Democracy, Development and the Rule of Law. She is the author of *Filming the Modern Middle East: Politics in the Cinemas of Hollywood and the Arab World* (2006) and of *Lebanese Cinema: Imagining the Civil War and Beyond* (2008), both from I.B.Tauris.

LINA KHATIB

Image Politics in the Middle East

THE ROLE OF THE VISUAL IN POLITICAL STRUGGLE

I.B. TAURIS

LONDON · NEW YORK

Published in 2013 by I.B.Tauris & Co Ltd
6 Salem Road, London W2 4BU
175 Fifth Avenue, New York NY 10010
www.ibtauris.com

Distributed in the United States and Canada
Exclusively by Palgrave Macmillan
175 Fifth Avenue, New York NY 10010

ISBN: 978 1 84885 281 5 (HB)
      978 1 84885 282 2 (PB)

A full CIP record for this book is available from the British Library
A full CIP record is available from the Library of Congress

Library of Congress Catalog Card Number: available

Typeset by Newgen Publishers, Chennai
Printed and bound by TJ International Ltd, Padstow, Cornwall

FSC
www.fsc.org

MIX
Paper from
responsible sources
FSC® C013056

This book is dedicated to my great teachers,

Samir Khalaf, for making me fall in love with cities, starting with my own,
and forever changing the way I "see" urban space and its relationship
with people, politics, and history,

Patricia Nabti, for the inspiration and creativity and for teaching
me the importance of perseverance,

Nabil Dajani, for your non-wavering belief in my work
and the optimism you bestow upon it,

and Paula Saukko, for your guidance, moral support,
and leading by example that have shaped the scholar I have become.

Contents

Illustrations

Acknowledgments

This book would not have been completed without a Small Research Grant from the British Academy that funded most of the fieldwork, and a Research Project Grant from the Leverhulme Trust that funded work on Chapter 2.

Research that formed the seed of this book started in 2005, stirred by the image explosion that Lebanon and Egypt had been witnessing through visually saturated political campaigns, leading to fieldwork in those and other Middle Eastern countries in the years that followed. The Green Movement in Iran and then the Arab Spring came to both affirm the primacy of the image in processes of political struggle in the Middle East and to consolidate the fact that the use of the visual in this context is part of a longer-term process of political expression that had started well before those protest movements. I am indebted to the Middle Eastern people who have inspired this work, and hope that this book is a small step towards acknowledgement of the need to document their efforts. The book itself offers just a snapshot of the rich discursive field of political expression in the Middle East; more research ought to be done to do the field justice.

I am obliged to the following fantastic group of people who dedicated time and resources without which research for this book would not have happened: in Egypt, Amr Gharbeia, Iman Hamam, Nora Younis, Gamal Eid, Wael Abbas, Ahmed Sherif and Ghada Shahbander; in Iran, Majid Karimi, Hadi Khaniki, Amirali Ghasemi, Mahmoud Bakhshi Moakhar, Homayoun Askari Sirizi, Aram Asgari, Simin Motamedarya, Esmail Yazdanpour, Bita Aziminezhadan and Arash Hanaei; in the UK, Tarik Sabry, Mohsen Biparva, Golriz Kolahi, Dalia Mustafa, Kay Dickinson, Anoush Ehteshami, Hossein Salimi and Francis Robinson; in the USA, Mona Eltahawy and Hamid Dabashi; in Lebanon, Hikmat El Khatib, Rana Issa, Omayma Abdel-Latif, Romy Lynn Attieh and Khaled Ramadan; in Syria, Khalid Ali; and in Palestine, Rich Wiles, for a breathtaking photographic collection. Thanks also to Neil Smith, Ben Rowswell, Hisham Issa, Samia Issa, Tareq Al-Samman, Tarek Zeidan, Sarina Beges and Lina Mikdashi for helping with images. Credit for the photographs of Qaddafi-era images in public spaces in Libya (taken in 2008) goes to Musa Mansour and Hussain Muftah – what a shame you eventually chose to be on the wrong side of history.

I express much gratitude to my hardworking research assistants. At Stanford University, Elizabeth Buckner: I would not have managed to finish this book without your meticulous and rigorous work – and Steve Monroe: thanks for the background research on Kifaya and the Green Movement; Jacqueline Barkett and Mona El Hamdani at the University of Southern California (USC): thanks for helping with re-searching Chapter 2. I also thank USC's Center on Public Diplomacy under the directorship of Philip Seib, for granting me a non-resident research fellowship at CPD from 2010–2012, and publishing a work-ing paper based on Chapter 2 in the series CPD Perspectives on Public Diplomacy in February 2012.

Thanks are due also to Larry Diamond at Stanford University, who generously supported this project through granting me encourage-ment, writing up time, much needed academic empathy and wonder-ful collegial support, and Philippa Brewster, my editor at I.B.Tauris, for being so patient and passionate.

Last but not least, I am grateful for the encouragement, com-ments and belief in this work by my dear friend and colleague Dina Matar, and for the moral support and intellectual exchanges of Nabeel Khoury, Zahera Harb, Kamran Rastegar, Radwan Ziadeh, Maha Issa, Kamal Samhan, Marwan Kraidy, Fadi El-Khatib, Adam Ganz, Gail Pearce, Mandy Merck, Gideon Koppel and Ryan Johnson.

Introduction: The Visual in Political Struggle

Politics in the Middle East is now *seen*. The image has claimed a central place in the processes through which political dynamics are communicated and experienced in the region. States, non-state actors, oppositional groups and ordinary people are engaging in political struggle through the image, and the media, especially the visual media, are not only mediators in this context, they are also political actors, deliberately using images to exert political influence. The image is at the heart of political struggle, which has become an endless process of images battling, reversing, erasing and replacing other images. As Groys argues, "[t]he desire to get rid of any image can be realized only through a new image – the image of a critique of the image."[1] Political struggle, then, is an inherently visually productive process. It is also itself visual to a large degree: It is a struggle over presence, over visibility. For authoritarian states, political power means having control over visual production and consumption. For political oppositions, democratic representation merges with visual representation. For people, possessing political agency means possessing the ability to be seen, not only heard.

The visual manifests itself in several forms in processes of political struggle: as a mass media image; a digital image; a cartoon; a piece of art; a physical space or object; an ephemeral image on paper, a wall or another physical medium; and as a human embodiment. It can also be a conceptual image, a visual idea. All those forms merge and interact, so that it is no longer possible to look at an image in any one form in isolation from the others. While the visual is not new as a component of visual struggle in the Middle East, its rise has accelerated since the attacks of September 11, 2001, so that key political moments in the last decade are mainly remembered as images and images of images: the Twin Towers collapsing, Osama bin Laden's video messages, the Separation Wall in Palestine, the toppling of the statue of Saddam Hussein in Baghdad, Abu Ghraib, the Cedar Revolution in Lebanon, Saddam Hussein's execution, the mobile phone video of Imad al-Kabir, the

1

Green Movement in Iran and the extraordinary visual rush that was the Arab Spring.

The Middle East has become a site of struggle over the construction of social and political reality through competing images. In this competition, one political actor's carefully self-constructed image can be erased by a new, oppositional image. The lasting image of bin Laden is not the video image of him giving speeches defying the West, but the mental image of him sitting in a house in Pakistan, smoking marijuana and watching pornography. The lasting image of the United States' war on Iraq is not the televised, staged image of the toppling of the statue of Saddam Hussein in Baghdad, but the photographs of tortured prisoners in Abu Ghraib. The lasting image of Saddam Hussein is not that of the public monuments in Iraq which embedded his likeness, handwriting and even blood, but the mobile phone video of his hanging. The lasting image of Israel's Separation Wall is not the wall itself but Banksy's graffiti challenging the physical supremacy of the wall with symbolism. The lasting image of the Hosni Mubarak era is not that of Barack Obama giving a "historic" speech in Cairo in 2009, but of government thugs attacking peaceful protesters in Tahrir Square on camel and horseback.

Fig. 1. A mural by Banksy on the Separation Wall in Palestine in September 2008. Photo by Rich Wiles.

This book aims to provide a snapshot of the role and dynamics of the image in processes of political struggle in the region from the second half of the past decade and into the present (2005 to today). It acknowledges images as constructs infused with meanings, attributes and projected perceptions.[2] As such, and although it mainly focuses on the role of visual representations, it also alludes to the image as a mental attribute.[3] David Morgan provides a useful definition of visual culture, which forms the basis of this book's analytical approach. He says,

> Visual culture is what images, acts of seeing, and attendant intellectual, emotional, and perceptual sensibilities do to build, maintain, or transform the worlds in which people live. The study of visual culture is the analysis and interpretation of images and the ways of seeing (gazes) that configure the agents, practices, conceptualities, and institutions that put images to work.[4]

This book is therefore concerned with image content in a variety of mediums, from television to the internet to street art, as well as the political meanings and practices by individuals, states and non-state political actors surrounding those images, be they practices of production or perception. The book argues that to understand political dynamics in the Middle East, one needs to take into account the role of the image in those dynamics, and to understand image dynamics in the Middle East, one needs to examine all those mediums and practices simultaneously.

The argument in this book does not separate "hard politics" from "soft politics" in its understanding of the role of the image in politics, for those two spheres are intertwined. It also does not separate the cultural from the political. Existing scholarship has examined the link *between* culture – especially popular culture – and politics, arguing for example that sometimes politics takes a popular cultural form (such as in the case of politicians who are regarded as celebrities) and that politics often *incorporates* elements of popular culture such as image making and performance.[5] This book argues that in the Middle East (as is elsewhere), often there is no longer a distinction between the cultural and the political spheres; it is not just that popular culture and politics feed off each other – very often, popular culture is politics. The image-making act can itself be a political act. As Lisa Wedeen argues, "[p]olitics is not merely about material interests but also about contests over the symbolic world, over the management and appropriation of meaning."[6] It is those contests over the symbolic world that the book aims to unearth. Focusing on case studies from Lebanon, Iran, Egypt, Syria and Libya, the book discusses images of and by states, political actors, artists, the media and ordinary people. The book's primary data has been collected mainly through trips by the author to Lebanon, Iran, Egypt and Syria between 2005 and 2011 and commissioned photography in Libya. The book's key argument is that there is a "visually epistemological sense of politics" in the Middle East that demands attention, and the book itself is a modest effort to document some of this visual knowledge as well as analyze its dynamics.[7]

Perhaps the first communication channel that comes to mind when thinking about image politics in the Middle East is the media, particularly after the Arab Spring. As Simon Cottle writes about this period,

> new social media and mainstream media often appear to have performed in tandem, with social media variously acting as a watchdog of state controlled national media, alerting international news media to growing opposition and dissent events and providing raw images of these for wider dissemination. International news media, in turn, including Al Jazeera, have distributed the flood of disturbing scenes and reports of the uprisings now easily accessed via Google's YouTube and boomeranged them back into the countries concerned. Mainstream newspapers and news broadcasters in their online variants also increasingly incorporate direct links to these new social media, effectively acting as a portal to their updating communication flows and near live-streaming of images direct from the protests themselves. This moving complex of interpenetrating communication flows and their political efficacy across the different uprisings deserves careful documentation and comparative analysis.[8]

The media space of the Arab Spring was not a mere space of remediation, "the representation of one medium in another,"[9] but a hypermedia space, as defined by Marwan Kraidy:

> Hypermedia space is a broadly defined symbolic field created by interactions between multiple media, from micro text-messaging to region-wide satellite broadcasting. The

term "hypermedia" captures the technological convergence and media saturation that characterize many contemporary societies, while emphasizing the speed and convergence of communication processes. The "interoperatibility of once-discrete media...linked together into a single seamless web of digital-electronic-telecommunications" (Deibert, 1997, pp. 114–115) creates a space with many "points of access" that are personalized, mobile, non-conspicuous and networked, and therefore not easily subjected to overt social or political control...Arab hypermedia space is constituted by various types of communicators (citizens, consumers, activists, etc) using email, mobile telephony, text messaging, digital cameras, electronic newspapers, and satellite television. This space's non-hierarchical nature invites a rethinking of Arab information dynamics.[10]

Kraidy argues that this hypermedia space is changing the relationship between states and citizens in the Arab world and blurring the boundaries between popular culture and politics, and between producers and consumers.[11] Etling et al. echo this, highlighting that there is now a

collision of old realities and new technologies taking place in the Arab world, and a surprising number of elements intertwine in them: abuse of power, legitimacy of authority, the power of television, the ubiquity of video cameras, feedback between blogs and the press, traditional vs. modern sensibilities, freedom of expression, the power of online voices, and the scope of political arenas – local, national, pan-Arab, pan-Muslim, global. At stake in this collision are both the symbolic construction and the hard power of "The Public" across the region. Notable is the seamless combination of modes of communication into a single system: face-to-face interaction (including cattle prods), mobile phones, television, newspapers, and multiple genres of Internet sites (blogs, forums, chat rooms, video sharing, photo sharing, etc.). Increasingly, these comprise an emerging networked public sphere, in which the power of elites to control the public agenda and bracket the range of allowable opinions is seriously challenged.[12]

The Arab Spring also went beyond this notion of hypermedia space as it saw a central role for the physicality of people and places. Sonia Livingstone argues that as the boundaries between interpersonal and mass forms of communication disappear, "everything is mediated."[13] But mediation still means that the body and the media are seen as two separate entities, even as bodies sometimes perform for the media. During the Arab Spring, the media were not just mediators in social and political interactions; the media were the individuals. Each person on the street in Tahrir Square or Daraa was an image creator and "broadcaster" of political messages. This broadcasting of messages, whether verbal or visual or both, did occur often using third-party communication tools like the internet or mobile phones or the carrying of placards, but it also occurred through performance by the body, through visible presence, through being in a space.

Silverstone argued that "politics, like experience, can no longer even be thought outside a media frame."[14] The last decade, particularly its second half, has witnessed a change in political culture in the Middle East as this culture became more visual in form. Amin defines political culture as "the values, norms, beliefs, sentiments and understandings of how power and authority operate within a particular political system. Generally, political culture sets informal and unwritten ground rules as to how the political process is to be performed."[15] Political culture in the Middle East is not just mediated, it is also mediatized. Mediatization "refers to the process through which mediated cultural products have gained importance as cultural referents and hence contribute to the development and maintenance of cultural communities."[16] It also refers to "both the (institutionalized as well as technologically composed) specificity of different media *and* their contents as moments of influence on other 'fields' or 'systems' of culture and society."[17] This mediatization has had three consequences in relation to political culture. First, it has resulted in the rise of the recognizable Middle East politician[18] who is almost a celebrity (like Hassan Nasrallah).[19] Second, it has resulted in symbolism becoming an established means of conveying political messages for states and oppositions alike (for example, through the staging of symbolic events like pro- and anti-regime public rallies).[20]

The third result is a change in the way political communication dynamics are conceived. Traditionally, political communication theorists conceived of citizens as being more on the receiving end of political communication messages, where those messages are sent by the state through the media.[21] Political communication theory has now moved beyond the state-citizen binary to incorporate other political actors, and beyond one-way communication to include non-linear exchanges, yet it remains focused on the media, mainly the mass media and later the internet, as a go-between. The Arab Spring is a reminder of the limitation of this approach. Rami Khouri argues that the four most important communication channels during the Egyptian January 25 Revolution were al-Jazeera, mobile phones, mosques and public spaces, as word of mouth worked hand in hand with digital communication.[22] The process of political communication today has therefore moved beyond the media, especially the press and broadcasting, and has become an all-encompassing collection of communicative processes occurring in physical, electronic, non-electronic virtual and embodied spaces. Television and radio broadcasts are now supplemented by internet campaigns, staged actions in public space, the wearing of symbolic attire, the production and consumption of merchandise, posters and other symbolic objects. Political communication dynamics must take into account the role of the citizen as an individual and as an agent in all those visual processes.

States and non-state political actors also have embraced visual processes in their image management strategies, particularly as they struggle against political opponents in an image-saturated world. Those image management strategies, ranging from propaganda to public diplomacy, rely on images for legitimation (of the self) and delegitimation (of "others"), mobilization and demobilization and empowerment and disempowerment.[23] Images, domestic and foreign policies in the Middle East can no longer be separated; none is simply dependent on the other, they all both influence and produce one another.[24]

Authoritarian states in the Middle East are particularly reliant on the image as a tool for "the engineering of consent."[25] Henri Lefebvre divides oppressive societies into three levels. The first is the "repressive society," characterized by poverty and an exploitative class that maintains its authority through ideological persuasion and compulsion. The second is the "over-repressive society," which, in addition to the above, uses language to deaden opposition, and "relies more on the self-repression inherent in organized everyday life."[26] The third is the "terrorist society," where "compulsion and the illusion of freedom converge...In a terrorist society terror is diffuse, violence is always latent, pressure is exerted from all sides on its members...terror cannot be located, for it comes from everywhere and from every specific thing."[27] Images testify to the progression of authoritarian states in the Middle East to this third level, as images have become a way in which terror is diffused. Terror is diffused through a simultaneous process of production and reception of images by the state. The citizen in this kind of society is always the object of the gaze of the state, whether physically (through human and electronic surveillance) or symbolically (through the watchful eye of the leader's image in public and private space) or both (through being made to perform in pro-regime spectacles).[28]

Lisa Wedeen argues that this kind of state "attempts to control the symbolic world, that is, to manipulate and manage systems of signification...official rhetoric and images operate as a form of power in their own right, helping to reinforce obedience and sustain the conditions under which regimes rule...'successful' rhetoric and symbols produce 'legitimacy', 'charisma', or 'hegemony' for the regime."[29] One way in which this is done is through the aestheticization of politics and political life.[30] An example is the reliance on staged pro-regime public rallies in places like Iran and Syria.[31] Walter Benjamin argues that mass movements are particularly suited to the eye of the camera, and thus have great propaganda potential.[32] The staged rallies are a way for despotic regimes to communicate power, approval, credibility and obedience. As Lefebvre puts it,

> The signal commands, controls behavior...and...can be grouped in codes...thus forming systems of compulsion. This shift to signals...involves the subjection of the senses to compulsions and a general conditioning of everyday life...Signals and codes provide practical systems for the *manipulation* of people and things.[33]

Hypermedia space allows despotic regimes and rulers to extend their control over the symbolic world into a public diplomacy message. This dynamic was particularly seen during the Arab Spring, when state television in Syria was keen on broadcasting footage of huge pro-regime rallies that was directed both at the Syrians and at foreign powers. This reliance on the image as visual evidence is an illustration of the belief that, in the words of American Civil War photographer Mathew Brady, "the camera is the eye of history."[34]

Yet, as Susan Sontag reminds us, "to photograph [is] to compose."[35] Ironically, it was Syrian president Bashar al-Assad who had once agreed with Sontag in his criticism of the camera's representation of anti-Syrian rallies in Lebanon during the Cedar Revolution in 2005, saying that close camera angles made the demonstration sizes appear larger than they were. The response by the demonstrators at the time was to organize a huge rally in which they carried placards instructing the television cameras to "zoom out and count." The camera, in this context, provides an arena "in which symbolic contests are carried out among competing sponsors of meaning."[36] The fact of composition erases the innocence of the image, complicating the projected images of despotic regimes even before they are received. Another complication arises because there is a difference between projected images and perceived images.[37] As Barthes puts it, "the language of the image is not merely the totality of utterances emitted...it is also the totality of utterances received."[38] The images projected by the Syrian, Libyan, Iranian, Egyptian, Tunisian and other authoritarian regimes in the Middle East in recent years have been subject to rejection and reversal by citizens who strived to reclaim a position of political agency. And while the process of rejection and reversal did not manage to topple the regime in Iran – not yet – it is an ongoing process that should be taken into account when one thinks of political struggle in Iran and other authoritarian states in the region. As Lefebvre argues, a terrorist society "cannot maintain itself for long; it aims at stability, consolidation, at preserving its conditions and at its own survival, but when it reaches its ends it explodes."[39]

The Arab Spring is an example of this process of gradual visual rejection and reversal leading to an explosion of the status quo. This process is in turn a reminder of Manuel Castells' conception of power in the network society, in which he argues that "political institutions are not the site of power any longer. The real power is the power of instrumental flows, and cultural codes, embedded in networks."[40] In the mediatized age, Arab citizens have become part of a network society in which cultural codes flow, and their acts of image reversal and subversion – which, before 2011, had taken place quietly, such as through contemporary art, and loudly, such as through movements like Kifaya – paved the way for the Arab Spring.

The Arab Spring was itself a field in which cultural codes flowed. The domino effect of the uprisings speaks of images as possessing the potential to activate the viewer, not because they impose a uniform meaning – images are always open to interpretation, negotiation and rejection – but because the image can be an empowering agent, enabling citizens to perform a meta-narrative of political agency.[41] As Joel Handler puts it, "[p]rogressive forces have to act *as if* the walls will come tumbling down...this is a meta-narrative – a construction of human nature that transcends context."[42] Images also make events more intimate and create further identification with them for the viewer. Sontag argues that the absence of well-known images documenting atrocities makes those atrocities seem more remote.[43] By the same token, the presence of images documenting revolution in a neighboring country makes the concept of revolution less remote. As Sontag puts it, "a photograph has only one language and is destined potentially for all."[44] Photographic images, whether through still cameras or video, brought the Arab Spring closer to audiences within and outside the immediate locales of the protests, acting as "a means of making 'real' (or 'more real') matters that the privileged and the mere safe might prefer to ignore."[45] It is undeniable, then, that the visual media played a role in creating the domino effect of uprisings during the Arab Spring. In this the media were not mere reflectors of social change, they were also themselves mediators and part-creators of social change.[46]

But media images were only one kind of image in the visual sphere of the Arab Spring. They were joined by physical images of bodies and places, in other words, physical presence. Asef Bayat argues that the "art of presence" is about the *active* use of public space by subjects who, in the modern states, are allowed to use it only *passively* – through walking, driving, watching – or in other ways that the state dictates."[47] Being present in public space in an "active" way as defined by Bayat is a visual political act. This visual complexity means that image politics in the context of the uprisings is about images *in* the Arab Spring (such as protest posters and protesters performing in public space), *of* the Arab Spring (such as of the presence of protesters in Tahrir Square) and produced *by* the Arab Spring (such as murals in Cairo). What links all three modes is the presence of intentionality in the act of creating the visual, the inherent acknowledgement of the potential power of the image. Images *in* the Arab Spring acted as political weapons: People carried placards and recorded videos on their mobile phones to declare political demands, and their presence (and actions) in public space was itself a visual political act. Images *of* the Arab Spring served as a visual record as well as a catalyst for others to join the action. The images produced *by* the Arab Spring are somewhat different. The Egyptian revolution, in particular, is noted for triggering a new visual field in Egypt, that of street art. The creation of images in public space as a way of claiming political power and marking territory is an established mechanism;

one only needs to think of the visual discursive space of Palestine for a vivid illustration of this. But in Egypt under the Mubarak regime, the authority to create an oppositional image in space, including to freely perform this role through the body, was denied to the citizen. The appearance of murals all over Cairo after the January 25 Revolution is, then, a way to let the body and the art make a "permanent" statement about public visibility. As Groys argues, "[a]rt and politics are initially connected in one fundamental respect: both are realms in which a struggle for recognition is being waged."[48] Through street art, the previously disenfranchised are waging a war of presence.

This war of presence has also led to another visual process in Egypt and Libya, the creation of exhibitions and museums commemorating the uprisings. In Egypt, an effort is being made to collect and display artifacts from the January 25 Revolution like tear gas canisters, protest signs and bullet casings at the American University in Cairo[49], while in Libya, two exhibitions in Misrata and Benghazi in the summer of 2011 also displayed weapons and paraphernalia as well as specially commissioned art about the battle between the rebels and the regime. This process of museumification can be related to two factors. First, the museum is an example of power in the public realm, as objects on display in a museum call attention to themselves as important. Museums are therefore a sign of agency for citizens; choosing what to include, what is important, is a sign of reclaiming power in the public realm. Second, as Levi-Strauss argues, cultures without museums "feel the threat of oblivion, of a complete loss of historical memory."[50] Museums are a way for citizens to cement the memories of revolution in history. What is notable about those museums is that they mainly harbor collections of visuals. Susan Sontag says that the act of remembering is increasingly taking on a more visual form, becoming more about the recall of pictures rather than of stories.[51] She adds that "[i]n an era of information overload, the photograph provides a quick way of apprehending something and a compact form for memorizing it."[52] The image, then, is a way for citizens to reclaim national and popular memory from the authoritarian state.

The embodied performances of protesters in public space, digital images, visual art, television images and other visual forms transformed the Arab Spring into a spectacle. But the Arab Spring is not just an event experienced through established kinds of images. It has itself crystallized the production of a new kind of image, which I call the floating image. The face of Khaled Said, the 28-year old man who was killed wrongfully by the Egyptian police in 2010, is the ultimate example of the floating image. Khaled Said's face with its multiple meanings, references, mediations, reincarnations and presences illustrates how the floating image combines the characteristics of other kinds of images. Like a floating signifier, the floating image's "initial meaning has been appropriated for a purpose that has no connection to the original context of its creation."[53] Like a meta-image, it is an image referencing other images.[54] Like a hyper-image, it blurs the line between what is real and what is represented. Like a hypermedia image[55], it floats between different nodes of representation, but unlike the hypermedia image, those nodes of representation go beyond the media sphere, as they include "physical" representations in offline space too. The floating image is a "strong image," one of those images with the "ability to originate, to multiply, and to distribute themselves...immediately and anonymously, without any curatorial control."[56] It is in possession of agency, not needing outside help to be seen. It imposes its identity by the sheer fact of its presence. The floating image, then, blends the dynamics of images in political struggle in the Middle East with the political agency of the region's people. It is the ultimate product of image politics in the Middle East.

PART I

REVOLUTIONARY ILLUSIONS

I

The Visual Legacy of the Cedar Revolution in Lebanon

The assassination of former Prime Minister Rafic Hariri on 14 February 2005 was a visual landmark for Lebanon. It catalyzed a series of public rallies in downtown Beirut calling for the withdrawal of Syrian troops from Lebanese soil, culminating in the establishment of two rival Lebanese political blocs, pro-Syrian March 8 and anti-Syrian March 14, and an image war between them. Image-conscious rallies were vital visual communicators of political stance during what came to be known as the Cedar Revolution, paving the way for a new era in Lebanese politics marked by the heightening of the role of the visual.

Prior to 2005, the visual in Lebanese politics had seen its manifestation mainly through the use of political posters, which different factions used to commemorate their martyrs and deeds, and to demark territory.[1] As Sune Haugbolle observes, since the days of the Lebanese Civil War (and even before), geographical zones in Lebanon have been visually marked through the presence of posters (as well as other public space markers like graffiti) belonging to particular groups, transforming those zones into "pure" "Hizbullah," "Kataeb," "Amal" or "Progressive Socialist Party" areas, while excluding "others."[2] Posters in Lebanon thus perform the role of symbolic, sectarian, political and physical boundary markers. This process of multiple exclusions can be read as a product of the "fragmentation of the social into a multiplicity of hegemonic formations" in Lebanon, whereby there is no centralized hegemonic force, but where, instead, each political-sectarian group constitutes its own "regime of truth."[3]

Hariri's assassination magnified this dynamic but also added to it new visual political formations. This chapter discusses the three main roles that the image has been playing in Lebanese politics since the Cedar Revolution: as a marker of political identity, as a political rallying tool and as a weapon against political rivals. The chapter argues that the importance of the Cedar Revolution in Lebanon lies in how it catalyzed a new style of politics in the Middle East that is marked by deliberate visual saturation.

The image as a political identity marker

The assassination of Hariri almost immediately created public markers for two rival political communities in Lebanon: Hizbullah and its allies, who were pro-Syrian, and who came to be known as the March 8 coalition, and Hariri's own Future Movement and its allies, the March 14 coalition, who believed that Syria was behind the assassination and called for the withdrawal of Syrian troops from Lebanon through the implementation of UN Resolution 1559, in addition to establishing a tribunal investigating the assassination. The rivalry between the two coalitions was played out both in the media and in public space, as they both attempted to present themselves as political blocs driven by wide popular support. This political competition resulted in the production of images acting as political identity markers both for the coalitions themselves and their followers.

Perhaps the first key image created through this competition was that of Rafic Hariri himself. Before his assassination, Hariri personified the "Big Man" style of political leadership, "characterized by authority derived from personal efforts and abilities through the allocation and reallocation of private resources."[4] Well before becoming Prime Minister, Hariri's clout was established as a result of his economic and philanthropic work in Lebanon that he funded through wealth accumulated while he worked as an ultra-successful businessman in Saudi Arabia. Hariri channelled his personal resources, mainly his economic capital and his high-profile international contacts, into a rising profile as a political player in Lebanon, which was cemented with the role he played in brokering the Taef Agreement in 1989 that ended the Lebanese Civil War. After his assassination, his political party and its allies sought to transform his image into an icon. Betsky et al. argue that icons act as anchors of meaning in a world of continual change.[5] With uncertainty shaking the Lebanese street, both in terms of who might have been responsible for the assassination and where the country would be headed afterwards, Hariri as an icon served to ground the political demands of his party and its allies and reassure their supporters. This icon stood for freedom, justice and development. A photo book produced by Dar Annahar in 2005 titled *The Beirut Spring*, to commemorate the popular uprising catalyzed by Hariri's death, presented Hariri as "the martyr of the nation." Photos of Hariri appeared all over Beirut, coupled with slogans inciting people to action. "I leave in God's will this beloved country [in your custody]," declared one poster. As such, Hariri the icon was calling on people to continue his legacy.

People responded to this political call in February 2005 by taking to the streets to commemorate his death, meeting every Monday in downtown Beirut while wearing t-shirts bearing his image or carrying his photos, and calling for the truth behind his assassination to be found. They eventually settled in Martyrs' Square, where Hariri was buried, creating a protest camp calling for the resignation of the pro-Syrian government. Future Television, the channel owned by Hariri, suspended its normal schedule to dedicate full-time coverage to Hariri's assassination and its aftermath. Several programs about his philanthropy, development work in Lebanon and political achievements were aired, in which Hariri was framed as a man of the people who gained the respect of world leaders.

Hariri's grave became an additional landmark in downtown Beirut. Situated next to the grand al-Amin mosque that Rafic Hariri had been building in Martyrs' Square, the grave itself is housed within a large tent transforming the place into at once a shrine for Hariri as well as a space for the communication of political messages. The grave-as-shrine is heavily reliant on visual imagery: It displays the last photos taken of Hariri alive, and in a nearby street, "footprints" are installed in the ground in downtown Beirut chronicling his last walk in the area. A large painting by Antoine Braidy on one side of the grave tent titled "The Phoenix" embeds Hariri in the iconic Martyrs' Square statue, and depicts the statue's martyrs alive, with one of them handing over the Lebanese flag to Hariri, thus marking him as the carrier of the legacy of those who died for Lebanon, and entering the country's national mythology. The space also utilizes intertextuality to frame Hariri as a popular leader. Above the grave, a large panoramic collage shows photos of Hariri's family as well as ordinary people clad in black, crying and praying on the day of his funeral.

The grave-as-political communicator has its messages communicated through posters that are frequently changed to comment on the political situation of the present moment. After the withdrawal of Syrian troops from Lebanon following the mass rallies protesting

Fig. 2. Painting by Antoine Braidy at Rafic Hariri's grave in downtown Beirut.

Hariri's death, the grave tent had on one side a banner with Hariri's photo and the words: "With you: He taught, he built, he liberated," referencing Hariri's education foundation and his effort to rebuild Lebanon's infrastructure after the civil war, and crediting him with posthumously liberating the country from Syria. The slogan was a message directed at Hizbullah, which had laid a monopoly over the label "liberation" as it applied it solely to its own effort to liberate Lebanon from Israel, which culminated in the withdrawal of Israeli troops in 2000 after almost two decades of occupying southern Lebanon. Another banner at the gravesite shows a photo of the mass gathering in Martyrs' Square on the day of Hariri's funeral, with the slogan "They feared you so they killed you." A stone plaque at the site is carved with the words "For the sake of Lebanon," and next to it official documents from the Special Tribunal for Lebanon set up by the United Nations to investigate Hariri's murder are displayed, a direct message about Hariri's supporters' not giving up on this cause.

For three weeks after Hariri's death, his rivals watched both the growing mass rallies in downtown Beirut and the pro-Hariri broadcasts on Future Television. They responded by organizing a mass rally of their own on 8 March 2005, in which people declared their allegiance to Syria yet also called for the truth behind Hariri's assassination to be found, thereby appropriating the image of the pro-Hariri Monday gatherings. This appropriation also took the form of declared patriotism. The Hariri supporters had used the Lebanese flag as a visual marker, signaling Hariri's contribution to Lebanon, but also framing their political demand as being in the country's interest. The March 8 protest saw a similar use of the Lebanese flag, framing the political demand of maintaining ties with Syria in their existing form as being in the interest of Lebanon. The flag, then, became a contested visual marker of a claimed national cause.

Fig. 3. A billboard on the road to southern Lebanon depicting the 14 March 2005 demonstration in downtown Beirut and the caption "Thank you, Lebanon." Photo taken on 31 August 2008.

The use of the Lebanese flag by Hariri's supporters was part of a process of value definition that first established core values (freedom, sovereignty, independence), and then aggregated those values under one national symbol.[6] But the flag was also part of the creation of what Assem Nasr calls a "Lebanese identity brand."[7] This brand was about Lebanon as a cosmopolitan, life-loving, unified country, and its visual expression was seen in political advertisements on television as well as in images and paraphernalia that started emerging after Hariri's camp organized a rival mass rally on 14 March 2005, which lent the political coalition its name. The March 14 rally resembled a carnival[8] where the Lebanese flag became an embodied marker, worn by people as a scarf, a hat or a cape, drawn on their faces and bodies, and embedded in various items of clothing and accessories. Political declarations thus merged with patriotic ones and became a fashion statement.[9]

The flag also appeared on merchandise that was being sold in downtown Beirut, from personal accessories to food. Those objects became quotidian communicators of political identity. This process was not accidental; March 14's public rally was in part due to the utilization of a public relations company, Quantum Communications, which designed the logos, slogans and objects used on the day of the demonstration, branding it "Independence '05." Red was the

Fig. 4. March 8 demonstration in downtown Beirut in 2005. Photo by Assafir.

background color of choice for the objects carrying this slogan, which was written in white, a direct reference to the colors of the Lebanese flag. Barak argues that this appropriation of national symbols served as a challenge to pro-Syrian state leaders, who were "referred to as part of the 'security regime' or 'security network' that usurped the country and the political society."[10] The 14th of March, then, can be seen as the day that marked the transformation of Lebanese politics into "merchandised politics."[11]

This merchandised politics is built on an ideology of consumption that was embodied in the paraphernalia; a citizen could literally "consume" the objects on sale. This consumption of objects can be located within a wider framework that has dominated Lebanon since the end of the civil war. As Nasr argues,

> Consumption emerges as a form of resistance for the people of Lebanon to the direction in which their country is heading: further conflict and turmoil. Accumulating items, such as clothing, cars...etc., which gives us the illusion of living in a cosmopolitan sphere, is the only vehicle to overcome the forces that hinder our development and unity as a nation.[12]

Future Television built on this framework though airing publicity videos encouraging the Lebanese people to shop as a show of support for the Lebanese economy.

As such, the publicity was also encouraging the simultaneous production and consumption of signs in everyday life. Citizens were to consume the publicity messages, and in turn, engage in the act of shopping as a symbolic patriotic act akin to participating in public rallies. Lefebvre argues that publicity "is based on the imaginary existence of things; it evokes them and involves a rhetoric and a poetry superimposed on the art of consuming and inherent in its image; a rhetoric that is not restricted to language but invades experience."[13] The Lebanese were encouraged to become "prosumers,"[14] producing and consuming patriotism, national unity and a stable economy as signs in their daily experience. But this hyperreality[15] rendered their performance of patriotism, through participating in public rallies and consuming national signs, a form of mimicry[16]: People shaped their daily behavior to resemble that of patriotic citizens. It was as if Lebanon were a country marked by national unity. This was seen most acutely in the proliferation of symbols about sectarian harmony.

Participants in the public rallies often carried a cross and a Quran together, or painted the images of those religious symbols on their cheeks or bought an intertwined crescent and cross on a string from one of the market stalls set up in Martyrs' Square to wear as a necklace. The media also focused on those images, zooming in their cameras on nuns and sheikhs praying together at Hariri's grave in Martyrs' Square. This communicative activity, both the actual gathering at the grave and its mediation, reproduced the public space of Martyrs' Square as a site for the performance of the Lebanese identity brand.[17]

The Independence '05 phase in Lebanese history did see genuine, spontaneous mass rallying of people who demanded a better future for Lebanon. But those people became ready prosumers of signs designed by politicians who appeared to be peddling the same ideals the people demanded. Those signs, as cultural commodities, were not entirely created by the people at the grassroots level. They were also a product of political marketing that was partly aimed at directing the political process in Lebanon towards maintaining the interests of pre-existing political groups. Michel de Certeau argues that "cultural commodities serve the class of those who create them and are bought by the mass of those who gain the least from them."[18] The Independence Intifada, as this phase came to be known, was not a purely bottom-up protest movement aimed at allowing new political blood to be injected into the stale Lebanese political sphere. It appeared like one, and even appropriated the term "revolution," mainly in reference to the colored revolutions in Eastern Europe, as it was also tagged the "Cedar Revolution" in reference to Lebanon's national tree, but it was merely the phase during which a new *style* of politics emerged in Lebanon, not new politics.

The image as a political rallying tool

The Cedar Revolution marked the start of a political environment in Lebanon that constructs the citizen as a postmodern consumer of signs.[19] Lebanese politics has since become based on a culture of consumption of symbolic goods, and politicians have become "disseminators of symbolic production...cultural intermediaries, who provide [those] symbolic goods and services" to steer people in particular political directions.[20] During the Cedar Revolution, political groups in Lebanon attempted to appeal to citizens through images invoking the past or promising a brighter future. The first took place through the dissemination of images in public space, and the second through the professionalization of politics, though the two processes were often intertwined.

In April 2005, the March 14 coalition set up a large exhibition in downtown Beirut commemorating Hariri's contribution to the rebuilding of Lebanon after the Civil War. Hariri was the owner of Solidere, the company responsible for the reconstruction of downtown Beirut, whose identity was so linked with the area that some people had started referring to downtown Beirut as "Solidere." A large section in the exhibition displayed "before and after" photographs of buildings, streets and neighborhoods in Beirut, mainly in the downtown area, presenting visual evidence of Hariri's post-war reconstruction work. The use of photographs was a visual way of directing memory. As Susan Sontag argues,

> sentiment is more likely to crystallize around a photograph than around a verbal slogan. And photographs help construct – and revise – our sense of a more distant past...Photographs that everyone recognizes are now a constituent part of what a society chooses to think about, or declares that it has chosen to think about.[21]

Gone were the various criticisms that had been hauled at Solidere for its destruction of archaeological sites in downtown Beirut to pave the way for building modern edifices; in their place was a glorification of the work of Hariri and an attempt at carving a positive, whitewashed memory of the man's deeds in the Lebanese mind.

The March 14 coalition also orchestrated the celebration of the 30th anniversary of the Lebanese Civil War on 13 April 2005. This celebration is important to pause at because remembering the civil war had been a contentious issue in Lebanon as the country preferred to engage in mass national amnesia, both on the popular and official levels, as a way of dealing with the trauma of the war.[22] It was only through civil society and the arts that the civil war was commemorated, and those commemorations were often regarded as marginal efforts. Yet Hariri's status as a peace broker, coupled with his assassination's bomb being the biggest explosion Lebanon had witnessed since the war, as well as the looming threat of political instability, presented an opportunity for the March 14 coalition to utilize the memory of the war as a political rallying tool. This utilization was a process of memory creation, not resurrection, because, as

Susan Sontag argues, collective memory is a fiction. "Strictly speaking, there is no such thing as collective memory...But there is collective instruction."[23] In this, Sontag is addressing the way people are told what is important through the creation of public archives and commemorative images and events.

Sune Haugbolle takes a similar stance to Sontag's in his analysis of the commemoration of the 30th anniversary of the civil war in Lebanon, highlighting the way "collective instruction" is a means of political influence; he says: "over the last ten years, memory of the war has become an idiom for political change, and recapturing history a means of recapturing influence."[24] Haugbolle warns that representations of war memory in Lebanon are not a simple expression of "the memory of the people," but are elite expressions, as those representations are driven by particular political and social positions by particular groups.[25] The things that civil society had fought for, remembrance and responsibility, which had been directed at the war and its legacy, were now channelled towards the demands of March 14.[26] The anniversary commemoration, then, was a way for members of the March 14 coalition to recapture political clout.

This invocation of memory as an act of power was expressed visually. The civil war commemoration took the form of a carnival in downtown Beirut, with music, poetry, art displays and several market stalls selling flag-tagged paraphernalia.[27] People descended upon Martyrs' Square in another performance of national unity. A huge map of Lebanon titled "Lebanon, the mosaic" was displayed, which had geographical areas color-coded according to their sectarian make up. The aim of the mosaic was to appropriate and subvert the sectarianism of the civil war through celebrating the unity-in-diversity of Lebanon. Haugbolle argues that this focus on sectarian unity and national symbols was an act of drawing on "the *idea* of a common civilian memory of the civil war,"[28] thereby adding another layer to the performative function of the commemoration, as it became another occasion for the production and consumption of signs. It was also a political message implying that people from all backgrounds in Lebanon supported March 14 and its cause.

This image of support became increasingly important as March 14 faced a number of political hurdles in the years to come. Although the Lebanese government did step down as a result of the 2005 rallies, and March 14 won the majority of seats in parliament in that year's ensuing election, shortly after, Hizbullah and its allies rose as serious political rivals who managed to paralyze the government on more than one occasion. Their rising popularity threatened to snatch the parliamentary majority from March 14. As Lebanon prepared for its next election in 2009, March 14 needed to channel its image of a popular movement into concrete votes. To do so, the coalition shifted from acting as a cultural broker and producer of images to being, in addition, a commodity for consumption, to be consumed not on the basis of its use-value but on the basis of the image it projected. This awareness of the importance of the image was understandable as, during elections, "voters respond more to their perceptions than to objective realities about...candidates."[29] March 14 set out to use a number of professionally designed visual promotional instruments to try to cultivate attractive personas for its candidates to win the election, from billboards in the streets to mass and social media messages. Thus March 14's professionalization of political packaging should be understood as a response to political need.[30]

One may wonder why any political group in Lebanon would bother with professional political marketing, considering that voting in Lebanon is traditionally done on the basis of sectarian and clan affiliations and loyalties rather than on the basis of political programs. The answer is partly that political marketing techniques, in the form of posters, chants and door-to-door campaigning, are established forms in Lebanon, though before the Cedar Revolution, they had an amateurish feel. This, to a degree, was because there was little need to do more to appeal to voters; very rarely in Lebanon have people deviated from following a particular leader, with such loyalty often being passed down through generations. But the answer to the question on professionalization is also about the when, not just the why. It partly lies in that the professionalization of political advocacy is a characteristic of politics in the media age[31], when changes in macro-level structures "(media, technologies, social structures) lead to an adaptive behavior on the micro-level."[32] It is also because March 14's political marketing was not aimed just at rallying its own supporters, it was also a performance directed at March 8 and its backers (namely Syria), as well as at March 14's own allies abroad, and even the world at large. For the first targeted group, it was political showmanship; for the second, it was a form of public diplomacy, meant to gather support for the international tribunal investigating Hariri's assassination, and to rally Western allies around a friendly coalition that would "save" Lebanon from the shackles of Syria and Iran.

Speaking to the outside world necessitates speaking in a language that can be understood by this audience, and the outside world that March 14 was targeting speaks the language of professionalized political marketing. The global use of techniques like branding and personification of politics is a response to "the proliferation of...personalized social realities" that are centered on "image tribes...constructed through consumer fantasies" across the globe.[33] Some have characterized this professionalization as being an example of the "Americanization" of politics, considering that this style of politics originated in the USA. However, as Negrine and Papathanassopoulos argue, practices like hiring media and PR professionals are about adapting tools from a variety of sources to suit domestic needs, rather than direct copying of American methods.[34] The rise of professionalization of politics in Lebanon therefore is an example of non-directional convergence of political communication processes around the world, where those communication processes are shaped by the specific cultures and contexts surrounding the political processes they act within.[35]

The 2009 parliamentary election saw political marketing in Lebanon merge product-oriented and sales-oriented approaches. Although the election's main actors were coalitions of people and political groups rather than political parties only, Lees-Marshmant's categorization of political parties is useful in understanding this merger. She labels a product-oriented party as one that "argues for what it stands for and believes in. It assumes that voters will realize its ideas are the right ones and therefore vote for it. This type of party refuses to change its ideas or product even if it fails to gain electoral or membership support."[36] A sales-oriented party, on the other hand, "employs the latest advertising and communication techniques to persuade others that it is right. A Sales-Oriented Party does not change its behavior to suit what people want, but tries to make them want what it offers."[37] Both March 8 and March 14 adopted elements of those two approaches.

Both camps distinguished themselves through the use of color. Blue was the trademark color of the Future Movement, becoming the defining color of the March 14 camp, while in the March 8 camp, Hizbullah's was yellow, Amal's was green and the Free Patriotic Movement's was orange (an adoption of the color of the Ukrainian revolution), leading the coalition to adopt a rainbow as its symbol (which it had been using since 2006). Both campaigns utilized billboards with messages in different languages, English, Arabic and French, though the Free Patriotic Movement was the one most reliant on French slogans. Both campaigns relied on the social media to attract voters, with some candidates setting up their own websites or Twitter accounts. Both were also reliant on PR companies and political consultants who were "power brokers" advancing each camp's political interests, but who presented the coalitions as "advocates for popular empowerment."[38] The "media-shaped images" of each coalition became their defining political symbols,[39] selling the image of a truly competitive and historic election whose result might tip Lebanon either in the direction of the West or the Syria/Iran axis. The election narrative was a simple one of good versus evil, glossing over the complex reality of politics in Lebanon. It was also a spectacular narrative played out through the media to appeal to a foreign audience. The election became another example of hyperreality, in which "[e]ach situation must be turned into a spectacle to become real."[40]

The narrative was also one with rival heroes. On the March 14 front, Rafic Hariri's son, Saad, who became his political heir, was tipped to become Lebanon's new prime minister if his camp won the election, while on the March 8 front, Free Patriotic Movement leader Michel Aoun had hopes for eventually claiming the presidency, and thus recognized the importance of presenting himself as the most popular Christian leader in Lebanon through the election. The rivalry between the two men marked a new era in Lebanon characterized by the mediated personification of politics, favoring "more eclectic, fluid, issue-specific and personality-bound forms of political recognition and engagement... [and where] people... vote for persons and their ideas rather than for political parties and their programs."[41] This mediated personification added another layer to the visual saturation of Lebanon's political landscape. The focus on the visual made the political sphere in Lebanon an example of Debord's "society of the spectacle."[42] Jansson writes, "the society of the spectacle is a social arrangement marked by an extreme preoccupation with how things appear... the spectacle is most clearly manifested in the fact that the use-value of commodities is judged to an increasing extent according to their style and surface."[43] In this society, "everyone aspires to become an image."[44]

Michel Aoun painted a picture of a shrewd leader who had the upper hand in his relationship with Hizbullah and Syria (partly an attempt at reconciling his pro-Syrian stance with his previous antagonism towards Syria in the 1990s). His visit to Damascus in December 2008 was presented to the outside world in quasi-presidential terms, as he arrived on Syrian president Bashar al-Assad's private plane, and received a red-carpet welcome in the presidential palace. The transformation in his relationship with Syria was one of the two main "changes" that his election campaign was calling for (the other one was changing the government from a March 14- to a March 8-dominated one). As such, one billboard in his election campaign depicted a blue layer peeled to reveal an orange layer, along with the words: "There is no future without change" (a direct reference to Hariri's Future Movement). Aoun also fully adopted the color of his party in his public appearances, often wearing an orange tie, shirt or cap, or a combination of them. In election rallies, Aoun resurrected his image as a populist leader, which he had propagated during the early 1990s before his exile to Paris after the end of the civil war. He also fully utilized his own television station, Orange TV, which he had launched in July 2007 to guarantee media coverage for himself, as the mouthpiece of his election campaign.

Saad Hariri's public image was different. The son of an assassinated popular leader whose popularity soared further after his death, Saad Hariri represented the underdog, the wronged victim of gross injustice who had to win the election so that justice could prevail. Hariri was not a charismatic figure, not experienced in politics, and, having been educated abroad, was not fluent in classical Arabic. Although Michel Aoun also gave his speeches in colloquial Lebanese, Saad Hariri bore a heavier load as, being a Muslim Sunni, he was tipped to become the next prime minister, and thus was expected to be able to give speeches in classical Arabic. Yet his victimized image directed people to overlook his shortcomings, and to "take pity" on him. The popular discourse was that his supporters should vote in the election "for the sake of Saad," and a number of election posters depicted him with the picture of his father Rafic Hariri above his head, looking out for his son. Saad Hariri also had guaranteed media coverage with the family-owned Future TV.

With Aoun and Hariri giving their political campaigns a face and a name, the "distance between the leader and people" narrowed.[45] Both leaders, lacking in genuine charisma, turned "to the mass media in order to attempt to manufacture pseudocharisma in its place."[46] The media can create star status, and both men used this to cultivate legitimacy for themselves as they strove to appear larger than life and beyond the ordinary individual.[47] Both *performed* the role of charismatic leaders, echoing Gibbins and Reimber's statement that, "[t]he art of politics [has become] the art of performance."[48] Glassman argues that one barrier to the manufacturing of charisma

Fig. 5. A banner in Saida (Sidon) in southern Lebanon depicting Rafic and Saad Hariri and proclaiming "No matter how long your absence from us is, your Saad's being with us makes us patient." Photo taken on 12 September 2010.

through the media is the presence of different groups and classes in any given society, which makes it difficult for any one leader to charismatize all members of the society.[49] Yet in the case of Aoun and Saad Hariri, because of Lebanon's political architecture which zones voting along sectarian and geographical lines, they sought not to sway undecided voters to their side, but merely to get their supporters to actually vote.

The use of the media and political marketing in the election campaign appears, at first glance, as a direct example of "mediatized politics," "politics that…has become dependent in its central functions on mass media, and is continuously shaped by interactions with mass media."[50] The concept of mediatized politics stems from political communication theory that has traditionally been weaved around the idea of political advocates competing to get their messages across through media outputs.[51] However, in Lebanon, the media actually are owned by politicians directly or are affiliated with political parties, which means that this traditional way of thinking about mass media interactions does not wholly apply. The situation is not the reverse, in which the media are dependent on politics, but a case in which media and politics are one. Political competition is not about access to media outlets, except through actually owning one. Thus, media images in Lebanon are part of the political battles on the ground and they are directly controlled by political actors. Yet one way in which the post-Cedar Revolution political landscape in Lebanon is an example of "mediatized politics" is the way it is characterized by "the displacement of political values by those of the media system."[52] Politics has become showbiz-like, formed around celebrity-like figures (Michael Aoun; Saad Hariri) and performance (Hassan Nasrallah).[53]

The image as a political weapon

In this media environment, it is to be expected that media outlets belonging to competing political factions become fields of political battle, and this is particularly the case with television, Lebanon's most prominent medium. Lebanon has been witnessing political on-air rivalry since the days of the civil war in the mid-1980s, when the trend of each political group establishing its own television station started. The trend has escalated now to the degree that rival television channels, particularly Hizbullah's al-Manar and the Future Movement's Future Television, have started to quote and re-broadcast clips from each other's programs, with added commentary to discredit one another. When Hizbullah members took over West Beirut in May 2008, in the worst case of politically driven street violence that Lebanon had witnessed since the end of the civil war, two of their targets were the offices of Future Television and its sister newspaper al-Mostaqbal. The latter was looted, while the former was burnt. This physical attack on media outlets can be read as an attempt to stifle the political competitor's point of view through preventing it from disseminating its own version of the news, but also as a symbolic attack as the media outlets are part of the political package of parties.

But image battles have also taken milder forms. During the Cedar Revolution, both March 8 and March 14 competed to present their mass rallies as gathering the largest number of people, not just to each other, but also to the world. The demonstration on 14 March, which reportedly gathered one million people, was partly motivated by a comment by Syrian president Bashar al-Assad, who had accused the television cameras of "zooming in" on pro-Hariri rallies to make them look like they had more people than they actually did. During the 14 March rally, people carried signs telling the television cameras to "zoom out and count." Television ceased to be a one-way medium as people attempted to frame their own broad-casted image.[54]

The image battles were also gendered. The foreign media were particularly interested in capturing images of young, fashionable Lebanese women who were taking part in the rallies (such as *Newsweek*'s 14 March 2005 cover that had the headline "People Power" and *The Economist*'s 5 March 2005 cover headlined "Democracy Stirs in the Middle East," both of which featured photos of attractive young women carried on the shoulders of young men at the pro-Hariri rallies), a framework welcomed by March 14 as it bolstered the cosmopolitan and "modern" image that it wanted to send to the world. In late 2006, March 8 orchestrated a fresh series of public rallies calling for the March 14-dominated government to resign, a move partly driven by the establishment of the UN's Special Tribunal for Lebanon to investigate Hariri's death that was expected to point the finger at Syria, and by the perceived "anti-Hizbullah" stance that the government had taken during the July 2006 war with Israel, which was catalyzed by Hizbullah's kidnapping of two Israeli soldiers across the Lebanese border on 12 July 2006. The rallies featured a significant presence of (often scantily-clad) young Christian and Muslim women carrying the Hizbullah flag, wearing Hizbullah t-shirts or carrying the photo of Hizbullah leader Hassan Nasrallah. By appropriating what had become one of the dominant images of the March 14 rallies, March 8 was sending a message that it also was cosmopolitan and "modern."

This appropriation became more pronounced when March 8 set up a protest camp in downtown Beirut in December 2006 calling for the fall of the government. The camp and its related protests deliberately carried a striking visual resemblance to the popular rallies of the Cedar Revolution of 2005. There was a carnivalesque tent city, the motif of the flag was dominant and there even was a Christmas tree erected in the protest camp as a sign of Muslim-Christian harmony. In doing so, Hizbullah attempted to control the narrative of the protests as being about spontaneous, bottom-up action of the diverse population of Lebanon.[55] Through this visual competition, March 8 tried to cultivate a sense of legitimacy and credibility for itself as the "true" representative of the will of the people and as a symbol of a unified Lebanon.

March 14 responded in early 2007 through a billboard campaign titled "I Love Life," an indirect message implying that Hizbullah loves death and martyrdom. The campaign's website listed its mission as

Fig. 6. Lebanese Opposition protest on 1 December 2006 in Riad Solh Square in Beirut. Photo by Assafir-Abbas Salman.

follows: *"We understand the Culture of Life, as opposed to the Culture of Death, as a deep, well-developed sense capable of discerning true values and interpreting authentic needs in our communities and society."*[56] The phrases "discerning true values" and "interpreting authentic needs" were a direct response to March 8's self-styling as the "true" representative of the will of the people. The campaign was composed of a series of billboards with a plain red background, a white heart with green olive leaves at the top and the words "I Love Life" written in white, thereby using the colors of the Lebanese flag. The billboards carried life-affirming messages like "I have a class" and "I am going to work." March 8 was quick to launch a rival campaign, which appropriated the visuals of the "I Love Life" billboards but added to them the March 8 rainbow flag, the signature "The Lebanese Opposition" and rejectionist slogans like "undictated," and "in all its colors." March 8's supporters also launched an email campaign in February 2007 that circulated images that used the same plain red background as the "I Love Life" billboards but replaced the upbeat slogans with ones like "I'm going to take drugs" and "I'm going to fuck your sister." If the Cedar Revolution was a political movement driven by signs, the post-Cedar Revolution political landscape became defined by signs.

Fig. 7. March 8 "We Want to Live" ("without debt" and "with honour") banners in Beirut in 2008 responding to March 14's "I Love Life" campaign. Behind the banners is a billboard featuring Hassan Nasrallah quoting his statement "The age of defeats has gone." Photo by Assafir.

This trend has changed the way politics is performed in Lebanon as visual political battles have become ordinary. A characteristic of those battles is their intertextuality and reliance on already recognizable images. During the parliamentary election campaign of 2009, such battles took place on the internet, with the proliferation of videos on YouTube ridiculing virtually all of Lebanon's political leaders, and digital images disseminating clear political messages. An example is an anti-March 8 picture representing a coffin that merges in its design the logos of Hizbullah and the Free Patriotic Movement, with Lebanon as the casualty of this alliance. The battles also took place in physical space. An election billboard by the Lebanese Forces, a member of the March 14 coalition, rallied people to vote for its candidates through presenting a photo of a man burning tyres during Hizbullah's demonstration on 7 May 2008, when Hizbullah violently took over West Beirut in an attempt to force the government to fall. The billboard's written message said: "Your vote changes the whole picture." Another Lebanese Forces billboard directly commented on March 8's statement that the coalition was working on establishing a "third republic" in Lebanon by presenting the Lebanese flag as yellow in color, meaning that a March 8 win would create a Hizbullah republic.

Fig. 8. Lebanese Forces parliamentary elections billboard proclaiming "Your vote changes the whole picture." Photo taken on 17 April 2009.

Women as symbolic battlegrounds became prominent again in the parliamentary election campaigns in 2009, when the Free Patriotic Movement launched a series of billboards that featured the photo of a young, attractive woman along with the slogan "Soit belle et vote" (be beautiful and vote). The billboard's intended message, a supposed subversion of the French saying "be beautiful and shut up," ended up becoming a sexist statement, not helped by the fact that the Free Patriotic Movement did not nominate any female candidates for the election and did not address women's rights in its political statements. March 14 responded by launching a rival campaign featuring a billboard with another attractive young woman along with the slogan "Soit egale et vote" (be equal and vote). Yet March 14's response was equally rejected since, even though the coalition backed female candidates, women's rights also did not feature as a prominent item on its agenda and the billboard equally presented women as an object of the gaze.

The Feminist Collective, a civil society group, responded online to both camps by rejecting both their messages. It created an image through photoshopping the original billboard image, so that the word "belle" was scratched and replaced with the word "intelligente," and adding "blanc" after "vote," so that the slogan was now "Be intelligent and vote blank," under which they added, "No one is concerned about your rights." Sarcastic pro-March 14 responses followed online. One image superimposed the photograph of the woman in the original billboard, photoshopped so that she appeared to be wearing a chador, on the background photo of chador-clad women at a Hizbullah rally, along with the slogan "Your face after voting," with the word "voting" written in orange, implying that a March 8 win in the election would turn Lebanon into another Iran. Another had the image of the woman replaced with that of Free Patriotic Movement leader Michel Aoun, with the FPM trademark orange swoosh covering his mouth, along with the slogan "Soi intelligent et tais toi" (be intelligent and shut up). This image toing and froing was the ultimate example of how the image embodied the absence of use-value in those election campaigns.

The endurance of the image

The Cedar Revolution was an important political moment in the Middle East. It marked the rebirth of public action as a method of attempting to cause political change. Although it did not have a lasting political legacy, as Lebanon regressed under (indirect) Syrian control in the years that followed, it did mark the start of an era of Middle Eastern citizens' publicly and collectively claiming their right to freedom from tyranny. But the Cedar Revolution's larger contribution was not a political one, it was a visual one. Since 2005, a new political dynamic has been spreading throughout the region. Images now are established political identity markers, political rallying tools and political weapons in Lebanon and beyond. Patriotism as an embodied performance has been witnessed across protest sites in Egypt, Syria and Yemen. Politicians have become acutely aware that how they are perceived plays a role. The image has permeated formal and informal politics. Both political and civil society campaigns have become intentionally image-reliant. Political actors attempt to colonize physical space through images, while the internet has become the space to visually express political views that do not have a place in the offline world. Online and offline images also intertwine and comment on each other. The Lebanese flag transformed from a national emblem to a floating image, producing different meanings in multiple virtual and physical spaces. This enduring power of the image is what defines the way Middle Eastern politics now is seen.

2

Hizbullah: Image Management and Political Survival

Image management has become a crucial component of political life in the twenty-first century. States, politicians and non-state actors are all realizing the importance of the way they are viewed by others – constituents and opponents alike – in political battles. Yet while significant attention has been given to the way individual politicians manage their image, mainly during elections[1], and to a lesser degree, to image management by states[2], non-state political organizations remain relatively overlooked.

Regard for non-state actors in this context is often given to organizations like NGOs when they are viewed as being useful partners supporting government public diplomacy efforts[3], or, in the context of the Middle East, to international terrorist organizations like al-Qaeda[4], a group that has attracted significant attention on this front due to its reliance on the internet and on video (of leaders like Osama bin Laden and of terrorist operations, the spectacle of September 11, 2001 notwithstanding) to disseminate its messages.[5] Therefore, the consideration that has been given in recent years to the way Islamist groups, as non-state political actors[6], engage in image management is normally presented under the umbrella of radicalization and propaganda.[7] When it comes to processes of political marketing, however, attention is driven away from such groups, partly because literature on political marketing has focused mainly on practices and styles of political parties and individuals during election campaigns.

But non-state political organizations from a wide spectrum often do have image management strategies, and this trend is growing in a world in which the image has started to play an increasing role in politics. Among Islamist groups in the Middle East and worldwide, it is the Lebanese political party Hizbullah that stands out as a group with a long history of image management. Hizbullah has been remarkable for its consistent attention to the need to reach out to constituents, and intimidate enemies[8], through a sophisticated communication strategy that has run parallel to the group's political evolution ever since its inception in 1982. Hizbullah has evolved over the years, especially since the July war of 2006, into a prime user of professionalized political campaigns characterized by "excessive personalization, a political star system, mass media impression management and an increasing negativity."[9] In doing so, Hizbullah has followed the "shopping model" of political campaigning,[10] adopting certain elements of "Americanized" politics while infusing them with local elements, resulting in hybridized practices and styles.

Hizbullah's image management merges both propaganda and political marketing. As Margaret Scammell argues:

> Propaganda...tends to begin from the premise that the "product" is sacrosanct, while public opinion is malleable and can be won over to the propagandists' cause. Political marketing starts from the other side of the communication equation and says that the product is malleable and may be changed according to "consumer" wants.[11]

This duality in Hizbullah's image management means that it transcends public diplomacy. It does not just target outside/foreign audiences, but domestic ones too, and it not only aims to attract and engage those audiences, but also to construct a menacing image to deter enemies. This combination of the attractive and the menacing in image management has allowed the group to establish credibility among different target audiences, including enemies, and to transform itself from an Islamist militia operating outside the Lebanese political system into a key player in the Lebanese political scene. As such, image management for Hizbullah can be viewed as a tool supporting the group's political survival as it navigates a changing political landscape in Lebanon and abroad.[12]

Hizbullah's image management strategy is multiplatform and operates through several communication means at once. The group has its own newspaper, *al-Intiqad* (formerly, *al-Ahd*), its own satellite television station (al-Manar), several websites, including one for al-Manar offered in multiple languages (Arabic, English, French), its own radio station (al-Nour) and produces children's games, merchandise, books, computer games, as well as using posters and billboards, in addition to mass rallies, as methods of communicating with its multiple audiences.[13] Its leader, Hassan Nasrallah, has established a reputation for delivering attention-grabbing speeches. Since the group's rise, it has become more skillful at combining those different communication means creatively. Messages in different mediums reference and reinforce each other, and text, spoken words and visuals combine seamlessly to make the messages memorable in the minds of their audiences.

As such, one can describe Hizbullah's image management strategy as a constant process of strategic communication, based on "developing a set of comprehensive messages and planning a series of symbolic events and photo opportunities to reinforce them."[14] Hizbullah's image management strategy is an example of Blumenthal's "permanent campaign." As he puts it, "the permanent campaign is a process of continuing transformation. It never stops, but continues once its practitioners take power."[15] The aim of the permanent campaign is to sustain legitimacy and credibility. To do so, Hizbullah follows Blumenthal's statement: "Credibility is verified by winning, staying in power. And legitimacy is confused with popularity."[16]

In what follows, Hizbullah's image management strategy since the July 2006 war will be examined, with a focus on Hizbullah's image that targets Lebanese and Arab audiences. One must remember that Hizbullah also has a developed psy-ops and propaganda strategy aimed squarely at Israel and which targets Israeli citizens as well as the Israeli military, which is part of what Zahera Harb calls "liberation propaganda."[17] This chapter will not address this strategy in detail. Rather, the sections that follow aim to highlight the key elements of Hizbullah's image management strategy, particularly visual ones, and to relate them to the political context within which Hizbullah operates.

The evolution of Hizbullah's image

Hizbullah's image management strategy has seen the group's image evolve over the past three decades. This image has several constants: Hizbullah as an ally of Iran; its role as a resistance group (to Israel); and its being a religious party representative of the Shiite community in Lebanon. But it also has changed, namely in moving from appealing almost exclusively to the Shiites in Lebanon to addressing a global audience; from operating as a group outside the Lebanese state to a key player within the state, in the process adopting a nationalist tag; and in alternating between a victimized image and a heroic one. The evolution of this image can be understood within the context of the relationship between organizations and the environment. As Dutton and Dukerich argue, organizational actions, decisions and responses adapt to changes in the external environment, while patterns of organizational action also have a modifying impact on this environment.[18] Hizbullah's image management strategy is a process of negotiation between the group's political aims and the changing political environment in Lebanon and the Middle East. The group's main political aim, to establish itself as the key political player in Lebanon, has been approached with a long-term vision by Hizbullah[19] as a process that would take decades to be achieved, which necessitates ensuring that Hizbullah's image at each stage in the process is responsive to the political dynamics of the time. At the same time, the image itself is crafted to effect a favorable change in those dynamics.

Visual products have played an important role in this evolving image management strategy. Created as an anti-Israeli Islamist militia following the invasion of Lebanon by Israel in 1982, Hizbullah's early image management visual products had two key characteristics. First, they were infused with Palestinian and Iranian references. The Iranian influence was particularly seen in the visual style of Hizbullah's posters that it used to disseminate its ideological and military messages, using the same logos and aesthetics as those used by Iranian state organizations like Bonyad-e Shahid (which Hizbullah launched in Lebanon under the Arabic name "Mo'assasat al-Shahid"). This borrowing is not surprising as Hizbullah itself is a product of the Iranian Republican Guard, utilizing the same Iranian institutions and with continuing Iranian patronage; moreover, the adoption of Iranian revolutionary aesthetics came at a time that coincided with the Iran–Iraq war, which produced similar visual outputs in Iran. This naturalized introduction of Iranian aesthetics into Lebanon can be seen as an attempt at normalizing Hizbullah's links with Iran, so that aspects of Iranian cultural expression blend into Lebanese ones.

The Palestinian influence manifested itself in two key ways: through Hizbullah's use of heroic videos, and through invoking the liberation of Palestine as one of the group's key drivers. Hizbullah is one of the first Islamist groups to record its "martyrdom operations" on video. Beyond the mere recording of personal testimonies by would-be martyrs (which were pioneered in Lebanon by anti-Israeli occupation National Resistance Front groups like the Communist Party and the Syrian Social Nationalist Party in the early 1980s), Hizbullah's videos contained footage of actual anti-Israeli operations.[20] Very early on, Hizbullah had learnt that establishing credibility, popularity and a lasting legacy would be supported by video "evidence," a lesson passed on from the Palestinian Liberation Organization, which had been a keen producer of "resistance" propaganda films in the 1970s, films that were in turn inspired by the idea of Third Cinema and the camera as a weapon that emerged from Latin American revolutionary contexts.[21] The videos are an example of Hizbullah's direct mediation of how its operations would be remembered. As Groys argues, contemporary warriors no longer need artists to represent their heroic acts; warriors themselves have started to act as artists through creating videos with recognizable aesthetics.[22] In this sense, they themselves become the mediators between reality and memory, often creating iconic images that become part of the collective imagination.

The group's commitment to Palestine is an ongoing attribute, and it is publicly communicated through visual outputs and spectacles like the organization of elaborate Jerusalem Day parades every year[23], as well as through invoking the liberation of Palestine constantly in Hizbullah rhetoric. Although this can be read as an appeal to the hearts and minds of Palestinians, and even Arabs at large – as the Arab-Israeli conflict is perhaps the most defining conflict of its kind for Arab citizens – it was not until the liberation of southern Lebanon in 2000 that Hizbullah was able to cement its reputation as a credible resistance force in the eyes of Arab citizens. Yet it could be argued that without having planted the seeds of credibility early, Hizbullah may not have been able to achieve its iconic status in the region.

The second characteristic is that early Hizbullah videos, posters, rhetoric and public rallies were heavily invested in Shiite religious references. Hizbullah emerged out of the context of the marginalization of the Shiites in Lebanon (particularly in the South) and the drive for self-empowerment for the community that was instigated by Imam Musa Sadr in the 1970s, as well as the ideology of the Islamic Republic of Iran.[24] Hizbullah's main audience in its early years was the Lebanese Shiites. Hizbullah's communication products were primarily aimed at rallying support for the group among this core community, promising it a rise to a brighter future. In this way, Hizbullah's image in the early and mid-1980s aimed at carving a space for the group in the hearts and minds of the Shiites. The visuals were raw and crude, but this spoke to the double abjection of the Shiites at the time, a community denied political, social and economic support by the Lebanese state and attacked by Israel, since most Shiites in Lebanon come from the Israel-bordering South.[25] Hizbullah adopted this marginalization framework along similar lines to those used by Lebanon's earlier Shiite movement Amal (set up by Sadr), but added to this victimized image one of prowess. With the group calling itself the "Party of God," religion was another marker of credibility within the community, and Hizbullah branded its anti-Israeli operations as a jihad in the path of God.

With the end of the Lebanese Civil War that was sealed with the signing of the Taef Agreement of 1989 (which Hizbullah was not part of), Hizbullah found itself in a limited political space that was too small for its growing ambitions. Having amassed a considerable degree of support within the Shiite community, the group decided to enter formal local Lebanese politics for the first time, running for municipal and parliamentary elections in 1992. This necessitated a change in the image of Hizbullah, adding a nationalist layer to it in order to appeal to communities beyond the Shiites. To do so, Hizbullah partly relied on a PR campaign to market itself in nationalist terms.[26] Hizbullah was no longer just a Shiite group. It now became a Lebanese group. Its resistance operations in southern Lebanon were now not just about liberating the people of the South, but also about liberating Lebanon as a nation-state. Hizbullah started infusing its communication messages with more references to Lebanon, and its political and media strategy succeeded as the group won a significant number of seats in the first post-war parliamentary election in 1992. This era also saw Hizbullah establish its own terrestrial television station, al-Manar, which started broadcasting in 1991. Al-Manar allowed Hizbullah to communicate directly with the wider Lebanese audience, which was crucial for establishing itself as a key political party. Al-Manar was characterized by Hizbullah as the "resistance channel,"[27] consolidating Hizbullah's image as a defender of Lebanon against Israeli aggression.

Hizbullah's image as a Lebanese nationalist group was bolstered with the withdrawal of Israeli troops from Lebanon in 2000 after 18 years of occupation. The liberation of southern Lebanon was widely credited to Hizbullah's resistance operations, allowing the group to sustain the nationalist tag and to claim further clout in the local Lebanese political scene.[28] Hizbullah achieved this through altering its image from the liberator of Lebanon to the protector of the country.[29] The liberation also marked the beginning of claiming a space in the pan-Arab imagination, especially as it coincided with the Second Palestinian Intifada, which Hizbullah was quick to embrace. The group had launched the satellite channel of its al-Manar television station that year, allowing it to communicate its messages to a regional audience in the Middle East. All those factors allowed Hizbullah to appropriate the label "the resistance," so that "the resistance" has become another name for "Hizbullah"; this labeling is a way of cultivating legitimacy, so that resistance connotations come up every time Hizbullah is mentioned or even thought about, no matter what the context. In adopting this label, Hizbullah also can be seen as using an international framework to appeal to global audiences, as it has branded itself a resistance movement on par with anti-colonial ones in Africa and Latin America.

This label was challenged during the Cedar Revolution of 2005 following the assassination of former Prime Minister Rafic Hariri on 14 February 2005. Widely regarded as an assassination orchestrated by Hizbullah's ally Syria, Hariri's death formed a key challenge for Hizbullah, as mass public mourning for the former prime minister became a daily ritual in downtown Beirut. As presented in Chapter 1, the assassination also resulted in the creation of the March 14 political coalition in Lebanon that challenged Hizbullah and marketed itself strongly in patriotic terms, calling for the withdrawal of Syrian troops from Lebanese soil following UN Resolution 1559. Hizbullah once more found itself in a position in which further engagement in local Lebanese politics was a necessity. Hizbullah competed with the March 14 coalition in the parliamentary election that ensued in May 2005, allying itself with a Christian political party, the Free Patriotic Movement, in a bid to sustain its Lebanese nationalist tag and to hold on to its political power. Hizbullah was keen to use the Lebanese flag alongside its own flag in its rallies and television broadcasts as a visual indicator of its nationalist sentiment.[30]

Attention to the Cedar Revolution went beyond Lebanon. Arab citizens as well as international observers mostly praised the street protests calling for freedom, sovereignty and independence (from Syrian control),[31] and Hizbullah's attempts at presenting a nationalist image while being a firm supporter of Syria started to look less than convincing. Hizbullah responded by attempting to redefine public discourse about the meaning of foreign intervention. It orchestrated a rally in downtown Beirut on 8 March 2005 where placards stating "No to foreign intervention" were carried, and where "foreign intervention" came to mean American intervention, but not Syrian or Iranian. This message was also mirrored in the media messages that Hizbullah employed, whether through Nasrallah's speeches or al-Manar broadcasts. This redefinition of "foreign" served to legitimize Hizbullah's connections with Iran and Syria.

In using the spectacle of a rally as a tool to create this redefinition, Hizbullah can be said to have followed Lisa Wedeen's argument that "ideologues use spectacles to revise resonant symbols so as to convey current political messages."[32] Wedeen also argues that "spectacles are taken simultaneously to represent dominance and to operate as a means of dominating."[33] The March 8 rally, then, was also a means for Hizbullah to display its power and exercise it over "others." Through it, the group asserted its dominance over its political opponents. As a spectacle, the rally served as a visual anchor for political ideas that framed the ways Hizbullah's supporters, part of the rally's intended audiences, defined themselves[34]; as Wedeen argues, spectacles are a way of disciplining the bodies of people through enacting political obedience.[35] The March 8 rally began a phase of stepped up public and private measures by Hizbullah to ensure the undivided loyalty of its followers and the intimidation of its rivals.

Hizbullah, in turn, became acutely aware of the need to perform to a regional audience, and even an international one. The Cedar Revolution's visual saturation was embraced by Hizbullah, and since 2005, Hizbullah's secretary general, Hassan Nasrallah, has become the public face of the group in the Arab world and outside, with carefully crafted speeches targeting multiple audiences and a charismatic image[36]; and the group's communication strategy has become a multiplatform one on a wider scale. But it was the July 2006 war that marked a key transformation in Hizbullah's image.

When Hizbullah first emerged as a paramilitary group, its primary target audiences were Israel and Lebanese Shiites. As the group's political aims widened, so did its target audience. Although Hizbullah had been addressing Arab audiences through its al-Manar satellite television channel since 2000, before the 2006 war, this address was presented by a local Lebanese Shiite paramilitary group that was nevertheless a key participant in Lebanese politics.

The group's main appeal to Arab audiences was through its con-stantly expressed support for the Palestinian cause.[37] Israel's reac-tion to Hizbullah's kidnapping of two IDF (Israel Defense Forces) soldiers on 12 July 2006 changed this image. Israel launched a mili-tary campaign targeting not just Hizbullah strongholds in southern Lebanon and southern Beirut, but also vital Lebanese infrastruc-tural sites, from bridges to power plants to Beirut's only lighthouse. Israel's attacks resulted in the death of more than 1,200 people in Lebanon, most of them civilians, and the displacement of one mil-lion people, a quarter of the Lebanese population.[38] The 2006 war saw Hizbullah once again market itself as Lebanon's savior from Israeli aggression, but went beyond that: The 24-hour coverage of the war on pan-Arab satellite television widened Hizbullah's network of audiences, and helped Hizbullah transform its image into that of a primarily *Arab* paramilitary group.[39] That Hizbullah emerged defi-ant after the war allowed the group to develop itself as a heroic brand across the Arab world. Nasrallah became the new Gamal Abdel Nasser, a pan-Arab leader, and Hizbullah came to be widely viewed as the only Arab actor that has succeeded in resisting Israel and "defeating" it in war.[40]

Hizbullah as a brand

Hizbullah's double "victory," according to its own rhetoric, made the group a household name in the Arab world. It strove to cultivate a sense of legitimacy based on this power, and this combination of power and legitimacy paved the way for Hizbullah's rising authority in Lebanon and its popularity in the Arab world.[41] The group worked hard on getting closer to Arab audiences by utilizing all its communi-cation tools at once. Mass rallies were organized and televised live to celebrate the 2006 victory, when Nasrallah gave speeches that often merged classical Arabic (to appeal to Arab audiences) with the Lebanese dialect (to appeal to the local audience). Flyers, ban-ners and billboards were created to commemorate the war. Al-Manar broadcast music videos dedicated to the war[42] and *al-Intiqad* news-paper carried images from the twice-liberated South on its front pages. Even merchandise commemorating the war was created. A key characteristic of those communication tools is that they were marked by a high degree of intertextuality and uniformity of mes-sage.[43] As such, they have helped construct Hizbullah as an identifi-able brand.

Stuart Agres defines a brand as "an asset of differentiating promises that links a product to its consumers."[44] The associative aspect of brands is particularly important: Strong brands have strong bonds with their target audiences. As Peter van Ham argues, brands serve as emotional appeals to people, granting them a sense of belonging and security.[45] Logos, in particular, serve as visual reminders to followers of their affinity with the brand, cultivating their sense of loyalty. The Hizbullah flag, with a distinct canary yellow background and the image of a rifle held high by an arm extending from the words "Hizb Allah" in Arabic, acts as one such marker of identity and pride for Hizbullah's followers.

Hizbullah was aware of the importance of engaging with its wider audience after the war on a more personal, everyday basis to sustain brand loyalty.[46] It therefore created war memorabilia like t-shirts and baseball caps bearing its logo and the color of its flag, as well as the picture of Nasrallah. It also issued merchandise that included a dart board featuring Israeli government officials and Israeli towns that the player was invited to throw darts at, and a new computer game ("Special Force 2: Tale of the Truthful Pledge") that allowed players to battle Israeli soldiers in the southern Lebanese villages affected by the 2006 war. As the game's designer said, the game aimed to make players "feel the victory as if they were taking part in attacks they were cheering for from far."[47] All those products can be seen as material efforts to associate Hizbullah's image with specific, definite values (defiance, heroism) in the eyes of its audience, no matter how much the values are actually related to Hizbullah's "real characteristics,"[48] because, as Falkowski and Cwalina argue, "it is sufficient [for a brand] that [the values associated with it] have a definite meaning for the recipient."[49]

Aaker writes that the strength of brands lies in brand awareness, perceived quality, brand loyalty and brand association.[50] Hizbullah's brand after 2006 scored high on all four levels. Brand awareness is not just about recognition of a brand name, but also its dominance in someone's mind over other brands. Hizbullah worked to achieve this through repetition of its victory messages across all media, which turned slogans like "the most honorable of people" (in reference to Nasrallah) and "The Divine Victory" (in reference to the 2006 war) into everyday expressions. The perception of quality was easy to achieve following the "victory" outcome of the 2006 war, but Hizbullah was keen to emphasize added value. Addressing audiences in the victory rally in September 2006, Nasrallah promised that those houses destroyed

Fig. 9. Pro-Hizbullah dart board depicting Israeli towns and politicians as targets on sale in Beirut in December 2009.

in the war would be rebuilt even better than they were before.[51] This promise can be connected with ensuring continued loyalty, as those who suffered great losses during the war could be seen as the most likely to enter a lukewarm relationship with Hizbullah. The group was keen to showcase people's loyalty through rallying thousands to participate in its victory celebrations. Loyalty was also communicated through cultivating the expression "fida al-sayyed" (meaning, a sacrifice to Sayyed Hassan Nasrallah), which was mouthed by those whose homes were destroyed or who lost loved ones during the war whenever they appeared in the media, to indicate that all those losses were worth it as long as Nasrallah prevailed, an expression of utmost loyalty to the brand no matter how dire the circumstances. This kind of rhetoric is what differentiates Nasrallah from most other Arab leaders. He is not merely the *head* of an institution who derives his authority from coercion,[52] he is a *leader* whom people follow because they "want to."[53] This bond with Nasrallah in turn strengthens Hizbullah's brand association, which refers to the emotional bonds that link a person to a brand. Such emotional bonds are important for Hizbullah because through them people internalize Hizbullah's principles. As Mueller argues, "[l]egitimating rationales, necessary to any system of domination, are effective only if their underlying principles have been internalized by the public, that is, collectively accepted as normative and thus as binding."[54]

The brand that Hizbullah intends people to form a bond with invokes certain positive connotations like justice, liberty, honor, defiance and heroism. Those connotations came to the fore during the 2006 war. The war was a media spectacle. While television coverage of the war in the Arab world highlighted the plight of civilians, al-Jazeera's coverage in particular was marked by taking a clear stance towards Hizbullah:[55] Hizbullah was branded "the resistance" and its fight against Israel was presented in David-versus-Goliath heroic terms. The channel's normal schedule was suspended as attention was focused on the small villages in southern Lebanon where the fiercest battles were taking place. There was little footage of actual Hizbullah fighters, but the rhetoric used in the newscasts painted a picture of larger-than-life, almost mythical action heroes. The news reports coupled graphic footage of Lebanese casualties with stories about Hizbullah's defense operations in the South. A similar, if more pronounced, image of Hizbullah could be seen on its own television channel, al-Manar. Merging footage of war-torn villages and civilians with those of Hizbullah fighters in the field, al-Manar disseminated a message of defiance that was bolstered when Israel destroyed the station's headquarters in southern Beirut on 16 July 2011, only for the channel to continue broadcasting from a secret location after a mere two-minute interruption to its live transmission. Al-Manar's feat came just two days after Hassan Nasrallah appeared on television promising victory against Israel:

> "The surprises that I have promised you will start now," Nasrallah said. "Now in the middle of the sea, facing Beirut, the Israeli warship that has attacked the infrastructure, people's homes and civilians. Look at it burning."[56]

The camera cut to what appeared to be live action of Hizbullah's attack on the warship. If there ever were an awe-inspiring symbolic action for Hizbullah's defiance during the war, that was it. The Hizbullah brand was sealed.

The divine image

The end of the war in August 2006 was labeled by Hizbullah a "Divine Victory" in a multimedia political marketing campaign. Bruce Newman lists three main components of political marketing: "Social Imagery," personality politics, and "Situational Contingency."[57] Hizbullah used all three in the Divine Victory campaign. Social imagery associated Hizbullah with issues relevant to its constituents; personality politics operated through Nasrallah's performances as discussed above; and situational contingency was used through presenting hypothetical scenarios that created the illusion that Hizbullah would be better able to deal with them than any other political/paramilitary entity. Writing about Bill Clinton's 1996 presidential election campaign, Bruce Newman highlights a key strategy for Clinton, which he terms "positioning strategy." He writes that this strategy constituted "his ability to convince voters that the American Dream was getting easier to achieve, that he was the person who would give them a sense of control over their own destinies, and that the 'age of opportunity' would make that happen for them."[58] Hizbullah followed a similar model in using situational contingency, as it aimed to convince its people that defeating Israel was getting easier to achieve, that Nasrallah was the person who would give them a sense of control over their own destinies and that, in Nasrallah's words, "the age of defeats has gone, and the age of victories has come."

But Hizbullah was also keen to market the 2006 war as a victory against Israel to an international audience. To achieve this, Hizbullah's image management strategy became more sophisticated and streamlined, relying on professionally designed visual products. No sooner had the war ended that Hizbullah planted 600 billboards in Lebanon that commemorated the group's achievements, the most prominent placed on the road from Beirut's international airport into the capital.[59] The billboards had several distinctive characteristics that marked a departure from Hizbullah's usual communication style.

First of all, as the billboards were meant for the cameras of the international media, they featured images and text in Arabic, English and French. While Hizbullah had used different languages in its communication messages before (namely through installing billboards in Hebrew on the Israeli border to intimidate the "enemy," and through al-Manar's multilingual website), this was the first time that the group had used foreign languages in this streamlined and self-knowing way.

Second, a clear distinction between Hizbullah's Divine Victory campaign and previous Hizbullah media campaigns is that the Divine Victory one was less dense, both visually and verbally.[60] *Newsweek* interviewed the creative director of the PR company Idea Creation that designed the campaign in 2006. In the interview, Mohammad Kawtharani revealed the intention behind this:

The international public "expects a clear and single message," he says. "That's the language of the media these days." So Hizbullah settled on the simple and catchy "Divine Victory" slogan, and repeated it over and over.[61]

Third, when using images of casualties, this time Hizbullah did not choose to display graphic violent images, which it had established a legacy of doing:

[N]ow that the war is over, says Kawtharani, publicizing what he calls the "more aggressive" visuals can be counterproductive...The West already considers Hizbullah a "bloody party," Kawtharani acknowledges. Continuing to publicize carnage would reinforce this image, especially among foreign audiences.[62]

A fourth distinction is the use of humor, something that Hassan Nasrallah had started employing in his speeches, and which was now translated into a visual form coupled with ironic text:

Some of Hizbullah's most common ads use a tactic that Kawtharani calls sending "double messages." One example: a red banner featuring the slogan *extremely accurate targets!* juxtaposed against the rubble of Beirut's southern suburbs. "In advertising, irony is part of the modern style," says Kawtharani. "The audience will receive the double message."[63]

The campaign is also worth examining for its appropriation of religious and patriotic frameworks that Hizbullah had used previously. All of the billboards had a red background, with the words "The Divine Victory" written in white and green – a reference to the colors of the Lebanese flag. They also featured a logo in the same colors written in a modern Arabic font that spelt the slogan "Victory from God" at the bottom. The same slogan, logo and colors also appeared on al-Manar, on Hizbullah's websites and on a variety of merchandise. The choice of words was deliberate: Hizbullah leader Hassan Nasrallah had, in April 2006, promised victory against Israel, as well as the release of Lebanese prisoners from Israeli jails (hence naming Hizbullah's operation on 12 July 2006 as "Operation Truthful Pledge"). Nasrallah's surname literally means "victory from God." So the media campaign that followed the 2006 war firmly placed the war as an achievement of Nasrallah himself, but it also elevated Nasrallah to a quasi-divine status, Lebanon's only savior.

The use of a religious framework for its activities, as stated earlier in this chapter, is a constant for Hizbullah. For example, Hizbullah's first anti-Israeli suicide bombing mission was called "Operation Khaibar" to connect it with the historic Battle of Khaibar when the Prophet Muhammad and his army took over a Jewish area. But "The Divine Victory" took this to another level, allowing Hizbullah to claim a position for itself above all other political parties in Lebanon. This use of religion makes Hizbullah's actions dogmatic and unchallengeable – to contest them would be equivalent to blasphemy. Indeed, in a later speech given by Hassan Nasrallah in 2008, he exclaimed, "This is the party of *God*! It is not a regular party. It is the party of *God*!" One can understand the need for this dogma as Hizbullah faced a degree of criticism in 2006 and after, both within and outside Lebanon, for recklessly dragging the country to war.

This criticism was also one reason behind Hizbullah's seeking narrative agency over the story of the war. As Hayden White argues, it is the presence of contest that produces narrativization of history.[64] Having narrative agency is important because being the narrator allows one control over how a story is presented, which elements of it to emphasize and which details to overlook. Narrativization is thus not only relevant in the context of competing with political opponents, but also in that of history. As Hegel wrote:

> In our language the term *History* unites the objective with the subjective side...it comprehends not less what has *happened*, than the *narration* of what has happened. This union of the two meanings we must regard as of a higher order than mere outward accident; we must suppose historical narrations to have appeared contemporaneously with historical deeds and events. It is an internal vital principle common to both that produces them synchronously.[65]

White elaborates by highlighting narration's relationship to historical reality, or "events that are offered as the proper content of historical discourse"[66]:

> The reality of these events does not consist in the fact they occurred but that, first of all, they were remembered, and second, that they are capable of finding a place in a

chronologically ordered sequence...The authority of the historical narrative is the authority of reality itself; the historical account endows this reality with form and thereby makes it desirable, imposing on its processes the formal coherency that only stories possess.[67]

Through this claim of authority over the writing of history, Hizbullah placed itself as the sole legitimate narrator of the story of the war. The story was about Hizbullah as the hero of the people, protecting them against aggression by a foreign villain (Israel) and its sidekick (the United States).

This multi-actor story of the war was featured on the billboards celebrating the Divine Victory, with individual billboards each focusing on Hizbullah, the Lebanese people, Israel and the USA. Hizbullah in the story is the protector of the nation and the people, the protagonist and hero, as seen in one billboard that carried the image of a rocket launcher and two Hizbullah fighters as well as the Hizbullah flag, with the caption "The arms of the mujahideen." The Lebanese people are the defiant victims. While some billboards depicted casualties, the majority acknowledged the steadfastness of the people of the South (Lebanon and Beirut). A billboard under this theme had the image of an old man with his fist raised in the air, standing in front of a burning bombed home, along with the caption "With the patience of the steadfast people." The Israeli army is not just the villain in the story, but also is the stooge. Several billboards belittled the Israeli army, such as one showing the picture of Israeli soldiers crying in a huddle, with the caption "It's Lebanon, you fools!" in Arabic and English. The United States is painted as a menacing Israeli accomplice in the war. A billboard showing a destroyed home had the caption "Made in USA" in English, while a red banner erected at the site of a destroyed building stated in English, "The New Middle Beast," in reference to Condoleezza Rice's speech on 21 July 2006 about the war representing the "birth pangs of a new Middle East." A notable feature of the representation of Hizbullah as a "character" in the story is that the faces of its fighters in the billboards are not shown. Instead, they are anonymous, almost mythical figures. This visual representation contrasts sharply with that of faces of Hizbullah martyrs displayed on posters commemorating their deaths, which have been a regular feature of Hizbullah's visual products in public space since its inception. By choosing to de-individualize its fighters, Hizbullah is appealing to the audience to identify with the group as a unified, larger-than-life entity, but also to imagine themselves as those heroic figures.[68] It is also reserving idealized personification for one individual: Hassan Nasrallah.

The personified image

Bergmann and Wickert write: "In difficult times, a charismatic leader helps to give a sense of direction both at the objective and emotional levels";[69] he is both "a director and a leading actor."[70] Nasrallah, as Hizbullah's leader and public face, plays this dual role. But the 2006 war gave him an additional one: He himself became "the platform" of Hizbullah.[71] Hassan Nasrallah is Hizbullah's first charismatic leader in the media age. As such, he can be seen as a product of the political and media environment in which he is serving as secretary general of the party. Nasrallah's unique image as a leader partly lies in the fact that his public persona is a mediated one but also in the fact that he possesses genuine charisma.[72] It is therefore useful to pay attention to those two aspects. On the mediation level, Corner and Pels argue that mediation projects political personhood in three different ways: iconically, vocally and through kinesis. All three revolve around style: the first referring to the image of the leader; the second to the manner in which he addresses the public (as well as what he says); and the third to his represented (and often choreographed) actions and interactions.[73] Nasrallah excels on all three stylistic levels. On the charismatic level, Hackman and Johnson list five behaviors that help followers attribute charisma to a leader: possessing a unique, yet attainable vision; acting in an unconventional manner; demonstrating personal risk taking; demonstrating confidence and expertise; and demonstrating personal power.[74] Again, Nasrallah's image draws on all five elements.

Hassan Nasrallah assumed the leadership of Hizbullah after the assassination of Secretary General Abbas Musawi on 16 February 1992. Nasrallah's image in the early years of his leadership was that of a modest and devout man, but this image evolved into a larger-than-life one. The seeds for his heroic image were planted when he lost his 18-year old son, Hadi, in a military operation against Israel on 12 September 1997. Not only did Nasrallah claim a great deal of credibility by having his eldest son serve as a Hizbullah fighter (which gave a huge moral boost to the group's followers), he was also remarkable in his public handling of the death. In a speech televised on al-Manar the day after Hadi's death, Nasrallah fiercely declared:

I thank God and praise Him for His great bounty, that He generously blessed my family by choosing one of its members for martyrdom, and accepted me and my family as members in the holy assembly of martyrs' families. I used to feel ashamed when visiting the fathers, mothers, wives, and children of martyrs, and I will stay feeling humble in front of them.[75]

Al-Manar's broadcast intercut Nasrallah's speech with footage of him visiting the families of martyrs, and with images of the attending audience in the hall where he was giving the speech, where the audience members twice responded to his statements by raising their fists in the air and chanting: "God is great. Khomeini is the leader. Victory to Islam. Death to Israel. Definitely [reaching] victory. Advancing till [we reach] Jerusalem," the standard chant that Hizbullah popularized in its public rallies, suggesting that his and their spirits had not been broken by this loss, and that their eyes were firmly fixed on their goals.

The liberation of the South on 25 May 2000 was another landmark for Nasrallah. The liberation marked the overriding of the Iranian discourse framing Hizbullah's actions by a Lebanese nationalist one, and the presentation of Nasrallah as an Arab hero. In his speech on the day of the liberation in 2000, Nasrallah addressed the Hizbullah flag-waving crowd in an open-air venue in the southern town of Bint Jbeil by standing in front of a large Lebanese flag and saying, "You have proven, and the resistance has proven – in harmony with the Lebanese government – that the people of Lebanon, and the Lebanese state, and the Lebanese resistance, and all the sects in Lebanon are worthy of victory."[76] He then dedicated the victory to the Arab people: "We dedicate this victory to our oppressed people in occupied Palestine, and to the peoples of our Arab and Islamic nation."[77] This appeal to non-Shiite Lebanese and Arabs at large marks a configuration of leadership that can be seen as a move away from traditional politics in the Middle East that is based on a leader firmly embedded within the immediate collective (such as tribal leaders). Instead, what Nasrallah represents is a sense of proximity that is based on an asymmetrical relationship between the leader and the led, but that nevertheless constructs the leader as "authentic" as the leader tries to bridge this asymmetry.[78]

Nasrallah's image as a charismatic pan-Arab leader was cemented by the end of the 2006 war. His "extraordinary" deed meant that he became victory personified. This served to both sustain his charismatic position and charismatize his followers. As Schweitzer argues, sustaining charismatic leadership is reliant on extraordinary deeds, and this is mainly demonstrated in times of war, when the leader gains possession of heroic charisma.[79] Hackman and Johnson add that through such deeds, charismatic leaders can in turn help their followers overcome feelings of inadequacy: "In validating a charismatic leader's extraordinary ability, followers may experience feelings of empowerment by submerging their own identities in that of a seemingly superior leader."[80] Through this two-step process, Nasrallah became a pan-Arab icon. Arab citizens demonstrated against the Israeli aggression towards Lebanon in 2006 in several countries in the region, and often, the image of Nasrallah was used in public space as an identity marker by those demonstrators. But it was the end of the war – and the "victory" – that marked a new visibility for Nasrallah. As Belt puts it, Nasrallah became "Islam's most noble [doer]."[81] Posters of Nasrallah were carried by people in Bahrain, songs praising him were sung in public gatherings in Egypt and Hizbullah souvenirs bearing his image could be bought alongside those of President Bashar al-Assad in Syria. Nasrallah represented a new hope for Arabs in the long battle against Israel, and he seemed the perfect candidate to fill the gap for a pan-Arab leader, which had existed since the death of Egyptian president Gamal Abdel Nasser in 1970. In Egypt in 2006, Nasrallah's picture was carried alongside that of Nasser[82]; the comparison with Nasser was pronounced not only because of Nasrallah's great deed in the 2006 war (which some saw as being on par with Nasser's nationalization of the Suez Canal in 1956, and which Hizbullah constantly framed as defeating the largest Israeli military operation against an Arab country[83]), but also because of Nasrallah's rhetorical style and charisma, as well as his ability to achieve parasocial intimacy with his followers.[84] Pels argues that parasocial intimacy between leaders and their followers disturbs the traditional political divide between elitism and populism. This disturbance is based on the linking of difference and familiarity; on one hand, "only through distance is the representer able to represent."[85] This is seen in Nasrallah's status as a larger-than-life person. On the other hand, as the representer speaks in the name of the represented, his representation implies a sense of proximity. Nasrallah is thus at once "one of us" and an untouchable star, displaying an "extraordinary ordinariness."[86]

This ambivalence was capitalized on by Hizbullah after the 2006 war through a "documentary" produced by al-Manar and distributed on

DVD called *Al-Abaya* (meaning "the cloak"). *Al-Abaya* used as its focus a Lebanese Shiite woman called Reem Haidar to construct "a film about the importance of mutual affinity and commitment between the leader and his people," as she states at the end of the film. Reem Haidar was an "ordinary" Lebanese woman who was interviewed on television as she walked to a café in Beirut two days into the 2006 war. She made one comment in the interview which turned her into a new "face" for Hizbullah:

> I want from Sayyed Hassan, when this mess is over, his cloak, that he sweated in while he was defending me and my children, my siblings, and my land. I want it so I can roll around in its sweat, and roll my children around in its sweat. Maybe its pieces can be distributed to people so they can acquire some of its generosity, honor and dignity.

Hassan Nasrallah's response after the war was to send Reem Haidar one of his cloaks, which she has displayed in her house "so that people can visit it and be blessed by it." *Al-Abaya* follows Reem as she talks to people from the areas destroyed in the war, intercutting her exchanges with monologues. The words she uses in the documentary echo those of Nasrallah. Talking to a woman whose home was destroyed in southern Beirut, Reem says, "those of us whose homes were not destroyed have been humbled by you." She then addresses the camera as she walks among the rubble: "I wish my home were here. Why is it only they who have received this honor?" The film ends with a scene in which Reem carefully takes Nasrallah's cloak out of its clear plastic trunk, spreads it as she gazes at it, with the camera zooming in on sections of the cloak, inviting us to share this intimate gaze, holds it in her arms twice and then carefully puts it back in its trunk.

Reem's verbal expressions and her embrace of the cloak construct Nasrallah as an object of almost erotic desire. If nuns are "the brides of Christ," women in the film express a unique affinity with Nasrallah as a man/superhuman/quasi-divine entity. The film is curious for choosing only women to speak specifically about their relationship with Nasrallah (the men interviewed in the film focus on other subjects related to the war and to Reem herself). It shows the women praising Nasrallah: An elderly woman recites a poem comparing him to the sun; a young woman declares that "what Sayyed Hassan has done could not have been done by any other human being or Arab leader"; another says "we have been blessed by God for existing in an era when Sayyed Hassan exists." This divine quality, according to Weber's theory of charisma, is part of how genuine charisma can exist: The leader must believe that he possesses a divine grace, and his followers must share this belief.[87] Through media images like the one invoked in this film, Nasrallah himself becomes a message defined by a heroic act. As Groys puts it, "[t]he heroic act transforms the hero's body from a medium into a message. Making the body the message requires above all an arena, a stage – or . . . a public created by the media."[88] The film then is an example of how Hizbullah uses the media to take its leader beyond familiarity and into the realm of intimacy, where he becomes internalized by the party's followers.[89]

The use of the hyper-image

The period following the 2006 war and its celebration was politically challenging for Hizbullah. The United Nations endorsed the establishment of a Special Tribunal for Lebanon to investigate the death of Rafic Hariri, according to a UN Resolution originally issued in March 2006. Hizbullah had lost the parliamentary elections of 2005, achieving only around 45 per cent of the seats with its allies. Empowered by the Divine Victory, Hizbullah's ministers and their allies resigned from the Cabinet in November 2006 in an attempt at halting the government's expected approval of the UN Resolution, and when that failed, on 1 December 2006, Hizbullah and its allies started a series of anti-government sit-ins in downtown Beirut that paralyzed life in the area, as well as the normal functioning of the government.

Hizbullah tried to place the sit-ins in a patriotic framework similar to the one used during the Cedar Revolution. The Lebanese flag was hung across the sit-in area and it was carried by the protesters. Tents were erected in Martyrs' Square, populated by young people, creating a quasi-carnivalesque atmosphere, and the Free Patriotic Movement ensured that its supporters were photographed alongside those of Hizbullah, an image of sectarian unity against a divisive government. The protest camp saw the use of political posters to discredit the government. One large poster depicted US Secretary of State Condoleezza Rice as a primary school teacher instructing Lebanese Prime Minister Fouad Siniora at the "School of the New Middle East" in courses on "corruption," "sectarianism," "the removal of sovereignty," "meddling with security" and "rigging elections." It also saw the erection of posters carrying the image of Nasrallah. The "Lebanese National Opposition" became the new title for the political coalition led by Hizbullah, and it took as its logo the sign of a rainbow, a reference to its claimed anti-sectarian agenda.

But the protest camp soon became a ghost town as most protesters left the area, although the tent city itself and the protest movement remained for almost 18 months, after which the tension escalated into a violent confrontation as Hizbullah took over the western area of Beirut, the stronghold of Hariri, in May 2008. The group needed to assert its political power. Establishing an image of grandeur and dominance was one way of communicating this. This image was targeted at both Israel and Hizbullah's opponents within Lebanon.

One element of this image was the almost mythical persona of Imad Mughniyeh. In contrast to the organic materiality of Nasrallah, Imad Mughniyeh, Hizbullah's head of external operations who was otherwise known as Haj Radwan, was an enigmatic figure whose existence Hizbullah had originally denied. His assassination in Damascus in February 2008 happened at a time when Hizbullah

Fig. 10. Anti-government poster featuring Condoleezza Rice and Prime Minister Fouad Siniora at the Lebanese Opposition's protest camp in downtown Beirut on 11 January 2008.

was presenting a defiant, anti-American and anti-Israeli image following the 2006 war, and his death became a useful tool, enabling Hizbullah to disseminate stories about him that benefited this defiant image. It was only after his death that Hizbullah claimed him as one of its own, and confirmed his responsibility for masterminding various attacks, some being attacks the group had never associated itself with before, like that on the American marines in Beirut in 1983. Mughniyeh's death was both operationally and symbolically useful for Hizbullah.

Very little was known about Mughniyeh in the public domain at the time of his death, not even the way he looked. But after his assassination, Hizbullah swiftly moved to add Mughniyeh to its public historical repertoire. To commemorate Martyrs' Day on 11 November 2008, the photo of Mughniyeh was added to those of Ahmad Kassir (Hizbullah's first martyr), and the assassinated Shiite notable Sheikh Ragheb Harb and former Hizbullah leader Abbas al-Musawi in a banner appearing on Hizbullah's website. He was given the title "Prince of the Caravan of Martyrs." Selected photos of him were uploaded on a special section of the website. And banners and billboards commemorating his death appeared on the road to Beirut's airport and elsewhere. The banners carried another title for Mughniyeh: "Leader of the Two Victories" (in reference to 2000 and 2006). Almost out of nowhere, the liberation of the South and the "defeat" of Israel in 2006 now had one mastermind.

Slogans were used to emphasize this. One banner of Mughniyeh in Beirut had his photo, in which he is wearing military fatigues and a baseball cap, in front of the Hizbullah logo, and it displayed the phrase: "The grace of conclusive victory." Another stated, "Our wound is the pulse of weapons." Another series of banners in the South had his photo with the phrases: "Karbala is my weapon"; "My blood is for Jerusalem"; "Our enemy is one: Israel"; "The key will is my will"; "Jerusalem is ours"; "[Our] position is a weapon – my position"; "My country is my spirit and blood"; "Palestine is my cause"; "Israel will be annihilated" and "My blood is victorious." In another set of yellow banners celebrating the release of the detainees and displaying the "Victory from God" logo used in the 2006 Divine Victory campaign, the impression of Mughniyeh surrounded by the halo of the sun was depicted along with the words "The liberation of detainees is the achievement of God with our hands."

An intriguing aspect of the phrases and slogans used in those banners is that none of them have been attributed to Imad Mughniyeh

Fig. 11. Banners of Imad Mughniyeh in southern Lebanon. Photo taken on 31 August 2008.

himself. Instead, they are a collection of pronouncements by other Hizbullah martyrs/leaders. "The key will" for example is a phrase from a statement once given by Abbas al-Musawi, when he said that "the key will is the preservation of the resistance." And "[Our] position is a weapon" was a statement by Shiite notable Sheikh Ragheb Harb, who was assassinated by Israel in 1985. By associating the image of Mughniyeh with the words of Hizbullah's martyred leaders, the story of Mughniyeh as another figure in the Hizbullah leadership was being weaved. This was cemented visually through banners showing the image of Nasrallah above that of Mughniyeh, as if looking out for him, a visual layout normally used by Hizbullah in representing the relationship between the Shiite Supreme Leader and the Hizbullah leader (in the hierarchy, the Supreme Leader [first Ruhollah Khomeini and now Ali Khamenei] is always highest and depicted visually as such).

But unlike other Hizbullah leaders, who had known public personas, Mughniyeh as a man was unknown. Hizbullah sought to create an individual persona for him by making his death the theme for celebrating the second anniversary of the Divine Victory in 2008. For the occasion, Hizbullah created an exhibition titled "Leader of the Two Victories" in a square in Nabatiyeh in southern Lebanon.

The exhibition was set against the backdrop of a huge banner displaying Mughinyeh's photo on the right and a coffin covered with an Israeli flag on the left with images of injured Israeli soldiers in the middle, under the phrase: "The martyr will remove them from existence." The exhibition featured items presented as having belonged to Mughniyeh: his rifle, clothes, shoes, prayer rug, cap and beads, hair brush, eyeglasses case, bag, torch and office chair and desk, upon which his now-trademark baseball cap was laid. As Laleh Khalili argues, such a display of quotidian "non-heroic" objects serves to lend the martyr familiarity in the eyes of the viewer.[90] In Mughinyeh's case, the display also serves to ground the myth in material reality.

Yet Mughniyeh's absence is a useful component in the myth, creating a hyper-image. As Fuery and Fuery argue, "[t]he hyper-image . . . can become the defining image for that which it comes to represent because it is such an extreme version . . . What we do not see [in hyper-images], however, are the people themselves."[91] In this way, the hyper-image of Mughniyeh has come to stand in for resistance as it is based on the absence of the man himself. Absence serves to keep the myth alive: "The hyper-image relies on absences to construct

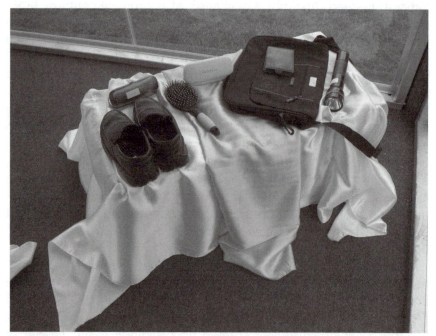

Fig. 12. Mughniyeh's personal objects on display in Nabatiyeh in southern Lebanon in 2008. Photo by Assafir.

and retain part of its power. Through these absences it seduces the spectator into a contributory role. In other words, the hyper-image self-perpetuates by convincing the spectator of its status."[92] In this way, "Imad Mughniyeh" becomes a postmodern tool for Hizbullah's image. It is a simulacra, a sign without a referent, whose existence is derived through referencing other signs.[93] The sign's usefulness is due to the fluidity of meaning that can be ascribed to it. As Baudrillard says, "simulation threatens the difference between 'true' and 'false', between 'real' and 'imaginary'."[94]

Through this elusiveness, "Imad Mughniyeh" functions as a hyper-image that Hizbullah can use to project whatever messages it wishes to disseminate. As Ajemian argues,

> the mystery surrounding Mughniyeh's life and activities provided a blank slate for Hezbollah's media apparatus to mold the myth of Mughniyeh through ceremony, discourse and imagery that frames his death, not as a defeat, but as an omen of victory that is part of a greater history of defiance.[95]

"Imad Mughniyeh" is a sign that serves "cultic purposes"; it continues to be invoked by Hizbullah in its public messages as a rallying, intimidating and legitimating tool, even though Hizbullah no longer relies on the physical/visual display of Mughniyeh's image in abundance. As Walter Benjamin argues, the presence of such signs "is more important than the fact that they are seen."[96]

A larger-than-life image

Mughniyeh's persona is part of a wider strategy to construct a larger-than-life image for Hizbullah in the post-2006 era. This image is manifested in a series of public visual displays. Three key displays form part of this strategy. The first is the organizing of public rallies and protests to commemorate the Divine Victory and the ensuing release of Lebanese prisoners from Israeli jails in July 2008. The second is the series of billboards that Hizbullah installs on the road from Beirut's international airport, which has now become an area for the exclusive display of Hizbullah messages, and in southern Lebanon. And the third is the establishment of a permanent visitor site in southern Lebanon called Mleeta, which opened in 2010, and which evolved out of a temporary exhibition in southern Beirut called Spider's Web that took place in 2007.

Public rallies have been a constant tool for Hizbullah since its inception. But after 2006, the rallies became larger in scale and more streamlined. Because of the threat to Nasrallah's life, most of his live addresses to the crowds have since had to be delivered through video on giant screens placed in football fields and other large community spaces. But there have been exceptions. The most notable one is the rally that took place in July 2008 to celebrate the release of Lebanese prisoners from Israeli jails, an occurrence that Nasrallah had "promised" as the outcome of Operation Truthful Pledge in 2006. Standing next to Samir Kuntar, Lebanon's longest serving prisoner in an Israeli jail who had been released after 29 years (and who hung a Hizbullah scarf around his neck at the rally), Nasrallah appeared in person for the first time in almost two years, and addressed the crowd using the same phrase he had coined in 2000 and which had become one of his trademark slogans: "The age of defeats has gone, and the age of victories has come." Behind them stood a huge yellow banner displaying the words "Operation Radwan." "Operation Radwan for the Release of Prisoners and the Return of Martyrs' Remains" was a shrewd choice of name for the event, as it referenced Imad Mughniyeh as the original planner of the operation, thereby immediately lending the event a larger-than-life status. Spectacular rallies have now become an established component of Hizbullah's image management strategies, used to comment on specific political developments.

The billboards that have been used to line the sides of the road to Beirut's international airport have varied over the years. In 2007, they retained the red, white and green colors of the Lebanese flag, but in later years, they reverted to the canary yellow of Hizbullah's flag, asserting the group's contribution to a "free" Lebanon, which serves as a message to Hizbullah's Lebanese political rivals. But the most striking visual display of power was through the opening of the Mleeta visitor center in spring 2010. Perched on a hill close to the Israeli border and overlooking several villages in southern Lebanon, the visitor center, under the title "Mleeta: The Story of the Earth to the Sky," is an ultramodern exhibition of Hizbullah's military operations and capabilities. Its message is a simple one: power – and as such, it is both an example of strategic warfare communication and internal propaganda.[97]

The exhibition is in two parts. An indoor space is dedicated to military information about Israel. A banner of Nasrallah raising his finger with the slogan, "If you hit, we hit" is placed facing the entrance. Another banner shows the map of Israel, on which key areas that could form military targets for Hizbullah are highlighted. Another map shows the location of Israel's military bases. Other banners display Israel's anti-aircraft missile capabilities, and information about Israeli drones and tanks. A flowchart illustrates the structure of the Israeli army. This part of the exhibition is a pure example of power in the Foucauldian sense, as a producer of knowledge.[98] It also places Hizbullah on an exalted level in relation to Israel, as it boasts the party's epistemological superiority over its enemy. This superiority is coupled with representing the "enemy" as weak. The indoor space contains Israeli military equipment displayed in glass cases. Stripped of its power, the equipment is rendered an exotic object to be gazed at. The space also harbors a banner dedicated to Israel's "special forces" that is illustrated with the photo of a distressed, wounded Israeli soldier supported by another. Another banner titled "The Israeli enemy army's battle ideology" is illustrated with a photo of seven Israeli soldiers crying. The display of such images is an example of political force today going back to the use of "the political sublime"[99] in the sense presented by Edmund Burke in 1756. Burke used the term "sublime" to refer to horrifying images, such as those of beheadings and torture in the pre-Enlightenment period, which invoke in the viewer a sense of intense emotion that is experienced as delight and awe.[100] The visitor to the Mleeta site is similarly invited to engage in delight and awe at Hizbullah's reducing the supposedly powerful Israeli army to a bunch of crying, injured men.

The second part of the exhibition is a vast outdoor space. A round, sunken area displays several Israeli military vehicles that Hizbullah took over after its many confrontations with the IDF. The vehicles are displayed in a way that signals impotence: One tank has its canon twisted, and military vehicles are placed upside down, tilted or embedded in rocks, their bombs scattered for viewers to stare at, becoming paralyzed, wounded, broken objects of the gaze. Tens of Israeli soldier helmets are arranged on the ground in a neat display, subjected to the ordering power of Hizbullah. Nearby, a path through the woods, where Hizbullah fighters engaged in live battles with Israeli soldiers, invites the visitor to walk in the fighters' footsteps, imagining their deeds and internalizing them. The path is lined with displays of Hizbullah's missile power, with signs showing photos of different missiles and descriptions of their capabilities, along with specimens of the actual missiles. The outdoor space is

العقيدة القتالية

لجيـش العـدو الإسـرائيـلي

Fig. 13. Banner at the Mleeta visitor center proclaiming "The Israeli enemy army's battle ideology." Photo taken on 12 September 2010.

immaculate and minimalist in its style, showing the aesthetic of war to full effect. It is a reminder of Marinetti's Futurist Manifesto of 1909:

> War is beautiful because it ushers in the dreamt-of metal-lization of the human body. War is beautiful because it enriches a meadow in bloom by adding the fiery orchids of machine-guns. War is beautiful because it combines rifle-fire, barrages of bullets, lulls in the firing, and the scents and smells of putrescence into a symphony. War is beautiful because it creates fresh architectures such as those of the large tank, geometrical flying formations, spirals of smoke rising from burning villages, and much else besides.[101]

Mleeta can be read as a propaganda site. Mowlana argues that the sociopolitical effect of propaganda is that it becomes autonomous, leaving no space outside the ideology it disseminates.[102] The presence of Mleeta in Lebanon is an attempt at expressing this totality of the commitment to militarization in Hizbullah's ideology. It is also a "permanent" record of symbolic victory which serves as a political

Fig. 14. An Israeli tank on display at the Mleeta visitor center in southern Lebanon in 2010.

and military deterrent. As Jervis argues, in relation to states, a "symbolic victory can lead others to see high resolve and risk-taking in a state's behavior. This image is apt to make other states retreat or act cautiously in conflicts with the first state."[103] If Hizbullah is viewed as a state metaphor in this way, Mleeta becomes a cautioning message to Hizbullah's political opponents within and outside Lebanon.

The victimized image

The image management strategy used by Hizbullah in reference to the points above has served to cultivate a high level of legitimacy for the group. Suchman defines legitimacy as "a generalized perception or assumption that the actions of an entity are desirable, proper, or appropriate within some socially constructed system of norms, values, beliefs, and definitions."[104] Hizbullah has cultivated this perception among the Shiites, the Lebanese at large and the Arabs by linking its behavior to shared beliefs among those different audiences, centered on ideas of freedom, dignity and justice. Hizbullah's supporters believe the group to be trustworthy, and the group in turn views this growing support as a sign that it could persevere in its chosen course of actions.

This sense of legitimacy was important for Hizbullah after it used its weapons against other Lebanese in May 2008. Hizbullah responded to criticism of its actions by framing the events as necessary to halt an American-backed conspiracy against it. This discourse was first declared by Hizbullah leader Hassan Nasrallah in a speech on 8 May 2008. Taking his cue from this speech, on 15 May, Hizbullah's political bureau chief Ibrahim al-Amin used this discourse strategically to defend Hizbullah's action on the ground, declaring that the events were necessary to prevent more serious events from occurring later on, meaning another civil war. Al-Amin created parallels between the May events and the 2006 war, expanding on Nasrallah's speech by implying that both events prevented further, bigger planned attacks on Hizbullah from being carried out.[105] This association between the two events also aimed at transferring the meaning of an event with positive connotations (the July 2006 war) onto a controversial one. This adaptation of discourse aimed to re-brand the May 2008 events as an act of self-defense (something stated by Nasrallah himself in his speech). Instead of being the aggressor that took over West Beirut, Hizbullah became the victim of an international conspiracy. The violence ended when Qatar intervened to mediate between all groups and orchestrated the signing of the Doha Accords that granted Hizbullah and its allies the right of veto in a newly formed cabinet headed by Saad Hariri, Rafic Hariri's son.

The events of May 2008 show how, in addition to the larger-than-life image that Hizbullah had created to cultivate legitimacy, it also resorted to victimization as an image management strategy to justify a departure from norms. This method of image management relied on a number of components. First, it used self-referential discourse that highly capitalized on Hizbullah's heroic legacy. Second, it used adaptable discourse that reframed events positively. Third, it relied on "support erosion"[106] to destroy public support for the STL, a key driver behind the 8 May violence, through equating Hizbullah's domestic opponents with Israel. Fourth, it made use of Hizbullah's legacy and legitimacy to "get away with" this departure from norms. As Suchman argues, "legitimacy is resilient to particular events, yet it is dependent on a history of events. An organization may occasionally depart from societal norms yet retain legitimacy because the departures are dismissed as unique."[107] Fifth, it relied on the strength of Hizbullah's brand to get through a controversial act. Peter van Ham argues: "Branding acquires its power because the right brand can surpass the actual product as a company's central asset."[108] In this case, the positive connotations invoked by Hizbullah's brand superseded the actual "product" it had become, a group involved in a violent attack on other Lebanese. Finally, it relied on Nasrallah's charisma, which had transformed the devotion of Hizbullah's followers into a sense of duty, leading those followers to obey his wishes regardless of the objective reality.[109] This is related to Nasrallah's having succeeded, as a charismatic leader, in building a relationship with his followers through presenting himself as a visionary, influencing his followers to the extent that they do not question his decisions or actions.[110]

The return to the discourse of victimization that began with the May 2008 events marked the start of a new phase in which victimization became a key tool for the group over the next three years as the Special Tribunal for Lebanon investigations took off, and leaked reports indicated that the tribunal would indict members of Hizbullah. Hizbullah engaged in a dedicated multiplatform media campaign to discredit the STL as an American and Israeli conspiracy against "the resistance." Al-Manar's and al-Intiqad's news coverage of STL developments consistently presented the court as non-credible, while criticizing the Hariri government which backed the tribunal. On 9 August 2010, Nasrallah gave a televised speech in which he attempted to show that Israel was actually responsible for the murder of Rafic Hariri. What is notable about this speech is that it utilized a number of visual tools. Nasrallah screened video footage intercepted from Israeli drones to show that Israel had followed closely the path taken by Hariri in his daily commute. The speech also included recorded reports using PowerPoint slides referencing Israeli statements about the STL as well as presenting key points about Lebanese collaborators with Israel. The reports and videos were intercut with Nasrallah's live commentary on them as he assumed the air of a professor or a legal investigator. In a reply to a journalist from the Iranian Arabic-language al-Alam television channel in the question and answer session that followed the two-hour speech, Nasrallah spoke directly about the necessity of image management:

> The main aim of the indictment is to tarnish the image of Hizbullah and to show Israel as being innocent. So there is a battle of public opinion. Some spent 500 million dollars – only in Lebanon, what they had spent in other countries or on other satellite stations they didn't say – [...] for the sake of tarnishing the image of Hizbullah. So there is a war of image,

of public image and public opinion. We are very cautious and we very much want to uncover the truth and we are also very much concerned, in waging this war of public opinion, to say that the resistance is subject to injustice.[111]

Hizbullah went on to "confirm" this injustice in October 2010 when two STL investigators visited a gynaecological clinic in southern Beirut to obtain some documents. The investigators were attacked by an angry mob of women and the incident was framed by Nasrallah as a response to an insult to women's honor. The attack was also presented by Hizbullah as a "spontaneous" reaction by wronged "ordinary people."[112] In doing so, Hizbullah extended the sense of victimization from itself to the Shiite community as a whole.

The challenge of the Arab Spring

Hizbullah's return to the victimization framework became a useful tool when the Arab uprisings started in December 2010. Hizbullah initially praised Arabs who had finally risen to claim their rights, especially that the Tunisian, Egyptian, Libyan and Bahraini uprisings were deemed to be useful occasions to advance Hizbullah's political position regionally. The first provided an opportunity to affirm Hizbullah's mistrust of the West. Following the fleeing of President Zine El-Abidine Ben Ali from Tunisia, and the refusal of European countries to host him, Hassan Nasrallah gave a televised speech on 16 January 2011 where he said he wanted to "congratulate the Tunisian people for their historic revolution as well as praise their bravery. But we must draw a lesson from that revolution. The lesson, above all, is this: the Ben Ali regime and its entourage have always served the interests of France, the United States, and the West in general, but now no Western power takes them in."[113] The second was an occasion to delight in the fall of a political nemesis. After Hosni Mubarak was forced to step down from the Egyptian presidency in February 2011, Hizbullah responded by issuing a statement in which it said it "congratulates the great people of Egypt on this historic and honorable victory, which is a direct result of their pioneering revolution."[114] This quick embrace was in no small part due to Mubarak's previous accusation of Hizbullah of masterminding planned attacks in Egypt aimed at destabilizing his regime, which led to the arrest of a member of the party in 2009.[115] The third was a ready made "revenge" against the regime that had kidnapped the prominent Shiite leader Imam Musa Sadr in the 1970s. It took less than a week from the start of anti-Muammar Qaddafi protests in Libya for Hizbullah Member of Parliament Hussein Moussawi to speak out, calling on the international community to rid Libya of Qaddafi, after its silence regarding the disappearance of Sadr in Libya in 1978, and condemning Qaddafi for slaughtering his people.[116] But Hizbullah reserved the most attention for the people of Bahrain, a Shiite majority country, as the protests began in Manama on 14 February 2011 and were met with a crackdown by the Sunni government. Careful not to invoke sectarianism, Hizbullah's discourse on Bahrain was cloaked in nationalist terms. Its website carried a banner declaring "Save the people of Bahrain," and Nasrallah blamed the Bahraini regime for painting the protests in sectarian terms. In doing so, Hizbullah was attempting to capitalize on an opportunity to reach out to a wide audience all over the Arab world.

But as the protests across the region gained momentum, Hizbullah's support became also driven by a sense of marginalization: The Arab Spring had stolen the limelight from Hizbullah as its status as the sole representative of Arab dignity had been shattered. Hizbullah's efforts faced a further challenge when anti-regime protests started in Syria, one of its key allies. Hizbullah took the Syrian government's line in blaming the protests on "foreign forces," and tried to spin the uprising as an American-Israeli conspiracy, using its familiar self-referential frameworks, a similar strategy to the one used to discredit the Green Movement in Iran in 2009. In an article on Hizbullah's main website on 28 June 2011, Naziha Saleh wrote:

> The US went back to its planning room to work on its ever existing project of the "New Middle East" – after the "Israeli" failure in achieving it in the July war 2006, and after the US failure in hitting the stability in Iran, which is considered as the supporter of the resistance. To choose Syria because it is the protector of the resistance and the only Arab country that still stands in the face of "Israel" for the Arab rights. In striking Syria, the US can achieve its goal and make the dream come true to isolate Iran geographically and politically after the UN economic sanctions resolution.[117]

Hizbullah paralleled this discourse about an American-Israeli plot with another audiovisual attack on the STL after indictments naming four Hizbullah members as involved in the murder of Hariri were issued in

July 2011. Nasrallah gave another speech on 2 July during which he displayed images of documents he claimed linked the tribunal with Israel.

The Arab Spring and the STL indictments presented a set of complex challenges for Hizbullah's image management strategy. Audiences across the Arab world were too concerned with the Arab Spring to pay much attention to Hizbullah, while the STL indictments created a sense of doubt about Hizbullah's trustworthiness in the eyes of some of its Lebanese and non-Lebanese supporters. Hizbullah attempted to spin the STL as an international conspiracy, leading the party to recycle its discourse of victimization. The fall of the regimes in Egypt and Tunisia also derailed the centrality of the image of Hizbullah as an Arab hero. With dignity and heroism having become within the reach of the average Arab citizen after the Arab Spring, victimization was the only avenue left for Hizbullah to stand out in a region that was witnessing a rise in individual agency outside the umbrella of political organizations, a factor that Hizbullah's image management strategy had never had to address before. Hizbullah tried to extend this framework of victimization to its Syrian ally, but this became harder to "sell" to Arab audiences as the flow of visual evidence from Syria attesting to the brutality of the regime against its people continued. A year after the start of the Syrian uprising, Hizbullah's Lebanese political opponents were speaking out loudly against its blind support of the Assad regime, with some comparing Hizbullah to the falling authoritarian regimes in the region[118], and others saying that the party has been blind to the transformations taking place in the Arab world, which will eventually result in a serious threat to its power.[119] As the international community as well as Arab citizens across the region took the side of the Syrian protesters, Hizbullah's utter support for the Assad regime became, at best, a source of embarrassment for a party that for the first time in its history seemed unable to adapt its political and communication strategies. The Arab Spring, then, put Hizbullah on a crossroads, not only stealing its limelight, but also testing its credibility in the Arab world, and consequently, its longevity.

Image management lessons

Hizbullah's image management trajectory offers a number of important lessons. First, image management strategy succeeds when a group can bridge the gap between the way it perceives itself and the way others perceive it, rather than remaining focused on the validity of its ideologies vis-à-vis those of others. The smaller the distance between those perceptions, the higher the degree of success of the image management strategy. Second, no image management strategy can succeed if it lacks credibility. Hizbullah has consistently relied on notions of justice and liberty to prove its legitimacy to its audiences, claiming to represent the voices of the people and to seek "justice" for victims of Israeli aggression, while branding itself as a "liberator" and "defender" of land and people. But this image was threatened as the Assad regime in Syria turned its weapons on its own people during the Arab Spring, as opposed to directing them towards the Israeli "enemy" in the occupied Golan Heights.

Finally, there is a need for a dynamic relationship between image management strategy and changing political contexts. Hizbullah's evolving image management strategy is part of the party's place within a larger political opportunity structure[120] where "fixed or permanent institutional features combine with more short-term, volatile, or conjectural factors to produce an overall particular opportunity structure."[121] Before the Arab Spring, Hizbullah had been largely successful at taking advantage of changes in the political environment to carve a favorable image, and simultaneously, to adapt its image according to changes in the environment. This highlights the fine balance that exists between political adaptability and reliability, which in turn generates trust. The Arab Spring has proven that this formula is perhaps the hardest to crack by any political group involved in image management, even a group with a long legacy of success like Hizbullah.

3

The Politics of (In)visibility in Iran

Iran is a country in seemingly permanent flux. Since the Islamic Revolution of 1979, Iran has been witnessing a tension between hard-line supporters of the regime and others who are either disillusioned with the path the Islamic Republic has taken or who feel alienated from what it represents. This struggle is both political and social, but it is also cultural; it is a struggle over the meaning of being Iranian, over cultural expression and over Iran's role and image in the Middle East and beyond. Since the election of Mahmoud Ahmadinejad in 2005, this tension has intensified as the regime's opponents, including supporters of the Reformists, felt that Iran had taken a step backwards into further conservatism and international isolation. But despite attempts by the Reformists as well as by Iranian liberals to express their opposition to state discourse and policies, it is the Iranian regime that has so far had the upper hand regarding public discourse and policy. Consequently, it is the regime that has had the most visibility in Iran; oppositional voices and images have been marginalized, and very often silenced.

The Green Movement in Iran, which started in 2009 as a reaction to the re-election of Ahmadinejad, which the Reformists saw as fraudulent, was the first time since the Islamic Revolution that the masses in Iran took to the streets in political protest against the regime on a large scale. It was an attempt at challenging the invisibility imposed on public oppositional discourse. For several months, the world's gaze turned to Iran, as the carefully managed image of the state was being challenged on a global scale: The social media transmitted images of protest from Tehran's streets to the whole world. And yet, the Iranian regime's brutal reaction to the Green Movement quelled the flow of such images as the state sought to monopolize politics as well as the realm of the visible once more.

This tension between visibility and invisibility manifests itself prominently in Iranian visual culture. In particular, state-sanctioned images like those in state art or images broadcast on state television present imaginings of the nation and its people that clash with those in images created by oppositional actors. Yet, while a significant body of literature exists on visual culture in Iran, from state art to contemporary art to publicly displayed artifacts, those different modes of visual representation are almost always addressed individually, without enough attention to the interplay of messages across different visual mediums. The aim of this chapter is to examine the clashing images of the state and oppositions in Iran through addressing all those modes together. Put together, the image of Ahmadinejad, images on Iranian state television, state-created posters and murals, cemetery and museum displays, contemporary art exhibits and Green Movement protest images reveal the power dynamics underlying those images as they comment on, reference and/or resist one another, demonstrating the central role that the image has been playing in Iranian politics since 2005. The chapter's content aims to highlight three key points. First, despite the authoritarian state's dominance over the public discursive field, authoritarian states only offer an illusion of totality. Their own crafted images often carry within them elements that undermine the very messages those images are meant to disseminate. Second, understanding the power dynamics underlying political struggles between the state and oppositional actors – in Iran and elsewhere – necessitates looking at the exchanges between the two sides across the online and offline worlds and across mediums and representations. In the case of Iran, this is not a dialogue, but a tense altercation whereby each side attempts to overcome the other. Looking at the role of the image in this altercation alerts us to the "hidden" strength of oppositional voices who resist through visual reversal, appropriation and presence. As such, and despite the dominance of the state and state discourse in Iran, there remain pockets of resistance that threaten to undermine the total authority of the ruling regime. Finally, the relative invisibility of oppositional actors in the public domain dominated by the authoritarian state does not mean that they are absent, or that they completely lack power. And that is why it is important to look beyond the traditional realm of "hard" politics to get a fuller picture of power struggles within authoritarian states.

Ahmadinejad's disenfranchised image

The election of Ahmadinejad came after two terms served by Reformist Mohamed Khatami during which Iran witnessed a degree of opening up on social and political levels, as well as promises of considerable economic progress. However, because of external factors like increasing oil prices and internal factors like the inability of the Reformists to organize themselves effectively, Khatami was limited in what he could achieve, and Iranians, particularly those in remote, rural areas, felt disillusioned with him. This sentiment was in no small part a product of tactics used by Khatami's conservative opponents to transform him "from a beacon of hope into an object of ridicule and the epitome of political impotence."[1] What added to the Reformists' isolation was their pursuit of reconciliation with the USA, which backfired with the rise of Bush-era neoconservatives, as the Reformists came to be associated with the Bush agenda. In addition, the conservatives in Iran crippled the Reformists' political power, with the Guardian Council severely limiting the number of Reformists who were allowed to run for Shura elections both in 2004 and in 2008 (leading the Reformists to eventually boycott the 2012 Shura elections).[2]

The Reformists also lost support among their own constituents. Khatami's victory in the 1997 presidential campaign was partly due to the role of small media, such as *Asterma* and *Salaam* newspapers, *Zanan* magazine, flyers, university bulletins and the local press and radio, which were all used to campaign for him. The importance of those small media lies in that they are the mass communication tools relied on by oppositional intellectuals, who are excluded from the mainstream media in Iran, to reach a wider public.[3] But by 2005, when Ahmadinejad was elected, those levels of support had disappeared. Khatami's media advisor, Hadi Khaniki, relates this to the lack of activism by intellectuals and non-governmental organizations (NGOs) who had previously acted as communication go-betweens linking Khatami with the people. In the Reformists' point of view, part of the blame laid with those elites in Iran who failed to connect them with the "masses."[4] But this lack of activism reflected a wider sentiment, as a large proportion of the Iranian population was disheartened when it did not see the vast improvements it had anticipated to witness after eight years of Reformist rule under Khatami.

Another hurdle for the Reformists was that their main appeal was to the urban middle class, particularly in Tehran, and they fell into the trap of primarily addressing those constituents in the 2005 presidential election at the expense of other social groups. According to Hadi Khaniki, the campaign messages used by the Reformists in the election were not accessible to the majority of the people. In an interview in 2008, he illustrated the difference between the Reformists' and conservatives' campaign messages at the time through reciting this metaphorical story: In a village where the inhabitants have low literacy, one man tried to communicate with the people through holding up a placard that spelt the word "snake," while another man simply held up an image of a snake.[5]

Unlike the Reformists, Ahmadinejad knew how to address those alienated masses. In his first presidential campaign, he used a tactic that had previously helped Khatami win the presidential election: He presented himself as coming from outside the "formal sphere" of politics.[6] Yes, he was the mayor of Tehran, but he was politically unknown. Ahmadinejad used this outsider status to manipulate the media. One time during his election campaign, while giving a live television interview, he suddenly announced, "Now that I'm talking to you, the electricity will be cut in some parts of the country to prevent my voice from being heard." Ahmadinejad created an image of himself as a victimized candidate who stood for the victimized in society. To emphasize this point, he deliberately did not use traditional political campaigning tools like political posters in abundance, saying he could not afford a professional campaign (although he did use promotional videos).[7] But he made sure that when he appeared in the media, he was represented interacting with the elderly and with villagers. In this sense, his campaign revolved around populist matters rather than political ones, and Ahmadinejad's image served to affiliate him with the "average" person on the street. He also announced an economic policy based on direct monetary handouts to the needy. In doing so, he appealed to the poor, who, as Bayat argues, are more interested in "strategies and associations that respond directly to their immediate concerns" than in political programs.[8] He also followed the regime line in invoking the Iran–Iraq war as a campaign rallying tool, referencing the war in one of his promotional videos.[9] Coupled with a background that associated him with the Basij, referencing the war was a legitimacy tool for Ahmadinejad, emphasizing his revolutionary credentials.

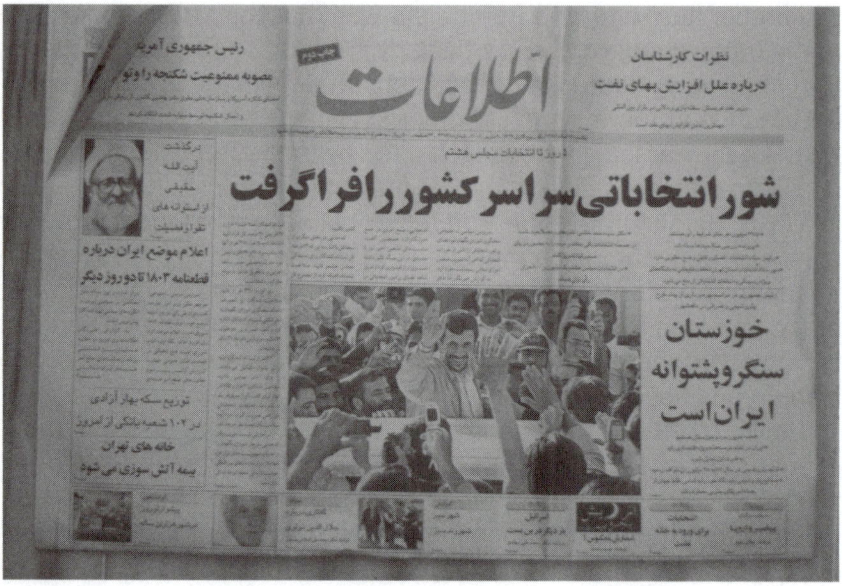

اطلاعات

نظرات کارشناسان
درباره علل افزایش بهای نفت

شور انتخاباتی سراسر کشور را فرا گرفت

اعلام موضع ایران درباره
قطعنامه ۱۸۰۳ تا دو روز دیگر

توزیع سکه بهار آزادی
در ۱۰۲ شعبه بانکی از امروز

خانه های تهران
بیمه آتش سوزی می شود

خوزستان
سنگر و پشتوانه
ایران است

Fig. 15. The front page of *Etela'at* newspaper on 9 March 2008 depicting Ahmadinejad being photographed by an adoring crowd in Iran.

Ahmadinejad continued this legacy after his election as president, weaving his image around three key themes: popularity, religion and resistance. He arranged for DVDs of his tours to provincial areas to be sold[10], and was keen to be photographed surrounded by ordinary people, especially if they were holding up their mobile phone cameras to take his photo. He reveled in disseminating photographs of himself with world leaders. Two such photos published in the Iranian photography magazine *Iran Aks* in 2008 show Ahmadinejad next to Bashar al-Assad and Hugo Chavez respectively, mirroring their body language. As such, he intended to project the image of a leader respected on a global scale (the irony of the choice of other leaders in the photographs notwithstanding). He also developed a reputation for excessive devoutness. In November 2005, he declared that the Hidden Imam Mahdi would appear in two years, and after his first speech at the United Nations, he excitedly spoke of how he was cloaked in the Imam's green halo during the speech.[11] While such pronouncements resulted in ridicule among many, they endeared the president to his core constituents who could identify with his earthy religiosity. He also cultivated an image as a leader who is defiant to Israel, giving speeches promising defeat over the "Zionist entity" and sponsoring public events such as a Holocaust denying conference

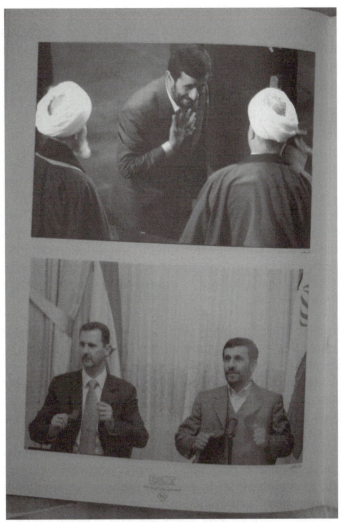

Fig. 16. Photos of Ahmadinejad, the lower with Assad of Syria, in *Iran Aks* magazine in March 2008.

in 2006 and an anti-Israeli cartoon competition in 2008. As such, Ahmadinejad was not only the creator of his own image, but also the producer of visual political statements in the public domain.

The image as a regime tool

Ahmadinejad's production of images falls comfortably within a wider context in Iran. Since its inception, the Islamic regime has been a prolific producer and user of images carrying religious and political meanings that are intended as a mechanism of control over the people, as well as a means of "selling" Iran's image abroad. One of the key arenas of image production and use for the Iranian regime is art. Art functions as political propaganda for totalitarian states, and Iran is no different.[12] Writing about the use of political posters during the Islamic Revolution, Haggai Ram writes that "the Revolution and its art were mutually constitutive."[13] As the 1979 Revolution in Iran was an Islamic one, Iranian state art is, not surprisingly, often infused with elements of Shiite Islamic aesthetic traditions. As Flaskerud writes about Shiism in Iran,

> [a]esthetic practices are an important arena for the construction and preservation of the religious community. In Iranian Shiism an image is perceived as a discursive field with which viewers can engage mentally and emotionally... Such cognitive processes can transform emotions and generate cultic behavior... Images... may serve to endorse religious dogma.[14]

Through associating political ideology with religious dogma in its propaganda, the Iranian regime cloaks its political ideology with an unchallengeable dogmatic air.

But state art is also secular. The state media in Iran, street art, photographs, cartoons, paintings, museum exhibitions and even cemeteries are all used as visual tools to disseminate state ideology. As Chelkowski says, "[b]y the 1980s, the Islamic Republic of Iran was in full semiotic control of the representation of itself, and serves as a dramatic example of how collectively held symbols – appearing in murals, graffiti, postage stamps, banknotes, posters, and primary-school textbook illustrations – were used to mobilize a people."[15] This use of images is still relevant in today's Iran, and until 2009, the images were largely characterized by a uniformity of discourse; the visual message that the Iranian regime was sending to its people was largely in harmony with that sent to those outside. The Green Movement challenged this harmony as the Iranian state strove to quell internal dissent while trying to cultivate a credible image abroad, particularly within the Arab and Islamic worlds.

The image of the Iran–Iraq war

One of the key themes in images created by the Iranian regime is that of the Iran–Iraq war. The eight-year war has become a defining component of the identity of the Islamic Republic, as it was a war triggered by the establishment of this Republic, which Iraq's then president Saddam Hussein saw as a political and military opportunity. Iraq's instigation of the war has resulted in its being known as "the imposed war" in Iran, a war that merges victimization, defense and heroism. The war is commemorated continuously in Iran, and this commemoration serves two main functions. First, it creates national cohesion. The war can be seen as an example of an invented, cohesive tradition, a tool of nationalism based on "collective group self-presentation."[16] Second, it serves as a method of political mobilization. As Gershoni and Jankowski argue, commemoration serves as "a powerful tool of social manipulation," a means to bring order and give purpose to the community by instilling its individuals with a shared sense of mission and molding them into an effective collectivity committed to the achievement of common goals."[17]

The war is remembered in several expressive arenas, keeping its memory alive in the minds of the Iranian public. This memory is important as it carries with it several layers of meaning: the image of the founder of the Iranian Islamic Republic, Ayatollah Ruhollah Khomeini, as a quasi-divine figure; the image of the current Supreme Leader Ali Khamenei as the carrier of the legacy of Khomeini; the sense of victimization by the Islamic state as it went under attack by its Arab neighbor; and the sense of sacrifice permeating Iranian society, where families from across the social spectrum have invested in the Islamic state through martyrs who died in the war. It is the latter two connotations that have driven the Iranian state to infuse the memory of the war with a sense of an imposed burden that has been kept alive through the decades as a rallying mechanism for the Iranian people.

Even prior to the parliamentary elections in Iran in 2008, which were the first since Ahmadinejad's ascendency to the presidency, the war was a visible tool on Iranian state television. Like in Ahmadinejad's election campaign, the war has been continuously used as a means to encourage people to vote, acting as a national solidarity symbol. In 2008, for example, state television broadcast several promos asking people to vote. The promos presented footage of men and women in chadors putting ballots in boxes or waiting in line to vote, as well as footage of both Khomeini and Khamenei voting. This footage was coupled with that of tanks during the Iran–Iraq war, soldiers launching rockets and martyrs, which were intercut with images of fields of red tulips symbolizing the martyrs. This collage also included footage of anti-American and anti-Israeli demonstrations juxtaposed with images of fertile, farmed land. Public rallies were organized to encourage people to vote during which the war featured prominently. In one rally in Isfahan in March 2008, posters featuring graphic images from the war, such as those of mutilated bodies of children, were laid out on the grass next to the Si-o-seh bridge. The posters featured the caption: "The Imposed War: Defense vs. Aggression." In this sense, the image of the war constructed a very particular national narrative that transformed the act of voting into a national duty sustaining the country's defense of itself against enemies. Moreover, the election sequences on Iranian television, while masquerading as being about urging people to vote, invariably told people who to vote for. Khamenei and the conservatives were presented in the sequences as the protectors of the legacy of the war, and by extension, of the Iranian state. Voting for their candidates, then, was implied to be an existential matter for the Iranian nation.

State visual art

The Iran–Iraq war is not only visually present in the media and election posters. It is also dominant in art created and sponsored by

Fig. 17. A poster in Tehran supporting the Shura elections, depicting Khomeini and Khamenei and proclaiming "Elections are a holy duty." Photo taken on 7 March 2008.

the Iranian regime. Visual art is one of the defining products of the Iranian revolution. As Chelkowski and Dabashi say in their study of this art, visual art constitutes "a powerful mechanism of persuasion" for the "self-generating myth of 'the Islamic Revolution'."[18] Writing about Nazi Germany, Boris Groys says that Hitler saw art as being heroic because it gives shape to reality, and that Hitler's vision of art was not focused on the production of "good" art, but on how this art can itself produce "the mass of viewers who will react correctly to this art even in the distant future."[19] Art, then, is a mechanism of productive power in the Foucauldian sense, through which the regime produces reality for its people, and at the same time, produces a lasting normative framework for interpreting state ideology.[20] As such, Iranian state art is an example of hegemony, an "order of signs and practices, relations and distinctions, images and epistemologies – drawn from a historically situated cultural field – that come to be taken for granted as the natural and received shape of the world and everything that inhabits it."[21]

Perhaps the best example of the way state visual art functions to create routinized ideology for the Iranian people is murals.[22] Cities in Iran, particularly Tehran, are densely populated with large murals, most of which have existed since the days of the Iran–Iraq war, when the Iranian government encouraged and sponsored the creation of this art form to "advertise, disseminate, and solidify the basic tenets of the Islamic republic."[23] Although the creation of murals has lessened significantly since the end of the war[24], this art form remains a means through which the Iranian regime communicates with people on an everyday basis. The murals subordinate public space to the power of the state, colonizing it with a dogmatic ideological message. This ideological message serves to situate Iran within a wider political context, as a state that resists American hegemony and supports the Palestinian cause. An example is a prominent mural in Tehran that represents the American flag, where the red stripes are shown to be dripping blood, and the stars are changed to falling bombs, and which is captioned with the words "Death to America" in a large font. This mural, as well as the site of the American embassy in Tehran, which has been occupied by the Basij since the storming and siege of the embassy in 1979, "are aimed at both a local and (putatively) American audience, [and] harness the combined power of word-and-image in order to transform the public domain into a virtual battleground for ideological supremacy."[25] Another example is Palestine Square in Tehran, which, in addition to its name, features a sculpture and murals denouncing Israel and affirming Iran's support for the Palestinians. Both the anti-American and pro-Palestinian messages are aimed at both an outside audience and at Iranians. For the former, the messages communicate defiance (US) and solidarity (Palestine). For the latter, the messages legitimize the regime's sponsorship of Palestinian groups like the Islamic Jihad by presenting Iran's patronage as a pillar of its political leadership in the Middle East.

Although they often rely on the interplay of word and image, the murals, as a mainly visual medium, "lend visual coherence to the political message expressed through the image."[26] This visual coherence is strengthened as most of the murals, despite the multiplicity of their aesthetic references, from Soviet-style patterns to Palestinian *fida'i* posters[27] to religious *pardeh*, and despite their stylistic evolution over time, still follow a harmonious aesthetic style that blends expressionism, vibrant colors and recognizable visual motifs like the use of red tulips to symbolize martyrs and halos around the heads of spiritual leaders. In this way, the murals also embody a particular aesthetic experience that privileges a defined mode of artistic expression and style.[28]

A key characteristic of the murals is that they visually convey the regime's merger of politics and religion. This is mainly seen in representations of the Supreme Leader (Khomeini, then Khamenei). The practice of placing rulers' portraits next to those of saints is an established method of cultivating legitimacy.[29] The image of Khomeini in the murals is the product of an effort by Iran's clergy to sacralize him after his death. Ansari argues that this effort was necessary to secure Khamenei's position as Khomeini's successor: "Charismatic succession could be secured and prolonged only if Khomeini's role was itself defined and historically secure."[30] The murals extend Khomeini's holiness to Khamenei. One mural shows the image of both men under a quote from the Quran instructing people to "obey God, obey the prophet, and obey your guardians." This holy message in the murals is mirrored in other visual forms. For example, a public information film produced by Iranian state television "sought to interpose the events of 1979 with the rise of Islam, drawing barely disguised parallels between Khomeini and the Prophet Muhammad and, perhaps more strikingly, between Imam Ali and Khamenei, whose first name was Ali, and who was now being introduced as 'the Ali of the Age'."[31] Having established the holy status of Khamenei, the regime in turn sought to use his image to direct political processes. During the Shura elections in 2008, public space in Iran was saturated with billboards featuring

Khamenei's picture, sometimes placed alongside that of Khomeini – a reminder of his status as the carrier of the legacy – but often on its own, coupled with written messages asking people to vote.

Another key characteristic of the murals is their focus on martyrs. The Iran–Iraq war left an estimated one million Iranians dead, and it is noted for its use of suicide operations by the Iranian army and Basij.[32] Murals of martyrs "serve to turn city walls and building surfaces into pictured metaphors for resistance, as well as dramatic icons of collective self-defiance in the face of devastation."[33] The murals commemorate both the victimization of the soldiers and their sacrifice through granting them a holy status endowed by Khomeini. One mural has the image of Khomeini looking over a poppy field in which a soldier's helmet is lying. Flags in the background carry the slogans "Death to America" and "We heed your call, Khomeini." Another commemorates Basij martyrs through representing a young man with a gun, again with the image of Khomeini at the top. A third depicts the Hidden Imam Mahdi, his face unseen as it is covered with a white cloth, cradling the body of a martyr. The mixing of messages invoking "God, nature, fate, life, [and] death" with political messages is normally seen as a way in which art "confronts finite, political power with images of the infinite."[34] Yet in Iran, this mixing is

Fig. 18. A faded mural depicting Khomeini and an Iranian martyr in Tehran. Photo taken on 8 March 2008.

not a confrontation; it is a way of merging "revolutionary realism" with "revolutionary romanticism,"[35] with the images of the infinite lending this quality to the regime's political power, and in turn, infusing the regime with "total social authority."[36]

The image of martyrs

The image of martyrs, then, is a key strategy for the Iranian regime to effect compliance. It is also a legitimating strategy, since contemporary representations of martyrdom in Iran are linked to those in Persian as well as Shiite literary and historical traditions[37]; in other words, the representations create legitimacy through the invocation, invention and appropriation of culturally resonant symbols.[38] In addition to the image of martyrs in television and film products, murals and posters, Iran is a prolific producer of quotidian products containing images of martyrs, from postcards to calendars. Such products are sold in the gift shops of places like the cemetery Behesht-e Zahra, the largest cemetery in Iran containing the graves of 200,000 people, most of whom martyrs from the Iran–Iraq war, and the Shohada Museum in Tehran, a museum primarily dedicated to the commemoration of martyrs.

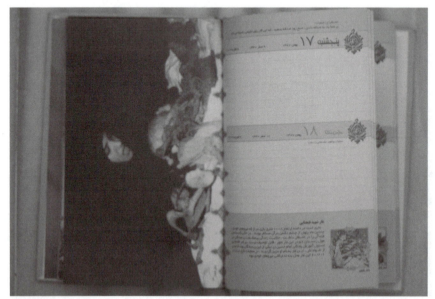

Fig. 19. A diary on sale at the gift shop of Behesht-e Zahra in March 2008, depicting a woman cradling the skeleton of a martyr.

Behesht-e Zahra is notable for being the site where Khomeini gave his first speech after returning to Iran from exile, and the exact location of the event is marked by a pedestal in the cemetery. Behind it, a giant billboard with Khomeini's image, his arm raised, greets the visitors, as a photo of crowds extending their arms towards him forms another part of the image, along with the colors of the Iranian flag, flowers (symbolizing the martyrs on earth) and birds (symbolizing them in heaven). The martyrs, then, are constructed as having sacrificed their lives for Khomeini, the nation and God. This link is brought to the present in another billboard in the cemetery that displays photos of the dead bodies of martyrs along with the picture of Khomeini and Khameini, both looking down and smiling. This display of dead bodies as a spectacle is part of a wider religious narrative tradition, including in Western-Christian history, through which suffering is understood.[39] But in Iran the spectacle of the dead body has a further meaning. A third billboard in Behesht-e Zahra features the photograph of another body of a martyr: Wrapped in a white shroud, but with the face and feet of the martyr showing, the body is laid out on the floor, covered with rose petals. Behind it a row of women in black chadors sit, some carrying the martyr's photos, and on either side of it, candles are lit. A caption in English, Arabic and Farsi presents a quote by Khomeini: "Marriage of the Good (people). A nation who [sic] considers martyrdom as its own prosperity is a vicoryius [sic, victorious] nation." As such, martyrdom is constructed as something to be celebrated, a source of power, transforming Behesht-e Zahra into a site of national pride. The entrance sign to the cemetery itself carries an Arabic statement by Imam Ali echoing this: "Life is in your death as conquerors and death is in your life as the oppressed."

The cemetery's visual messages are layered. On one hand, we have the graves of the martyrs themselves and the objects displayed on those graves, and on the other hand, we have the billboards discussed above, offering the visitor a particular framework through which to interpret the images of the martyrs buried there. It is customary for the relatives of the martyrs buried at Behesht-e Zahra to regularly visit the site to clean and decorate their graves and pray for their souls, especially during weekends and national and religious holidays. As such, the site of Behesht-e Zahra serves as a place of invented tradition that unites people in ritual.[40] In this function, it is linked with the site of the grave of Imam Khomeini in Tehran, which, despite his holy status, is a large complex with fast food and gift shops, where people go in their leisure time – more similar in its layout and function to a shopping mall than a holy shrine. Both sites are places for the routinization of state ideology. But Behesht-e Zahra goes further in that it invites people to internalize the culture of martyrdom. Several glass cabinets over individual graves, in addition to displaying photographs of the martyrs in life and/or death, prayer books, pictures of the Imams Hassan and Hussein, photos of the Supreme Leaders and the national flag, also display mirrors. The mirrors transform the visitor into a potential martyr, and as such, are another visual tool for the exercise of "total social control" by the state over the dead and the living.

The Shohada Museum is another site where the cult of martyrdom is kept alive. The museum was established by the Martyrs Foundation (Bonyad-e Shahid) in 1981, and mainly exhibits photos and artifacts from the Iran–Iraq war that commemorate the war's martyrs. The Martyrs Foundation is a parastatal organization whose work extends beyond Iran as it also supports Hizbullah, Hamas and the Palestinian Islamic Jihad, with branches in Lebanon and Palestine. Like Behesht-e Zahra, the Shohada Museum serves as a site of memory and acts as a public archive, and can thereby be seen as an attempt at defining reality.[41] But it also has a different function from Behesht-e Zahra. It "works" as an ideological tool in a different way from the cemetery

Fig. 20. Graves at Behesht-e Zahra in Iran. Photo taken on 8 March 2008.

because of its form, i.e., because it is a *museum*. As Crane argues, "we rely on museums...to get the past 'right'...Museums are not supposed to lie to us."[42]

What aids museums in the process of defining the past (and in casting its shadow on the present and the future) is that the museum space is a narrative space telling a story through the order in which objects are organized.[43] The Shohada Museum is a narrative space instructing the visitor in Iranian state ideology through the display of objects linked with martyrs. The narrative told about Iran's past, present and future in this space has several components: The nation's military prowess is symbolized through the display of plastic models of tanks and grenades; its martyrs are introduced as representatives of ordinary Iranians, and this is achieved through the display of personal objects belonging to the martyrs: prayer beads, prayer books (featuring the photos of Khomeini and Khamenei), a karate uniform, education certificates, civilian clothes, eyeglasses, watches, slippers, a walking cane; and the religious dimension ensuring the endurance of its ideology is invoked in a poster on display representing the Hidden Imam Mahdi (as a white ghost) standing behind a man in a wheelchair looking out an open window onto a

Fig. 21. A glass case displaying the photograph, personal objects and official statement of an Iran–Iraq war martyr at the Shohada Musum in Tehran. Photo taken on 9 March 2008.

stormy sky. The museum also has a section dedicated to the children who died during the war, both civilian children and child fighters. Baby clothes, toys, dolls, hair ribbons, school bags and books and photos of innocent faces merge with the photo of a small boy posing in a swimming costume behind two torpedoes. Writing about the representation of children in Chinese Cultural Revolution posters, Stephanie Donald says that children in those posters act as political messengers signifying a hopeful future.[44] In the Shohada museum, on the other hand, children symbolize both an oppressed past and a defiant, ruthless future.

In all the forms above, the narrative of martyrdom is repeated and self-referenced. One can read this repetition as part of a wider

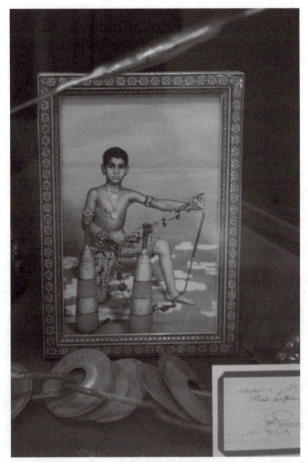

Fig. 22. A photo of a child martyr on display at the Shohada Museum in Tehran. Photo taken on 9 March 2008.

Shiite stylistic tradition. As Susan Sontag points out, the *ta'ziyeh* drama of the murder of Imam Hussein, which is performed repeatedly during Ashura and other religious occasions, does not lose its impact with the repetition; it is a narrative in which the *repetition* of the performance enhances the audience's engagement with it.[45] In other words, the power of martyr images lies in their repetition as it creates meanings that the viewer absorbs, anticipates and performs.

But there is a limit to the power of those images. In martyr imagery, displaying the dead has moved from the realm of the "other" (boosting the morale of one's fighters by showing them images of enemy casualties), to the realm of the self (boosting the morale by showing images of one's own casualties). Sontag writes that this visual display of images of martyrs is "intended to move and excite, and to instruct and exemplify."[46] More than just invoking a sense of victimization, the images also "invoke the miracle of survival."[47] The Shohada Museum displays several "before and after" photographs of martyrs, alive and then dead. The gift shop at Behesht-e Zahra also sells posters of dead soldiers, and calendars and postcards with graphic images of mutilated bodies. A striking photograph replicated in a number of products is that of a woman in a black chador cradling the skeleton of a person we can assume is her martyred son. The graphic images of dead bodies carry a shock value that can be seen as an incitement to compliance by the Iranian state. But the display of dead bodies of martyrs across visual forms, posters, murals, billboards, television promos, martyr "souvenirs," cemetery and museum displays, can have a desensitizing effect. As Sontag writes, "[s]hock can become familiar. Shock can wear off. Even if it doesn't, one can *not* look"; moreover, "[a]s one can become habituated to horror in real life, one can become habituated to the horror of certain images."[48]

Another limitation is that museums are constrained by their temporality. The longevity of objects on display inside the museum is an artificial one, a simulation of longevity, as those objects are subject to destruction (by accidents or time) or to being moved.[49] This temporality is also a feature of the murals on the streets of Iran. Most of the murals are faded, and a lot are obscured by trees that were obviously planted after the murals were painted, and which have grown to become natural curtains hiding the murals. The murals can be seen as visual symbols of a faded ideology that is removed from the present. But also, their daily presence in people's lives naturalizes

Fig. 23. "Before" and "after" photographs of a martyr displayed at the Shohada Museum in Tehran. Photo taken on 9 March 2008.

them to the degree of invisibility. And the very mirroring by the messages of the murals of those in the Shohada Museum, instead of reinforcing the messages, can be a limiting factor. This limitation is driven by the museum's form. As Groys argues:

> What is already presented in the museum is automatically regarded as belonging to the past, as already dead. If, outside the museum, we encounter something that makes us think of the forms, positions, and approaches already represented inside the museum, we do not see this something as real or alive, but rather as a dead copy of the dead past.[50]

The image of women

Women have traditionally been seen as symbols of the nation.[51] In Iran, women are part of the set of discourses used by the regime to present a progressive image of itself to the world and to its own people. The official line presented by state-sponsored images is a direct response to the stereotype of Islam as confining women to the private sphere; this response is a superficial one, relying on the message that women are not oppressed simply because they are not confined to the home.[52] This uniform discourse is reproduced in a variety of media, from television programs to films to photographic exhibitions, rendering those media visually coherent. In this section, I will focus on images of women displayed at the Shohada Museum, as it has a floor featuring an exhibition of photographs that form a good sample of regime images of Iranian women that exist in other mediums as well.

None of the women in the photographs in the Shohada Museum exhibition are depicted in the domestic arena. Instead, they are shown as active participants in public life. The photographs present women in these roles:

- Athletes (women in chador breaking a stack of wood at a martial arts competition; female rowers);
- Fighters (female parachutists; women writing graffiti alongside men during the Iran–Iraq war; female fighters carrying rifles during the Islamic Revolution);
- Political activists (women at a rally carrying photos of Khomeini; women at a demonstration against the ban on the veil in France, carrying placards spelling the word "Democracy" [in English] in the colors of the French flag; women at a pro-nuclear energy rally carrying a sign stating "Nuclear energy is our obvious right" [in English]);
- Political actors (female parliamentarians; women standing in line and carrying ballots as they wait to cast their votes);
- Medical workers (female nurses at a hospital; a female doctor in a white uniform fitting a man with an artificial limb);
- Musicians (female cello player at a classical musical concert, with the photo of Khamenei behind her).

The images in the Shohada museum mirror those displayed at the Museum of Contemporary Art in Tehran, which also has a smaller selection of photographs depicting women in public roles. A notable photograph in the collection is one of a female police officer veiled in black sitting at her desk, upon which a pair of handcuffs can be seen, as a male prisoner stands behind her in a cage.

Fig. 24. A photo of Iranian female athletes exhibited at the Shohada Museum in Tehran. Photo taken on 9 March 2008.

The images are highly aware of the symbolic dimension of women's dress and intend to acknowledge and subvert a "Western" conception of the veil as subjugating women.[53] They communicate a message in which Islam is presented as not being a barrier to women's achievements in the public domain. They are also aware of the public/private binary that governs "Western" stereotypes about Muslim women's relationship with men. However, the images fail to challenge those binaries. Instead of transgressing the binary through contesting it, the images simply move women from one side of the binary to the other. The photographs invariably *reinforce* the notion of Islam and veiling as a barrier, because it is as if they are saying that women are out in the public domain *despite* the veil and *despite* the political system being an Islamic one.

The women are moreover stripped of their political and social motivations and used as a tool to polish the image of the Iranian regime. The owner of a photograph is not the subject in it, but the person who took it. Regardless of whether the women in the photographs were posing for the camera or not, the photographs make them objects of the gaze and of a particular political framework that renders them powerless. This powerlessness becomes contradictory to the idea of political agency that the images are trying to convey. Take for example, the image of women voting. The photo assumes that the women are voting for regime candidates. Thus, the act of political participation is being repackaged to serve the ideological status quo that the women in the photo may well have been voting against. We do not know which names the ballots they are carrying have, or if they are blank. In other words, the photographs deny the women any chance of resistance by creating an illusion of agency. This illusion of agency serves to gloss over the subordinate status that women have under the Iranian regime. To reference just some basic examples, female singers are banned in Iran, and although more than 63% of university students in Iran are women (as one Iranian state promotional video boasts), women constitute only 12% of the Iranian work force.[54] It also serves to erase the struggle for equal rights that women in Iran are active in.[55] By presenting the condition of women in Iran as being unproblematic, the photographs both undermine women's own efforts and silence them. As Anne McClintock argues, "women are...constructed as the symbolic bearers of the nation but are denied any direct relation to national agency."[56]

The photos are symbolic of the dominant order in which women in Iran exist, and are a metaphor of the way authoritarian regimes approach the idea of citizenship. The citizen becomes an object owned by the state. There is a limit to this citizen's political will, but the citizen is expected to parade or to be paraded as a display of the regime's grace. Thus we can read the photograph of women parading in demonstrations, especially as they carry signs in English, as constructing the women as a display of the regime's power to outsiders. Being women, invoking the dominant Western discourse on women in Islamic countries (being hidden), they also become visual tools that aim at aiding the construction of legitimacy for the regime in the eyes of the West (though of course, judging by Iran's international political position, they have not been very successful in achieving this aim).

The photos are also undermined by their own sense of contradictory messages. Take for example, the photo of women demonstrating against the ban on the veil in French schools. That they are carrying placards in English demonstrates that their target audience is not just France, but the world. Holding up the word "Democracy," they are juxtaposing "Western" democracy with Iranian democracy, signaling that "real" democracy is "here." But the fact that they are veiled themselves makes this juxtaposition ironic. Iranian women must wear the veil because it is *imposed* by the state, yet in this demonstration they are protesting the veil's ban by another state. Both state practices meet in their subjugation of the bodies of women to political ideology.

This subjugation of women's bodies is also seen in another section of the Shohada Museum dedicated to Palestinian female suicide bombers. The display carries mostly official "martyrdom" photographs taken by the Islamic Jihad before the women's suicide operations, but a couple of images appear to be of the women as they lay dead. What is most striking about the display is its lack of political context. The images of the women are often juxtaposed with those of the coffins of Israeli soldiers, but there is no explanation (in the form of a sign or a placard) about which political group the women belong to. The only clue is in the scarves the women in the photos sometimes wear, which hint that they are members of the Islamic Jihad. In the absence of political context, the Iranian state is able to reduce the women into ideological tools. This is in line with Iran's stance towards the Palestinian-Israeli conflict, which is used both internally and externally as an ideological tool to reinforce the role of Iran as a legitimate political leader in the Middle East. The two discourses about women in the displays, of public life and of resistance, merge with and reinforce each other, blurring the line between the national and the regional. In this sense, the images of women can be seen as a method through which Iran is trying to preserve its internal status quo while carving a role for itself as a challenger to the political status quo in the Middle East, and also to the West.

Iran's exported image

The idealized image of women that the Iranian regime has created is part of a wider effort to export a favorable image of Iran. The Iranian state actively promotes "approved" visual art by Iranian women abroad through exhibitions and screenings of films by female artists at Iran's cultural centers.[57] Such activities are part of a multiplatform public diplomacy campaign involving the broadcast media, aid programs and cultural programs through which the Iranian state attempts to present an image of itself as an Islamic state that works, and as a "democratic" country. In a state video commemorating the anniversary of the Islamic Revolution that was screened at the Iran Light Cultural Center in London in February 2008, the voiceover proudly stated that Iran "presents a model of democracy for the world to emulate." The video also presented the holding of regular elections as a proof of Iran's true democratic practices. Of course, nothing was said about the country's vetting system of electoral candidates, which only allows those approved by the Guardian Council to actually run

Fig. 25. A banner featuring a female Palestinian suicide bomber at the Shohada Museum in Tehran. Photo taken on 9 March 2009.

for election. Securing large turnouts at elections is another "proof." In the Shura elections of 2008 and 2012, having a large voter turnout was presented as a show of national unity. On both occasions, Supreme Leader Ayatollah Ali Khamenei urged people to vote in order to present an image of Iranian solidarity and therefore regime legitimacy to the "enemies" abroad.[58]

But the March 2008 election was marked by an underlying discomfort. The government announced that no advertising for candidates was allowed on the streets in the period preceding the election. The Reformists interpreted that as an attempt to silence them; they believed that an election with a high participation rate would be one with a high Reformist success rate, especially in

95

Tehran, where they held the most support. Yet, despite the ban on individual campaign adverts, there were illegal candidate banners on the streets in Tehran, advertising the candidacy of conservatives. The Reformists said that the police only removed illegal banners for Reformist candidates. But most strikingly, the streets were full of billboards and posters featuring Supreme Leader Ali Khamenei. The slogan used on most billboards referenced a statement by Khamenei: "National unity, Muslim harmony." The use of images, slogans and historical references to secure a large turnout can then be read as an instrument for the conservatives to prove that they were still powerful.[59]

Until the Green Movement exploded on the international scene after Ahmadinejad's questionable re-election in 2009, Iran had largely succeeded in cultivating an image as a successful Islamic democracy in the eyes of some in the Arab world. That is partly because there was insufficient knowledge about internal Iranian politics in the Arab street. And because much of the Arab world did not elect its leaders, Iran gained from exporting an image of hosting competitive elections. This image was important for Iran as it aimed to expand its role in the Middle East, exploiting the decline of the influence of Saudi Arabia, and the rise of a Shiite current extending from the Gulf

Fig. 26. An Iran–Iraq war poster at a Shura elections rally in Isfahan on 13 March 2008.

through Iraq and into Syria and Lebanon. This shift in the balance of power allowed Iran to try appeal to Arabs, particularly in Lebanon and Syria, in a number of ways.

First, Iran tried to construct an image as a friend through the media. Since 2003, Iran has been broadcasting to the Arab world directly through the Arabic language television channel, al-Alam, which was established during the war on Iraq. The channel focuses on news from Iraq and Palestine but also monitors and reports on Israeli affairs. This was particularly the case during the Israeli attack on Lebanon in 2006, when the channel prioritized this issue in its news coverage and constructed Iran as a supporter of Lebanon in its crisis. When the uprising in Bahrain started in 2011, al-Alam dedicated significant air time to covering the events, focusing on the injustices imposed on Bahraini Shiites by the Bahraini regime.

Second, Iran attempted to construct an image as a favorable cultural and economic partner in Lebanon and Syria. In Syria, the Sayyida Zeinab shrine became a popular destination for Iranian pilgrims, and in Lebanon, the annual Iranian bazaar became a regular fixture where Iranian goods as well as cultural products like books were sold. Iran is also involved directly in health and reconstruction programs in Lebanon, like establishing the Bahman hospital and funding the rebuilding of areas destroyed by Israel in the 2006 war. Villages across southern Lebanon have benefited from Iranian money, and there is even an "Iran Garden" in the border town of Maroun al-Rass, which had seen some of the worst destruction in the war. Iran erected billboards all over the South marking its contribution. The billboards read: "The Zionist enemy destroys, the Islamic Republic of Iran builds."

Third, Iran tried to sell itself as a natural political partner. In Syria, posters featuring Bashar al-Assad, Hassan Nasrallah and Mahmoud Ahmadinejad together could be found on the streets of Damascus until the Syrian uprising of 2011, packaging Iran's alliance with Syria and Hizbullah as a resistant force against American imperialism and Zionism in the region. Iran's nuclear development program has been sold as a necessary component of maintaining sovereignty in the face of American pressure, used by Iran to cultivate an image of defiance that is deemed attractive to audiences across the Arab world. One striking feature of this image creation is a sculpture exhibited at the site of Imam Reza in Mashad, the holiest site in Iran, which is visited by pilgrims from across the globe. In the midst of the religious items on display in one of the site's museums, a glass case holds a green rock from which two hands extend upwards, while at the bottom, several test tubes with different colored powders are lined up. When I asked the tour guide accompanying me at the site about that particular display, he replied that Iran was proud of its nuclear development program.

As the chapter will later illustrate, the Green Movement served to undermine the Iranian state's exported image. This damage worsened after the Syrian uprising of 2011, when Iran did not only uphold an image of alliance to the Assad regime, but also provided logistical support to quell the Syrian revolution, emboldened by its own "success" in suppressing the Green Movement in 2009.

Oppositional art as a "free space" of visual resistance

Through the above discussion we can see that the Iranian regime has been trying to exercise a visual monopoly over *what* politics is visible and *how* this politics is represented. Oppositional representations are silenced in public space and in the media. But this silence is not total; the Green Movement drew the world's attention to oppositional visual representations both in public space (demonstrations) and in the media (blogs) in Iran's political sphere. But since before the Green Movement, visual resistance in Iran has also existed in a sphere that is often overlooked in analyses of political dynamics: art. Francesca Polletta argues against perceiving the cultural and political spheres as a dichotomy that separates culture from political structure and from the instrumental angle of protest.[60] Following this argument, it is important to pay attention to alternative representations created by Iran's contemporary artists, as those representations are firmly part of Iran's political sphere.

Of course, contemporary art is not alone as a visual communicator of oppositional politics. Independent film and blogs are now established forms of communicating resistance to the Iranian government's line[61], and independent Persian satellite television channels broadcasting from outside Iran in Farsi present a different version of the nation from that weaved through the state media. Iranian diaspora artists like Shirin Neshat and Marjane Satrapi are prolific producers of visual discourse that directly confronts the dominant discourse of the Iranian regime. But while those forms of visual resistance are often produced or consumed outside Iran (censorship being a key driver of this trend), oppositional visual representations that are both produced within Iran and are primarily and explicitly for domestic consumption are to be found within the blogging and the contemporary art scenes.[62] While it may be difficult to imagine how subversive artists have been able to display their work in the public domain in Iran, an explanation given by one of the artists in 2008 is that the government perceived this kind of art as a "safety valve," expressing resistant sentiment without posing a real threat. The art's impact was perceived by the state as limited, since only a small part of the population visits contemporary art galleries, and the art itself is often so symbolic in its suggestiveness that its messages may not be received automatically by a wide audience. This dismissal by the state ended up inadvertently supporting the creation and dissemination of resistant art.

This characterization of Iranian contemporary art as resistant art is not an absolute one, however. Iran's contemporary art movement (sometimes referred to as the New Art movement), which has partly been a product of the cultural opening up that occurred in Iran under Khatami's rule, is a vibrant scene, and several visual artists have achieved international acclaim. However, sometimes those artists' attempts to challenge the visual constructions of the regime end up achieving the opposite. Two key political implications exist. The first is that the attempt to challenge the regime's politics by ignoring it altogether and instead embracing "global" politics can result in "dislocated" art. As Iman Afsarian, an artist and member of the editorial board of the art journal *Herfeh Hunarmand*, put it in 2006:

> We are producing products that on many occasions have no connection with our needs or priorities. They cannot be lasting, because most of them have no connection with the artists' lived experience. A number of Iranian artists are living in the world of the internet, not in their own surroundings. Because of this, the "Twin Towers" is more interesting to them than events that are happening in their own country.[63]

But this statement must not be taken in an absolute sense either. As the artist Arash Hanaei said about his work "Abu Ghraib, or How to Engage in Dialogue," which recreates the scenes from Abu Ghraib using action men dolls, "Abu Ghraib images are more important than what happened in Abu Ghraib. We cannot talk about the Evin Prison," implying that the representation of events "outside" can be a metaphor for what is going on inside.[64]

The second implication is that attempts at appropriating state discourse can end up affirming exoticism, as exoticism is often what attracts the gaze of the coveted "other" and grants the artists international visibility. Afsarian says about artists engaging in such a practice,

> It sounds as if the only obsession for them is to be seen [in the West]; otherwise they do not exist... This might be a common problem for any artist anywhere. But I think here there is a difference, i.e., our artist needs to be seen by "others" not in his own society. In this scene he has to talk the "global" language which is New Art. He has to apply the latest artistic conventions and mix them with the popular political issues to be approved by them.[65]

An example of this is what artist Amirali Ghasemi calls "chador art," visual representations of Iranian women that focus on the chador as a symbolic marker of Iranian female identity. He says, "If you make work about women and religion, then you are almost guaranteed instant fame [in the West]."[66] The danger in this is that this kind of art, instead of presenting alternative meanings, ends up being complicit "with the dominant form by taking advantage of it."[67] The characterization of art as protest, then, does not apply to this kind of self-exoticizing art. It applies to the hub of committed artists whose political expression speaks to marginalized Iranians. It is not that those artists are unknown in the West, it is that their acclaim is not the result of courting the Western gaze through self-exoticism.

The fact that the artists oppose the regime also does not imply an automatic affiliation with oppositional political groups within Iran. What must be emphasized in the work of those artists is that they present an independent political vision. The artists are acutely aware of how their work could be appropriated for political purposes and some actively "self-curate" to prevent that from happening. Amirali Ghasemi, for example, said in 2008:

> I thought about creating a project on the use of web cameras in chat rooms, how people dress up etc. to talk through these cameras to people from the opposite sex. But I did not do it because I thought, the Reformists might use it as

an example of how Iranian society is progressing, or the conservatives might use it to clamp down on such activities and say how un-Islamic these practices are.[68]

In positioning themselves in a non-aligned space, the artists transform their art into an act of speaking, making the margin "a space of radical openness" that deconstructs political binaries.[69]

One artist whose work offers a sharp, oblique challenge to the status quo is Mahmoud Bakhshi Moakhar. In "Martyrs Kaleidoscope," Moakhar covered the unmarked graves of people who died under torture inflicted by the Iranian state with the Iranian flag, and digitally altered the images of the graves to make them aesthetically resemble images seen through the kaleidoscopes featuring pictures of holy sites that are commonly sold in Iranian souvenir shops. The project subverts dominant, government-created images of martyrs like the ones seen in Behesht-e Zahra, and calls for visibility of both those who died under torture – "they are martyrs too," says the artist – as well as the state's violence. In another project, "Air Pollution of Iran," he exhibited Iranian flags collected from public spaces, and which were all stained by pollution, a symbolic challenge of the sanitization of the image of the state that the regime presents to the world, and a message about the poisoned political atmosphere in Iran. The exhibition was closed down by the government after two days. In another project, "Farshfouroushi" (Carpet Bazaar), inspired by one of the entrances to the University of Tehran, where one has to step on the image of the American flag on the floor as one walks in, he created American flag carpets, placing one of them at the exhibition entrance, another hung on the wall and a third facing the *qibla* in Mecca, commenting obliquely on the political and religious rituals that the Iranian state imposes on its people.

Lisa Wedeen argues against the distinction between "resistant" art and "compliant" art that is often seen as acting as a "safety valve" for regimes. She sees this distinction as artificial because even "compliant" practices are ambiguous in their meanings and intentions.[70] It is this ambiguity that carries within it the seeds of protest. One of Moakhar's projects addresses the ambiguity of compliance. The project, "Rose Garden," featured a series of 64 dainty postcards featuring flowers. The project's ironic message was that this was the kind of art "approved" by the state, the "official art of Iran." Exhibiting this art becomes a form of critique that "passes" the censor yet undermines the power of the state under its very nose, a strategy mastered by Iranian artists who have had to find indirect ways of expressing oppositional politics. All of Moakhar's projects subvert dominant discourse on nationalism, religion and politics, and are infused with Iranian cultural signs because "I believe that you have to make work about your own [society's] problems."[71]

Another artist whose work challenges state discourse through appropriation is Homayoun Askari Sirizi. Three installations by him in consecutive years tell an evolving story. In 2005, shortly after the election of Ahmadinejad, Askari Sirizi worked on an exhibition titled "Test of Democracy." In this exhibition, he simply displayed, in a barren room, a post box, a ballot box, a charity donations box and a garbage can. Placing those four objects together in a neat line infused the act of placing a ballot in a box with banal connotations. This critique of democratic actions mirrored the wider malaise among liberals in Iran who had felt disappointed by the presidency's regressing towards further conservatism after the opening-up window offered during Khatami's period of rule. Askari Sirizi's work is an illustration of how, in the words of Groys,

> conceptual art...has demonstrated time and again its power by appropriating the iconoclastic gestures directed against it and by turning these gestures into new modes of art production. The modern artwork positioned itself as a paradox-object...as an image and as a critique of the image at the same time.[72]

Ahmadinejad's election brought Iran once again to the brink of confrontation with Israel, particularly after the July 2006 war between Hizbullah and Israel and the ongoing development of Iran's nuclear program. Askari Sirizi responded to this tension through an installation titled "A Preconceived War," a twist on the state's "The Imposed War." The installation consisted of a set of plastic containers laid side by side in a photographic dark room, containing "unfinished" photographs of war scenes. As one entered the room and proceeded to examine the content of the containers from right to left, one could make out images of bomb smoke and of urban destruction. The last container on the far left had a label with the caption "Unknown Martyr" in Farsi and English. Peering into the container, one would be confronted by his or her own image, as the container held not a photograph being developed, but a mirror. The installation thus appropriates the use of mirrors placed at martyrs' graves in Behesht-e

Fig. 27. "A Preconceived War" exhibition by Homayoun Askari Sirizi in 2006. Photo courtesy of the artist.

Zahra, which invite visitors to wish for the "gift" of martyrdom, lending the mirrors a new meaning as the message becomes one about the state leading its people to their deaths.

In another exhibition from November 2006 titled "Unofficial Methodology," Askari Sirizi displayed five plates on a wall that resembled pages from a medical ailments and surgery book. Each plate contained black and white photographs of human head organs, most in a state of decay. Underneath each set of organs, the artist provided a "methodology" for counting people. Plate VI had three photographs of eyes: one photograph of the site of a removed eye; one of two bruised eyes; and one of an infected eye. Underneath, the explanation stated:

"Head>Face>Eyes
Everyone has two eyes ordinarily.
Therefore, 70 counted eyes signify the existence of at least
35 people."

Plate V also displayed three photographs: the side of the head of a man, missing an ear; a severed ear; and the hastily stitched location of where an ear normally should be. The explanation below stated:

103

"Head>Face>Ears
There are two ears on both sides of human face [sic].
Therefore, counting 1000 ears indicates the existence of at
least 500 people."

The installation's disturbing images, paired with the detached-tone text, deliver a stark comment on what it means to be an Iranian citizen. People are stripped of their humanity as they are reduced to body parts. And the use of the words "at least" paints a harrowing picture of victims of torture or war who have lost organs, and whose experiences come to define the state as the instigator of this loss.

Askari Sirizi's 2007 exhibition took his criticism to a more overt level. The exhibition was in two parts. One part was called "Buridan's Society." In this installation, Askari Sirizi referenced the well-known philosophical tale about John Buridan's ass and the lack of free well. The installation displayed buckets of hay on one side of a barren room, and buckets of water on the other side, with the photograph of a donkey placed on the wall in the middle. In the philosophical tale, a hungry and thirsty donkey is condemned to starve because it is unable to choose between food and water. In Askari Sirizi's version, a photograph of bread is added to the wall on the left and one of philosophy, psychology and literature books to the wall on the right. The artist here took Buridan's idea further by not only implying that the Iranian people lack free will, but also that they have been reduced to a state in which they have to choose between basic survival and intellectual nourishment. The laws of nature dictate that living organisms normally aim to satisfy their basic needs before any other higher needs, and in this, Askari Sirizi's installation is a harsh critique of the reduction of the human being into a creature of basic needs under the current Iranian state. The Iranian state is implied to be a usurper of free and inquiring thought.

This critique was emphasized in the second installation in the exhibition, "U-turn to Utopia." The photo of the bottom of a donkey's hoof to which a horseshoe is attached stood at the center of a room, surrounded by road signs of U-turns, arranged in a semi-circle. The road signs started on the right with one signaling "Neo-fundamentalism Sq.," then moved to "Wellbeing St., Freedom St.," "Paradise Blvd., Garden of Grace," "Utopia St.," "Happiness St.," "Heaven St., Beautiful Town" and ended with the sign for "Evin Prison, Pleasant Land," which

Fig. 28. "Buridan's Society" exhibition by Homayoun Askari Sirizi in 2007. Photo courtesy of the artist.

also instructed drivers to reduce their speed. The installation is a clear critique of the historical development of Iran since the Islamic Revolution, hinting, through the visual motif of the curve of the letter "U," that the Revolution is leading people backwards and, as signalled through the last road sign's instruction to reduce speed while pointing to the Evin Prison, into a life of entrapment.

Within Iran, the oppositional politics of those artists has not expressed itself in populist spaces, but remains limited to niches inhabited by their marginalized voices. The artist Mahmoud Bakhshi Moakhar says that this marginalization is partly because the mainstream (state) media do not report on the art scene in Iran. Television does not cover independent art events and the newspapers do not have art listings.[73] Amirali Ghasemi agrees, saying that the arts page in a newspaper would be the first to be dropped if more space were needed to cover a political matter.[74] This state inattention has rendered this art scene in Iran invisible on the popular level. But the power of Iran's oppositional contemporary art creations is driven by precisely this invisibility. The artists exist in what Polletta terms "free spaces," "small-scale settings within a community or movement that are removed from the direct control of dominant groups, are voluntarily participated in, and are *generative of the cultural challenge that precedes political mobilization.*"[75] This placing of "free spaces" as a precedent for political mobilization is an important statement: While significant attention has been granted to the visual expressions of the Green Movement of 2009, Polleta's concept of "free spaces" alerts us to the indirect role played by contemporary art in paving the way for this public protest to be expressed. In other words, contemporary art contributed to the cultural-political infrastructure from which the Green Movement emerged.

The Green Movement as visual protest

Within this oppositional context, the Green Movement can be understood not just as a protest against the monopolization of politics by the Iranian regime, but also against the invisibility of political resistance. The movement was a spontaneous, bottom-up protest against what many Iranians saw as the stealing of their votes by the regime, catalyzing the slogan "Where is my vote?" that became the most prevalent statement witnessed/heard in the anti-fraud protests that began on 13 June 2009. The Green Movement was a movement about presence, and it was striking in its focus on the visual and on symbolism. For example, on 16 June, Reformist Mir-Hossein Mousavi, who had run against Ahmadinejad in the election, asked his supporters to march from Inqilab Square (Revolution Square) to Azadi Square (Freedom Square), a symbolic movement in space that sent a message about the Green Movement's political intentions.[76]

The Green Movement's visual dimension manifested itself in several arenas, lending the movement important visual characteristics. First, it was a color-branded movement, as it appropriated the color green. The movement started after supporters of Mir-Hossein Mousavi rejected his loss in the presidential election to Ahmadinejad. Mousavi had used the color green in his presidential campaign as a sign of adhering to Islamic principles while calling for reforming the Iranian regime. But the campaign was marred by weaknesses similar to those that had marred Khatami's in 2005. Dabashi describes Mousavi's presidential campaign as "full of necessary color symbolism but lacking in substance, in a clearly articulated platform...in reaching out to a wider spectrum of his constituency. His campaign was too elitist, trapped, in its visual paraphernalia, inside too excessive attention to Northern Tehran's sensibility."[77] Yet after Mousavi's

Fig. 29. Mousavi supporters at a rally in Tehran on 17 June 2009. Photo by AFP.

loss, this same visual paraphernalia was appropriated by his supporters to disseminate messages that went beyond Mousavi himself.
Even though Mousavi became the political face of the movement, the
movement was about claiming citizen rights. The color green was a
way for the protesters to affirm their own adherence to their heritage,
their own authenticity, signaling to the regime that they were Iranians
and Muslim too. Green was found everywhere, in ribbons worn by protesters around their heads and wrists, in women's headscarves and
in the bands tied around the arms of Iran's national football team in
a World Cup qualifier match against South Korea on 17 June. It was
the color of the models of a hand signaling the victory sign, another
visual symbol for the movement, that were created and carried in
demonstrations. It was also the color that online activists used to
mark their Facebook profile photos and tag their online visual messages, from photos to banners to posters.

This use of the online media was what lent the movement its
second visual characteristic. The Movement was an exercise in
using the capability of the online media to provide visual evidence
to achieve global visibility. Larry Diamond has argued that the online
media can function as a "liberation technology," aiding people in
their struggle for democracy.[78] Iran has one of the world's highest

Fig. 30. A Mousavi supporter in Tehran at a rally on 17 June 2009 carrying a picture of Iran's national football team players wearing green wristbands. Photo by AFP, originally released by Mehr News Agency.

proportions of bloggers, and this human/technological infrastructure was put to use to let people outside Iran, as well as those in other areas of the country, see what was going on within Tehran and other protest locations.[79] YouTube and other video sharing platforms were used not just to transmit footage of the growing number of people protesting (and who often carried signs in English as they were deliberately addressing a global audience), but also of incidents of state violence, such as videos of the Basij attacking people on the streets, recorded with mobile phone cameras. Those videos became valuable sources of "evidence" after the Iranian government prevented foreign correspondents from covering the protests through closing down media offices (al-Arabiya's for example), arresting journalists and accusing the media (CNN and the BBC) of being part of a Western anti-regime plot.

The third visual characteristic was the creation of an alternative image of the Iranian people. The Iranian state had monopolized this image, so that certain iconic representations – women wearing the chador, or Muslim clerics, for example – became automatic regime identifiers. Although the Western media, in particular, focused their

cameras on the fashionable young Iranian women among the protesters, who were pushing the boundaries of acceptable public dress
through colorful scarves, heavy make-up and a fair amount of defiant locks of hair on show, the movement attracted people from a
wider social spectrum. Zahra Rahnavard, Mousavi's chador-wearing
wife, was the most prominent female among Tehrani protesters,
while cleric Mohammad Ali Abtahi was another popular figure. Abtahi
was detained, accused of helping plot a velvet revolution. Using an
established visual technique normally favored by the regime, "before
and after" pictures of Abtahi were circulated online by Iran's youth-
ful bloggers, showing his physical deterioration after imprisonment.[80]
As such, the movement reclaimed the image of the Iranian people,
secular and pious, young and old, back from the regime.

The fourth visual characteristic was inter-image commentary. The
protesters "spoke back" to the regime through appropriating some
of the very visual discourses that the state uses to legitimate itself.
At one rally, the family of a famous Iran–Iraq war martyr, Amir Haj
Amiri, carried a photo of him dead, a familiar visual representation of
a martyr, to which they had added the caption "The family of martyr
Haj Amiri," to clarify their authenticity, along with a photo of Mousavi.
Protesters also used inter-image commentary to seize power from
the regime. At a rally in late June, a young woman held up a photograph of Iranian citizens being beaten up by the police in a previous
pro-Mousavi demonstration. The photograph here transformed the
police violence from a regime-controlled act into visual evidence, a
tool in the hands of the protesters.

One must remember that most people in the world have encoun-
tered the Green Movement through an image. Photos of the demonstrations mentioned in the above paragraph can be found on several
websites, and other images-featuring-images have appeared in the
broadcast media, print media and online media. Images of, from and
by the movement circulated freely through all those platforms. The
New York Times front page from Monday 22 June 2009, for example,
featured a photograph of the daughter of Reformist cleric Ali Akbar
Hashemi Rafsanjani at a demonstration, with eight members of the
public around her holding up their mobile phone cameras to capture
the event. As such, the Green Movement's fifth visual characteristic is
that it took place in a "hypermedia space." Kraidy and Mourad write:

Hypermedia space's importance resides in the ways in which
it combines mobility, interactivity and visibility. We can now

glimpse the contours of a theory of hypermedia in which mobile activists interactively activate inter-media configurations that connect media old and new, gaining visibility for their cause through a hypermedia space that is less controllable than social space and therefore potentially subversive of the prevalent mode of governance.[81]

This hypermedia space was mobilized at full speed on and after 20 June 2009, when a young Iranian woman, Neda Agha-Soltan, was shot dead as she passed by a demonstration in Tehran. Neda's death was captured through a mobile phone video, and the footage spread across the globe, through the mass media and the internet. Neda's blood-stained face became an iconic image[82], reproduced in art works, held up at subsequent demonstrations and transmitted via moving and still images, becoming a floating image. For several months after her death, Neda's image was reproduced repeatedly by various documentaries around the globe, making her death an international event.[83] Neda gave the movement its sixth visual characteristic: an ordinary, individual, innocent, human face. If Mousavi was the political face of the Green Movement, Neda was its popular face.

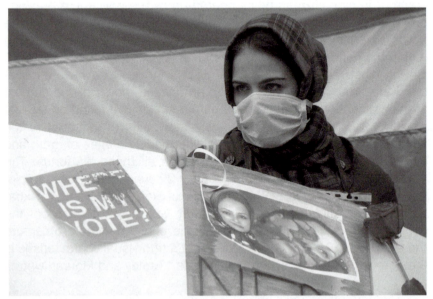

Fig. 31. An Iranian protester in Trieste, Italy on 25 June 2009, during the G8 Foreign Ministers' meeting, holding a portrait of "Neda." Photo by AFP–Giuseppe Cacace.

Neda's death served as a mobilizing tool as more people took to the streets in further protest. The protests started co-opting important commemorative dates normally used by the government to rally the masses: Jerusalem Day (18 September), the day of the taking over of the American embassy in 1979 (4 November) and National Student Day (7 December, commemorating the deaths of three students who died protesting Nixon's visit to Iran in 1953). This use of symbolic national days was coupled with organizing rallies on dates marking events defiant to or outside regime ideology, such as the anniversary of the student riots of 1999 (9 July), and the Festival of Fire, a ceremonious Zoroastrian traditional day (the rally was on 16 March 2010). As such, the protesters visually appropriated state symbols. As they marched in the streets lined by state murals, they rendered the murals powerless, and gave the movement its seventh visual characteristic: The movement was a spectacle, and, in the words of Hamid Dabashi: "The spectacle is no longer solely Islamic."[84]

The Green Movement also reversed the image of Ahmadinejad, with anti-Ahmadinejad protesters chanting "death to the dictator" and carrying defaced pictures of the president. The regime's response was to organize public rallies of its own in support of Ahmadinejad, both in Iran and abroad. A large pro-regime demonstration was staged on 30 December 2009, and it was presented as a spontaneous one, leading to the coining of a new Persian word among Iranian bloggers: khod-jushandeh, which Dabashi translates as "spontaneous-ed."[85] On 11 February 2010, the day of the anniversary of the 1979 Revolution, another pro-regime rally was organized in Iran, while on 13 October, the Iranian state, along with Hizbullah, orchestrated a popular public welcome of Ahmadinejad in Lebanon when he visited the country, where the Iranian president was thanked for Iran's reconstruction efforts in Lebanon and the Iranian state was praised as a supporter of Lebanon and Palestine. The visit came at a time when Iran was witnessing a rising influence in the Middle East, whether in Iraq, Bahrain or Lebanon, and thus it served to divert attention away from domestic issues and to Iran's regional role.

Yet the most striking visual response to the Green Movement by the Iranian regime was in another arena. The filmmaker Mohsen Makhmalbaf and the graphic novel artist Marjane Satrapi became the intellectual faces of the movement abroad, taking an active part in lobbying foreign countries to denounce the legitimacy of Ahmadinejad's re-election. The Iranian regime's response was to attempt to silence such image makers. On 1 March 2010, the filmmaker Jafar Panahi was arrested (for the second time), accused of making a film about the Green Movement. On 20 December 2010, Panahi was given a six-year prison sentence and a 20-year ban on making films. If the state could not stop the images themselves, it was trying to stifle image creators.

"It matters that these cameras stay on"

Examining what is traditionally thought of as "hard" politics shows that the Green Movement lost its battle against the Iranian regime. The crackdown on activists like Panahi or the Reformists' boycott of the 2012 Shura elections could be seen as illustrations of this. However, this framework presents a myopic view of power dynamics in Iran. Using the lens of culture as politics, which does not draw a line between "hard" and "soft" politics, complicates this view through revealing continuing efforts by oppositional actors to resist the government's attempts to transform their relative invisibility into actual absence. The story of the struggle for visibility by Iran's political oppositions, parties and individuals alike, is ongoing, and it is not likely to end completely as long as the current regime prevails, despite the regime's many efforts to suppress it. The more the regime steps up its suppression, the more oppositional voices find ways to resist. If the most striking visual response to the Green Movement by the Iranian regime was the sentencing of Jafar Panahi, Panahi's own visual response to his sentencing is even more awe inducing. His response was to secretly make This is Not a Film, which was smuggled to the Cannes Film Festival in May 2011. The "non-film" chronicles Panahi's life at home as he awaits his prison sentence. It is a statement of presence, both of Panahi as an oppositional figure and of itself as a piece of art whose mere existence defies the Iranian regime. At one point in the "non-film," Panahi's friend, documentarist Mojtaba Mirtahmasb, says to him, "Listen, Jafar. What matters is that this is documented. It matters that these cameras stay on."

In addition to this dual visual message about presence, the "non-film" sends a political message through overlapping visual layers. We see Panahi watch the news on television, where a report mentions that Ahmadinejad declared that fireworks are illegal. Panahi takes his iPhone and films fireworks exploding there and then outside his window. The iPhone video of fireworks becomes an image-within-an-image (the latter being the "non-film") responding to another image-within-an-image (the televised news report as seen through the "non-film") through recording a visual act of defiance (fireworks) whose own image (in the mobile phone recording) becomes part of another visual act of defiance (the "non-film" itself). The interlocking visual layers unite Panahi and those continuously engaged in small acts of defiance, sending a strong message that although the Green Movement did not result in the demise of the Iranian regime, the future of Iran will ultimately hold a different image from that of the present.

PART II

REVOLUTIONARY IMAGES

4

The Visual Rush of the Arab Spring

No political development in the Middle East has been as highly visual as the Arab Spring, the series of uprisings that began in Tunisia in December 2010 and spread across the Arab world in 2011. The image played multiple roles within the Arab Spring, and the Arab Spring itself was also a regional phenomenon partly instigated by the journey of the image into the heart of political struggle prior to the revolutions. Guy Debord writes in the *The Society of the Spectacle*, "[t]he spectacle is not a collection of images; rather, it is a social relationship between people that is mediated by images."[1] The image as a mediator of political critique is a product of "today's televisual public sphere," where

> states (in the persons/bodies of politicians) stage spectacles...certifying their status before the people/public and subaltern counterpublics participate through the performance of image events, employing the consequent publicity as a social medium through which to hold...states accountable, help form public opinion, and constitute their own identities as subaltern counterpublics. Critique through spectacle, not critique versus spectacle.[2]

The Arab Spring saw a manifestation of critique through spectacle, but it also went beyond this characterization. It was not just a phenomenon whereby opposing political actors (states versus peoples) *utilized* spectacle as a form of critique; it was also one that *produced* latent images, as well as *being* in itself a spectacle that was simultaneously watched and emulated. Focusing on Egypt, the aim of this chapter is to document the trajectory of the image from the period leading to the Arab Spring, through the Arab Spring itself, and to the immediate post-revolutionary period in Egypt, to highlight the role the image has been playing in processes of political struggle that render the Arab Spring part of a longer evolutionary political context.

The image as an instigator of protest

The Arab Spring can be traced back to December 2010, when Mohamed Bouazizi, a poor street vendor in Sidi Bouzid in Tunisia, set fire to himself in protest at his humiliation at the hands of a government official who accused him of selling vegetables without a licence. There is no visual record of Mohamed Bouazizi's self-immolation. Yet news of this extreme act of despair and protest spread fast through word of mouth, the pan-Arab media and the online media, leading to the organization of a series of protests in Sidi Bouzid that later spread to other Tunisian cities, becoming a national uprising. The Tunisian Jasmine Revolution led to the stepping down of Tunisian president Zine El-Abidine Ben Ali in January 2011 – an unprecedented move in the Arab world – and to the catalyzing of copycat uprisings across the region.

It is undeniable that the Tunisian online media played a role in the escalation of protests in Tunisia into a revolution. Tunisian opposition and protest websites have existed since 1998, when the "Takreez" distribution list appeared, which was followed by a number of sites with similar aims, like tunisnews.net, an independent news portal set up by Tunisian exiles to report on repression inside Tunisia, and reveiltunisien.org in 2002, a hub for Tunisian and French political activists.[3] This infrastructure, coupled with Facebook, YouTube and Twitter, was greatly utilized during the Jasmine Revolution, leading to a circular journey of images, from the online to the mass media and back to the online media. Tunisia's opposition websites, as well as the social media, served as tools of mass mobilization through posting videos of protesters attacking government buildings, victims of police shootings and mass rallies around Tunisia. The videos became a key source for al-Jazeera after the Tunisian government blocked the channel's on-the-ground reporting of the revolution. As Miladi points out, it was al-Jazeera's reliance on videos and images posted on YouTube and Facebook that fuelled Tunisians' increased use of the social media during the revolution.[4] The online media were also used to disseminate visual anti-regime material, like the video clip of the song *Rais Lebled* (O country's president) by Tunisian rapper Hamada Ben-Amor, which had been posted online in late 2010, leading to the rapper's arrest, and which became a mobilizing tool during the revolution.[5]

The Jasmine Revolution was not a "Twitter revolution" or a revolution caused by the social media. The online activism that had been building up prior to the revolution was part of a wider political context that saw different kinds of offline activism both within Tunisia and in the diaspora. And to reduce any of the Arab revolutions to being a product of one communication tool denies the complexity of the dynamics of those revolutions. But the Jasmine Revolution was a revolution characterized by extraordinary images that citizens across the Arab world witnessed through television and electronic screens: Arab citizens rising up against tyranny, and protesting to reclaim dignity.

News of Bouazizi's act resulted in similar self-immolations across the Arab world, from Egypt to Algeria to Mauritania. The sense of lost dignity that Bouazizi was protesting against was shared all over the region. Yet it was the image of a Ben Ali-free Tunisia that could be said to have catalyzed the Arab Spring. This image, which was created by the "local public" in Tunisia, transcended national borders.[6] Photos and videos of jubilant Tunisians celebrating their revolutionary achievement became a catalyst for other Arabs to rise against their tyrants, while those of the Tunisians protesting, resisting government crackdowns and defending and cleaning their neighborhoods as an act of community solidarity became a template for revolutionary public action. Of course, one could argue that the mere news of hearing about the success of the Tunisian revolution could have acted as a catalyst for other Arabs, yet, the role of the image was to bring other Arab citizens closer to this experience. People across the Arab world could visualize themselves in the place of the Tunisians as they watched the events develop on their screens in real time. Handler argues that "[p]rotest movements emerge when there is a transformation of both consciousness and behavior, when people believe that they have been wronged and develop a sense of efficacy."[7] The images from Tunisia helped cultivate this sense of efficacy among Arabs, acting as a visual signal of empowerment.

Arabs responded to this visual invitation through taking to the streets against their own tyrants. Egypt led the way, with a protest on 25 January, Police Day, chosen for its celebration of one of the regime's key oppressive apparatuses, during which protesters in Cairo's Tahrir Square honored the Tunisian revolution through carrying images characterized by intertextuality. Slogans from the Jasmine Revolution, "The people want the fall of the regime"

119

and "Degage" (Leave), were chanted and displayed on placards. A sign was held up that showed president Hosni Mubarak, carrying an umbrella to protect him from a barrage of hurled shoes, running towards a plane headed to Saudi Arabia, following Ben Ali's fate. A placard had the image of Mubarak with a shoe hurled directly at his face, under the caption "First it was Tunisia, and now it's Egypt." People carried hand-drawn Tunisian flags captioned with "May God let us be next."

The above snapshot points to a wider phenomenon during the Arab Spring: the merger of social movements and nonmovements. Unlike social movements, which are characterized by being organized collectives, Bayat defines nonmovements as "the collective actions of noncollective actors; they embody shared practices of large numbers of ordinary people whose fragmented but similar activities trigger much social change."[8] Bayat's list of key differences between the two tropes is useful, as the Arab Spring saw all the characteristics of social movements and nonmovements come into play at once. Bayat says:

> First, nonmovements ... tend to be action oriented ... Second, whereas in social movements leaders usually mobilize the constituencies to put pressure on authorities to meet their demands, in nonmovements actors directly practice what they claim, despite government sanctions. Thus, theirs is not a politics of protest, but of practice ... Third, unlike social movements, where actors are involved usually in *extraordinary* deeds of mobilization and protestation that go beyond the routine of daily life [...], the nonmovements are made up of practices that are merged into ... the *ordinary* practices of daily life.[9]

Bayat acknowledges that nonmovements can transform into social movements if the opportunity arises, and if a common threat to the individuals in nonmovements catalyzes collective action. However, the Arab Spring went beyond this as it created a new hybrid movement blending those characteristics. What was unique about it is that the "*common* practices of *everyday* life"[10] that had characterized resistance as a fragmented lived experience became the *same* practices used in centralized protest locales like Tahrir Square. This hybrid movement became a site "for the production and reception of cultural texts."[11]

Although, as just presented, this hybrid movement goes beyond social movement theory, Reed's framework on the role of culture in social movements provides a useful template for understanding the role of the image in the Arab Spring. Reed states that culture performs the following functions for social movements (and I add, the hybrid movement in the Arab Spring):

- Encourage. Individuals should feel the strength of the group...
- Empower. Individuals should feel their own strength...
- Harmonize. Smooth differences among diverse constituencies...
- Inform internally. Express or reinforce movement values, ideas and tactics...
- Inform externally. Express movement values, ideas and tactics to potential recruits, opponents and undecided bystanders...
- Enact movement goals. This entails art that actively intervenes directly to achieve values...
- Historicize. Invent, tell, and retell the history of the movement...
- Transform affect or tactics. Set a new emotional tone (for example, diffuse tension from anger to focused resistance, or from fear to calm resolve), or redirect the attention of the group (use a song of image to signal a new stage of a demonstration)...
- Critique movement ideology. Challenge dominant ideas, values, and tactics...
- Make room for pleasure. Provide respite from the rigors of movement work through aesthetic joy.[12]

The image during the Arab Spring performed all those roles. Yet in order to understand the visual dynamics during the Arab Spring, one needs to go back a few years to examine the battle between the state and the opposition (both social movements and nonmovements), particularly in Egypt, whose progression paved the way for the Egyptian revolution and the cascading Arab uprisings that followed. This battle has been occurring not just through formal politics, but also through popular cultural expressions and everyday experiences, and it has been following an upward trajectory. In 2005, the battle between the state and the opposition in Egypt was asymmetrical, but slowly, Egyptian citizens tipped the balance in their favor. It can be argued that the Egyptian revolution of 25 January was the product of this ongoing process of power struggle. The analysis that follows aims to capture two tropes in this progression: "the role of 'popular culture' as a site for the production of political meaning" and "the centrality of 'the everyday' to the Arab masses and their cultures," for, as Tarik

Sabry argues, one of the problematics of studying the Arab world has been that "Arab popular cultures and lived experiences remain, not only on the periphery of Arab intellectual discourse but also on the periphery of political discourses."[13] The analysis, then, is a small attempt at addressing this problematic.

Public space and the Egyptian state before the Arab Spring

The space of Cairo is populated by monuments and museums commemorating key moments in the nation's history. From the 6 October bridge to the 1973 War Panorama to the house of Saad Zaghloul, monuments and museums in Cairo offer a vision of Egypt as a leading Arab nation and a force of resistance to foreign occupation. What is key in the majority of monuments and museums in Cairo is the importance of place. Egypt's geography makes it a country bridging Africa and Asia, the Mediterranean and the Red Sea. But the country also has a historical legacy that endows its geography with symbolic meaning. It bridges the past and the present, Islam and Christianity, North Africa and the Levant. The Egyptian state made use of this rich legacy to construct visible forms of national belonging. Even the People's Assembly had its own museum to commemorate Egypt's "governing systems, legislations, regulations and treaties" throughout its history.[14] Pride in the national past, however, was also used as a tool to fill the gap created by the malaise of the present. Under Mubarak, Egypt was losing its status as a political leader in the Arab world, eclipsed by Saudi Arabia and Qatar. A large proportion of its population lived below the poverty line. Political dissent was growing among both Islamist and non-Islamist groups.

The Egyptian state's response to social, economic and political unrest remained constant ever since Mubarak came to power: to declare a "permanent" state of emergency. This state of emergency meant that Egypt became a space of exception, where the sovereign could invoke this law as a means of exclusion of those deemed to be a threat to the national space. Giorgio Agamben defines sovereignty as the ability to decide on the state of exception, the state that determines who is included and who is not.[15] Sovereignty, then, is based on the idea of exclusion, "the hidden foundation on which the entire political system rested."[16] But this dynamic presents a paradox; as Agamben asks, "What is the relation between politics and life, if life presents itself as what is included by means of an exclusion?"[17] This paradox of inclusion/exclusion is found in sovereignty because the sovereign is both inside and outside the judicial system: "the sovereign, having the legal power to suspend the validity of the law, legally places himself outside the law."[18] However, exclusion in the case of Mubarak's Egypt was not interpreted as having the "other" essentially "outside" and forgotten about. On the contrary, as Deleuze and Guattari argue, "[s]overeignty only rules over what it is capable of interiorizing."[19] Agamben cites Maurice Blanchot to illustrate this point, who says that it is a case of society's attempt to "confine the outside."[20]

Confining the outside in Egypt was performed in the literal sense, with the mass arrest of political dissidents such as members of the Muslim Brotherhood. But it was also done symbolically through the appropriation of space. By declaring political dissidents, from bloggers to journalists to Muslim Brotherhood supporters, a threat to the nation, the Egyptian authoritarian state attempted to create a uniform narrative of national belonging. With official discourse in Egypt relying heavily on the country's historical legacy, the various constructions in physical space commemorating this legacy became instruments in the hands of the state. Instead of instilling a sense of pride in the population, they became reminders of its dominant discourse. At best, they became an ironic sign of the difference between what had been and what could have been and the reality of the present.

The image of Mubarak as a modern president

Writing in 1989, Robert Springborg said that Egyptian president Hosni Mubarak had no charisma or social skills, with a stiff physical appearance and a degree of unease in front of television cameras and thus an unfortunate political persona. Mubarak was also protective of his private life – a departure from Sadat's and Nasser's openness about their personal feelings that had brought them closer to their people emotionally. Springborg concluded: "Mubarak gives the impression of being cut off from popular sentiments. He does not read public opinion well and has difficulty in articulating and encapsulating popular desires in appropriate words and actions."[21]

It is within this context that Mubarak launched his only presidential campaign in 2005, following international pressure, particularly from the United States, to hold competitive elections in Egypt. Voltmer argues that in countries where political actors do not have strong social ties with the people, "Americanized" politics, including media manipulation and spin, become the basis for electoral campaigns and winning over voters as a way of compensating for the lack of those ties.[22] Mubarak hired long-term National Democratic Party member and advertising executive Sami Abdel Aziz to design his campaign. Abdel Aziz sought to deliberately change the established image of Mubarak. He characterized the 2005 presidential campaign as "more professional, more personal, and multiplatform, using a variety of media at the same time, relying on integrated marketing communication."[23] The campaign featured public rallies, billboards and media appearances by Mubarak and his family. Abdel Aziz explained that Mubarak's campaign speeches were not allowed on state television, as a result of a ruling by the Minister of Information regulating election campaigns, yet they were broadcast on Dream TV and al-Mihwar, private channels owned by NDP members. Mubarak also recorded a three-part television interview with high-profile journalist Imad al-Din Adib that was broadcast on al-Arabiya. Mubarak's image in the interview, which was directed by film director Sherif Arafa, "was that of a fearless officer and statesman, a hero of the October 1973 War, who as President is successful in navigating his country's course with judgment and understanding, under difficult conditions."[24]

The campaign sought to market Mubarak as a modern, energetic, in-touch president who could appeal to a younger generation. The first speech that Mubarak gave in the campaign in the al-Azhar Park in Cairo featured the screening of a ten-minute film about how he and his wife got engaged.[25] It also featured videos showing NDP members projecting concern for their fellow citizens, and the park was scattered with young people wearing t-shirts and baseball caps carrying the slogan "Mubarak 2005." Collombier comments on the campaign's posters: "The President's image itself was carefully studied, polished, and renewed. Even propaganda posters spread out in the whole country showed the perfect leader: A President in his shirt sleeves, wearing a trendy tie, sitting at his desk, holding the businessman's very necessary accessory, a Mont-Blanc pen."[26] An intriguing fact is that Sami Abdel Aziz, the PR mastermind of the campaign, also designed the presidential campaign for one of Mubarak's rival candidates, No'man Gom'a of al-Wafd party. Abdel Aziz is Gom'a's son-in-law, and as such, needed to design both campaigns while remaining on good

Fig. 32. A poster in Cairo proclaiming "Congratulations, president. Your encouragement of us is the reason for our success. Congratulations to the Egyptian national team. Congratulations to all Egyptians." Photo taken on 21 March 2008.

terms with both men. As the National Democratic Party in Egypt had identified the middle class as the target audience that mattered in the election, Abdel Aziz's campaign for Gom'a was populist in tone, appealing to the lower classes. So while Mubarak's campaign used slick, photoshopped images of Mubarak looking a few years younger, wearing a shirt without a tie and corporate-style logos and slogans like "Mubarak 2005, your choice for the future," Gom'a's campaign simply featured his picture along with the sign of a blossoming tree to indicate that it is time for change. The campaign's slogan had a populist, emotive tone, and it was written in colloquial Egyptian: "With me, O people, let us seriously change Egypt."

Mubarak's campaign persona, however, did not completely override his characterization as the contemporary pharaoh of Egypt. Billboards showing his image surrounded with pharaonic ones were prevalent in Cairo, and his likeness was also embedded in the Panorama commemorating the 1973 war, fixing his image as a historic, national hero. His self-proclaimed "father of the people" status was symbolized through billboards showing him emerging from a pyramid of people from different walks of life. This representation was part of a wider move by the NDP to rebrand itself. In 2004, the

Fig. 33. An NDP poster of Mubarak in Cairo proclaiming "For the sake of democracy and stability." Photo taken on 24 March 2008.

party had launched a campaign tagged "New thinking, and reform priorities," which saw its visual representation in billboards depicting different "kinds" of Egyptian people: veiled and unveiled women, old people and children, men in modern and traditional clothes, branding the NDP as the legitimate representative of Egyptians. This use of images became a trend for the NDP as it strove to hold on to its power in the years that followed, presenting a "democratic façade" behind which hid an unchanging authoritarian regime.[27]

As Egypt prepared for parliamentary elections in 2010, the NDP was keen to polish the image of Mubarak as a global political leader. In September, when US president Barack Obama resurrected talks between the Israeli and Palestinian leadership, a faked image of

Fig. 34. Billboard in Cairo proclaiming "Mubarak, security for Egypt" and featuring panels captioned "Democracy," "Goodness," "Prosperity" and "Growth." Photo taken on 24 March 2008

Mubarak appeared in the pro-regime *al-Ahram* newspaper which showed Mubarak walking in front of Obama, Benjamin Netanyahu, King Abdullah of Jordan and Mahmoud Abbas during the talks, when the original, real photo actually shows Mubarak walking in the back of the crowd. With the presidential elections anticipated in 2011, the NDP also began a visual campaign to present Mubarak's son, Gamal, as a credible successor to his father. The campaign utilized several media platforms: live, online streaming of "townhall" meetings between Gamal Mubarak and students and business leaders; state television coverage of Gamal Mubarak's visits to poor villages; and interviews with the international media like CNN, in which Gamal Mubarak was presented as an expert on the economy who could revive Egypt's. In addition, from 2008 onwards, promotional posters and videos for Gamal Mubarak were created by his Future Generation Foundation to present "popular" approval of his anticipated presidency. This extreme reliance on manufactured images can be seen as a desperate attempt at filling a growing social void, which was only made more acute through developments like the wrongful killing of Khaled Said in June 2010 at the hands of the police, the blatantly fraudulent parliamentary elections in November 2010, which saw the NDP sweep the vast majority of seats and ongoing arrests and intimidation of political activists and reformers.

The image as a resistance tool

It is within the context of presidential election and succession that the Egyptian Movement for Change, Kifaya (meaning Enough) was born in 2004. Under the slogan, "No to renewal, no to hereditary succession, yes to electing the president of the republic," Kifaya was a gathering of intellectuals and activists who sought to bring about political change. Kifaya was a visually aware movement, relying in its street protests on branded stickers, balloons, banners and other visual products, all of which had a distinctive yellow background with a logo: the word "Kifaya" written in red in a modern Arabic font. Kifaya's "repeated public displays"[28] were a key method through which it disseminated its message. It organized its first anti-Mubarak demonstration in central Cairo on 12 December 2004, where protesters covered their mouths with yellow stickers bearing its logo[29] and launched an initiative titled *"al-shari' lana"* (the street is ours) on 2 June 2005 that emphasized that the streets belonged to the Egyptian citizens.[30] Later that month, the movement used the folkloric tradition of sweeping the floor of the Sayyida Zeinab mosque as a symbolic message to Egypt's security apparatus, with activists gathering at the mosque and calling on the Prophet's granddaughter to help fight injustice.[31] Kifaya thus planted the seed of citizens reclaiming their visibility in national space, as well as appropriating religious tradition as an oppositional political tool.

Kifaya's use of public displays was coupled with the use of photographs as a tool of resistance. During a demonstration against the constitutional referendum that would allow Mubarak to run for election, on 25 May 2005, protesters were attacked by thugs and the riot police. They responded by starting to photograph the police with their mobile phone cameras, and later made demonstration banners featuring those police photos. At those subsequent demonstrations, they also held up posters of the Minister of Interior with the slogan *"aqee-louh"* (remove him from office).[32] Utilizing "visual evidence" triggered a wider phenomenon of images documenting regime brutality and election fraud. Ghada Shahbander set up a grassroots election monitoring group called "Shayfeen.com" (We can see you), which documented, often through images, incidents of transgression. Shayfeen.com and the photographs taken by citizens were part of a new politics of seeing, presence and image reversal that transformed the citizen from a passive visual object into an empowered agent.

Those efforts were strengthened with the establishment of Wael Abbas' Misr Digital blog[33] in March 2005, which became an online political newspaper chronicling Kifaya's activities and the state's response to it. His reporting of stories was often accompanied by photographs, which gained him credibility.[34] Abbas' pioneering site was notable for helping break the taboo of speaking against regime brutality. His posting of pictures of people who had been attacked by the police encouraged other torture victims to start taking photos and videos of their injuries with their mobile phones and posting them on the internet. It also encouraged other activists to send Abbas photos they had taken for posting.[35] In January 2007 he started uploading mobile phone videos taken by the police as they tortured detained citizens, adding another layer of credibility to the image as visual evidence.[36] Abbas' Misr Digital catalyzed the rise of self-reporting and political blogging in Egypt, and a new symbiotic relationship between the press and the blogosphere.[37] Abbas explains that in the case of stories that the press could not report directly, he and the journalists would agree that he would break the story first on his blog, after which the press would simply report the story of him mentioning the original story, which proved to be a successful method of getting around censorship.[38]

Other bloggers started to follow Wael Abbas in using images online, not just posting photographs on blogs but also through social media sites like Flickr, such as the blogger Hossam el-Hamalawy, whose blog[39] and Flickr Photostream[40] constitute two of the most comprehensive photographic archives of public political life in Egypt since the Kifaya movement.[41] This rising role of the image was seminal for Kifaya. As Amr Gharbeia, one of the Egyptian bloggers, explains, "Kifaya found a space for expression on the internet after being physically restricted on the streets. Before, the police used to surround Kifaya protesters on a given street and no one would know what the police were doing."[42] The posting of online images created visibility about police brutality. In doing so, the electronic image pushed the boundaries of what could be represented in the public domain in Egypt. But the images went beyond being pieces of evidence. They also became tools of mobilization. As Etling et al. write, "Egyptian bloggers frequently use pictorial badges on their sites to show support for various campaigns, such as for freeing bloggers, calling for reform, or promoting social issues."[43] Amr and Ahmed Gharbeia were two bloggers who started the use of internet banners to organize offline protest campaigns, which became a standard mobilizing method.[44] In this way, the Egyptian blogosphere became an example of how technology "reflects and mirrors the culture in which it evolves rather than guiding and directing it."[45]

The Egyptian blogosphere was a space that allowed individual identities to be expressed while also fostering a sense of community among bloggers and activists.[46] Key bloggers like Wael Abbas became household names. The arrest of online activists also gave them recognition by other members of the blogging community, with online banners featuring their photographs and calling for their release becoming a standard method of expressing community support.[47] One of the most prominent cases is that of Israa Abdel Fattah, whose arrest following her calling for a national strike on 6 April 2008 in support of workers in Mahalla al-Kubra through a Facebook group made her an icon.[48] Her photograph was disseminated in cyberspace as well as in physical space, as she in turn became the face of online activism, and was given the nickname "Facebook Girl." This act led to the birth of the April 6 movement, an activist group that continues to play an important political role among Egypt's youth.

Cyberspace also became a space where the right of the disenfranchised individual was touted as a key demand, a departure from the dominant discourse on the disenfranchised that saw them as a mere mass. Imad al-Kabir, a bus driver whose torture by the police was captured on video and disseminated by Wael Abbas on his blog, eventually leading to the trial and conviction of the two policemen responsible, became an example of the rise of the individual as a social agent.[49] The image of the individual, then, marked a new era in the politics of mobilization in Egypt that was driven by the importance of individual dignity.

This use of the image was not limited to "secular" communities; the use of blogs by Kifaya and secular activists influenced the Muslim Brotherhood to use the same technique. Muslim Brotherhood blogs were notable for displaying the photographs of Brotherhood prisoners. This strategy allowed the Brotherhood to individualize its prisoners through individual online posters. The Brotherhood went further through launching one blog for every prisoner, which were normally run by the prisoners' children, and organized public displays like *iftar*s in Ramadan where red goody bags with the names of its prisoners were distributed.[50] The Brotherhood honed its visual outputs over the years, producing a variety of merchandise like baseball caps, stickers and posters carrying messages of its political demands. Often, those products appealed to an international audience as they relied on professional advertising standards, slogans in English and universalist emotional appeals such as through using the image of children as carriers of messages. The Brotherhood also relied on dramatic visual displays in public action, such as one protest against the trial of political prisoners in military jails that took place during the Cairo Conference in 2008, where Brotherhood university students demonstrated against such trials of their professors through posing for the media in a line with their hands tied and their mouths covered with tape.

The death of 28-year old Khaled Said in June 2010 at the hands of the Egyptian police was the epitome of the development of the image into a resistance tool. Said allegedly had posted on YouTube a piece of visual evidence, a video of Egyptian policemen profiteering from drugs. His death as a result of subsequent torture at the hands of the police catalyzed outrage among Egypt's youth. A Facebook group, "We Are All Khaled Said," was set up, on which "before and after" photographs of Said's face were posted as evidence of police brutality. The same images, captioned "Because of which offense was he killed?" were

Fig. 35. A Muslim Brotherhood demonstration against the trial of university professors in military courts at the Cairo Conference on 27 March 2008.

Fig. 36. A Muslim Brotherhood poster on display at the Cairo Conference on 27 March 2008.

carried by demonstrators who took to the streets to protest his death, turning Khaled Said into an icon of the disenfranchised individual among Egyptian youth.

Bloggers, Kifaya and Brotherhood activists were not the only creators of oppositional images in Egypt. Joining them were artists, who constituted what Bayat calls "passive networks" of "imagined solidarities,"[51] as those artists did not always deliberately engage in collective action, yet they formed a spontaneous network of resistant visual practices. Thus, whether collectively or individually, they did take part in practicing visual political critique. Some did participate in collective action, like the artist Mustafa Hussein, who created visual

Fig. 37. A youth demonstration in Cairo on 20 June 2010 against the killing of Khaled Said. Photo by AFP–Khaled Desouki.

material for use in public protests. One of his most recognized creations is a poster of Mubarak done in the color-saturated style of old Egyptian film posters. The poster featured the drawing of the head of Mubarak and the word *"Batel"* (void) written beneath it in the style of a film title.[52] In a blog post from 28 September 2005, Hussein wrote about the use of this poster during a Kifaya demonstration the previous day, which protested Mubarak's swearing in ceremony after his "victory" in the presidential election: "I couldn't stop bragging about my posters. I felt I don't need to shout any of the slogan [sic], I shouted already but visually!"[53] Cinematic references were also used by the cartoonist and photomontage artist Tantawy, who publishes his work online. In 2005, he created a spoof poster referencing the Egyptian action film *Mafia* (Sherif Arafa, 2002), which featured Hosni Mubarak, his wife and his son, Gamal, as the film cast, with Hosni Mubarak as the lead gangster, wearing a red shirt and black leather jacket, sporting a goatee beard, and carrying a hand gun. Another spoof poster referenced Youssef Chahine's film *Iskindiriya Kaman w Kaman*[54], in which the film title was changed to *Baltageyya Kaman w Kaman* (Thugs, again and again), and the picture of Mubarak carrying a large axe behind a strip of yellow tape marked with the words "crime scene" was featured. The poster also featured the introduction: "Starring Egypt's number one star, Hosni Mubarak, and a selection of NDP candidates."[55]

Other artists engaged in visual critique in more oblique ways. Magdi al-Shafe'i's graphic novel *Metro* (2008), Egypt's first of this genre, is one example, representing the state of mind of the disaffected youth in Egypt against the backdrop of the Kifaya movement. The novel does not send a direct political message. It has only one casual reference to Kifaya, and its most direct political statement is a piece of dialogue by its leading character, Mustafa, on page 53, where he says to his girlfriend Dina, "Newspapers are one of our biggest problems...I mean newspapers and television, and anything else that makes us get used to submission, on the basis that the situation is hopeless, that corruption will remain corruption and injustice will remain injustice, and that standing in a 50-metre-long cue is absolutely normal. I have stopped distracting myself through the current affairs pages and forgetting who the real criminal is, who has caused those cues in the first place." The novel's cover carries a covert message about the "real criminal," as it shows Mustafa in a Cairo street, behind whom can be seen, faintly in the background, a banner from Mubarak's 2005 campaign, declaring "For a better tomorrow, yes to Mubarak." Mustafa goes on a rampage against the socioeconomic status quo, symbolizing the rage within Egypt's activist youth. The novel can thus be read as part of the visual outputs of Egypt's politically active community of anti-regime youth. The novel acknowledges this connection, through being dedicated by its author to "the Egyptian bloggers, who make me feel that there is still light in the world."

Maha Mamoun, a contemporary artist based in Cairo, is another artist who engaged in visual critique through creating a photographic project in 2005 titled "Domestic Tourism." Two images from this exhibition stand out. In one, sailboats on the Nile are depicted with the image of Mubarak embedded on their sails. In another, an image of Cairo at night is photoshopped so that the advertisement billboards on the city's rooftops display an extreme close-up of Mubarak's mouth. Both images are critiques of the surveillance of national space in Egypt under the Mubarak regime. Ahmed Basiony is another artist whose work critiqued the Mubarak regime. In 2010, he staged a performance art event, titled "Thirty Days of Running in Place," in which, for one month, he ran in place for one hour each day in a specially constructed room in the Cairo Opera House while wearing a plastic suit embedded with digital sensors. The performance was an allegory of the lack of political progress in Egypt. Basiony was killed in a demonstration in Tahrir Square in February 2011, and the video of his Opera House performance was chosen as Egypt's official entry in that year's Venice Biennale, where it was juxtaposed with video footage of protests in Tahrir Square that had been shot by the artist prior to his death.

The image as part of revolutionary infrastructure

It has been argued that the existence of communities of political expression (such as those on the internet) can have a counter-mobilizing effect. Stanyer argues that it can be an example of "self-expressive political culture, one characterized by a plurality of voices talking *across each other*" as opposed to *to each other*.[56] He adds that "[t]his self-expressive culture is one where the public – at least perhaps the more educated and relatively wealthy – can and do move fleetingly from local issues to national and global issues, expressing opposition or support in a variety of ways, as and when they see fit, without having to move outside their immediate locale."[57] Indeed, the Kifaya movement, the Egyptian blogosphere and Egypt's contemporary art scene were accused of being primarily elitist, appealing to and engaging with only a small portion of the Egyptian population.

Yet this argument misses two things. First, it misses the cultural intimacy through which the visual products created by those actors spoke to local Egyptians from a wide social spectrum. Kifaya public displays like the sweeping of the Sayyida Zeinab mosque were firmly populist; Egyptian bloggers mostly blogged in Arabic, often using the Egyptian colloquial dialect; and oppositional visual art also is rooted firmly in the local cultural context. Hussein's and Tantawy's work references Egypt's most prominent cultural product, cinema; Mamoun's work references Egypt's most prominent cultural industry, tourism; and Basiouny's performance was set in one of Egypt's most prominent cultural settings, the Opera House, while al-Shafe'i's novel is written in colloquial Egyptian Arabic. This locality gives this art power. As Auyero argues, "[t]he embeddedness of contention in local context gives protest its power and meaning"; collective action is rooted "in 'normal' social relations...joint struggle takes place embedded, and often hidden, in the mundane structures of everyday life and usual politics."[58] A blog post from 30 September 2005 by the blogger Baheyya titled "The Color of Protest" acknowledged this use of visuals in grassroots political struggle on the level of everyday life. The post concluded: "Whether in protest slogans or street theatre or the proliferating samizdat, weighty political issues are twined with every-day concerns. Presidential powers are a street-level issue. Bread and freedom. Politics is life, life is politics."[59] More than half a decade later, Baheyya's post became a prophetic, self-reflexive statement about street politics in Egypt, as the January 25 Revolution was a carnival of local cultural expression, of politics as life.

Second, the argument misses the evolutionary dimension of political struggle. Three key elements of this evolution in Egypt are worth highlighting. First, the use of the internet itself should not be examined in an absolute sense. As Etling et al. argue, "[t]he Internet lays a good foundation for a battle of ideas, but it does not necessarily favor a winner."[60] Rather, the internet's use in politi-cal struggle is more oblique: "the Internet can empower political movements in the region, since it *provides an infrastructure* for expressing minority points of view, breaking gatekeeper monopo-lies on public voice, lowering barriers to political mobilization (even if symbolic), and building capacity for bottom-up contributions to the public agenda."[61] The fast transformation of the "We Are All Khaled Said" Facebook page into a platform for the expression of political demands is an illustration of this point. The "We Are All Khaled Said" Facebook page became a platform for airing political demands from campaigning against torture and electoral fraud to the lifting of emergency law.[62]

Another key element of the infrastructure that the internet has helped create is dialogue between Muslim Brotherhood youth activ-ists and their secular counterparts. Not only did secular bloggers support Brotherhood bloggers who had been detained through online banners and other forms of support, they also engaged in debates about their respective visions for Egypt. One such debate, which par-tially took a visual form, was between Muslim Brotherhood blogger Abdul Monem Mahmoud, who ran the popular Ana Ikhwan blog until he left the Brotherhood in 2009, and online "artivist" Ahmed Sherif.[63] In 2008, Sherif created a video in which he argued that Egyptians come from different walks of life, and criticized the Brotherhood for seeking to paint all of them in one color. Monem's response after being sent the video by Sherif was to post it on his blog and ask readers to com-ment on it. Monem used the video as a tool to publicly ask the ques-tions of whether the Muslim Brotherhood was succeeding in reaching out to different sectors of Egyptian society, what kind of message the Brotherhood was sending society and whether the Brotherhood was forcing its Islamist "color" on others.[64] This kind of tolerance, diversity and dialogue can be seen as the seed of the mutual support between the Muslim Brotherhood and secular protesters witnessed during the January 25 Revolution, when it was Brotherhood members who protected other protesters during violent confrontations with the police, and when both camps gave one another a platform to express their opinions in Tahrir Square.

Second, activists were constantly honing their visual skills. An account of this process is given by Maryam Ishani, who writes about one of the founders of the April 6 movement:

> Watching the Iranian protests of 2009, Samir was troubled by the poor quality of the videos taken by activists. Although compelling, the images were often too shaky and confusing to be used by international media outlets, thus limiting their impact. In early 2010, Samir led a small delegation of representatives to the United States for media training, particularly focused on video reporting…In one session, they learned about mapping tools, using open-source maps like Google Maps and UMapper to document protest events online and choose locations for potential demonstrations. Trainees examined their local streets and plotted good locations for photography…They were trained on how to convey their content out of the event site safely: running exercises where photographers would hand off small memory flash cards at frequent intervals, switch cameras with activists who would pose as innocent bystanders, and send in camera teams in waves instead of all at once. Another novel tactic was carrying a decoy memory card with photos of tourist sites on it to hand over to police.[65]

This account highlights several important developments: the way the media helped one activist community learn from another community in another location; awareness of the potential of the image as a resistance tool; recognition of the symbiosis between the online media and the mass media; and the linking of digital activism (such as through taking and distributing photographs) with offline activism. All those developments were subsequently used during the January 25 Revolution.

Third, activists learnt the importance of reaching out to communities beyond their own. One way of doing this was through mobile phones. Rafael argues that mobile phones "bring a new kind of crowd about, one that was thoroughly conscious of itself as a movement headed towards a common goal."[66] In the Egyptian case, mobile phones allowed activists to engage other activists beyond the online community, but they were also used to disseminate the message of the online media to a wider crowd. Audio recordings meant for downloading and circulation via mobile phones, such as those by Mahmoud Tawfic, became a means of reaching out to people beyond the internet. Mahmoud Tawfic's audio pieces mixed actual recordings and satirical commentary to critique issues like Mubarak's landslide victory in the 6 September 2005 election and fraud during the parliamentary elections of 9 November 2005. The pieces pushed boundaries by presenting the voices of the people declaring that "Mubarak is void" and giving eyewitness accounts of the presence of fraud in the elections. Another taboo was broken: criticizing the president in a public forum.

Ahmed Sherif took this further through creating videos meant for distribution online as well as via mobile phones. The videos, mainly accompanying satirical songs, commented on political developments and occasions like Imad al-Kabir's story, constitutional amendments and Mubarak's birthday. The videos sometimes used global cultural references such as the video "Dictatorship for Dummies" (which displayed text in English but in which the accompanying Arabic commentary translated "dummies" to the very Egyptian slang word "bahayem" [literally meaning cattle]), but they mostly used local cultural references like the folkloric song used in the 2005 video about Mubarak's birthday, in which the expression "abu'l fasal" was changed to "abu'l fasad" (meaning "father of corruption"). Explaining the way he distributed the videos, Sherif said, "When I released the mobile phone videos, I posted them on YouTube but also sent them 'manually' to a large mailing list of friends and sympathizers. I sent them as 3GP files (the appropriate MMS format for cell phones) so they would spread them within their own communities." Sherif's motive behind this strategy was twofold. First, as he put it, "I thought the Web 2.0, at large, could be extremely conductive, and serve the voicing of free opinions and even help the migration of free uncensored expression from the Web to other offline and more accessible media (print, radio, mp3 exchange . . .). I always bear in mind that less than 5 or 10% of the Egyptian population has access to the Internet." Second, "Video, in general (for songs or other purposes) is perfect in a country with so many people who can't read or write. I had always been hoping, from the very beginning, that these videos would reach these populations. It's probably just a dream, but who knows what might happen."[67] The notable feature of Ahmad Sherif's videos is that they were created for the purpose of jumping outside the online frame and becoming a quotidian tangible experience.

Finally, a key evolutionary element is that activists learnt the need to transcend the digital sphere. One way in which this was done was through the launch of a print publication in 2010 called *Wasla* (meaning the "link") by the Arab Network for Human Rights Information. Wasla published selected written Arabic and English language blog posts by Arab bloggers as well as images from blogs in a printed newspaper that was distributed for free, extending the reach of blogs into the offline community. *Wasla*'s name summarized the four key ways in which it acted as a link. First, *Wasla* acted as a link between bloggers and readers who were not well versed in the language of the internet. Its first issue, published in April 2010, had a technical section explaining what Twitter was, and its second issue from May 2010 featured an article about whether blogs could be considered a new literary genre. Second, *Wasla* was a link between the worlds of the acceptable and the unacceptable in the public domain, pushing the boundaries of what issues could be discussed publicly. Its inaugural issue carried a post from the blog *Yawmiyat Emraa Mithlya* (Diaries of a Lesbian) as well as a two-page spread chronicling an incident of police brutality against a man and his daughters in Egypt, where one of the headlines stated that one of the daughters was threatened with rape. Third, *Wasla* was a link between the different Arab blogging communities. Its April 2010 issue carried a story about the arrest of a Moroccan blogger who was jailed for blogging about demonstrations, and its May 2010 issue contained textual and visual entries by bloggers in Tunisia, Kuwait and Lebanon. Finally, *Wasla* linked visual representations normally only found on the internet to the world of print publications. Issue 2 contained two blog posts on Egypt's *"baltagiyya"* (government thugs), illustrated with photographs of those thugs attacking civilians. Due to censorship measures, such photographs would not have found a space in Egypt's mainstream press. In those ways, *Wasla* helped set the tone for a heightened interplay of those four factors when the Arab uprisings began.

Another way in which activists transcended the digital sphere was through beginning to work on offline mobilization tactics. As Faris cites in an article from 2008, "[i]n the aftermath of the failed May 4th follow up strike [which was called for through Facebook that year], Hossam El-Hamalawy lectured his fellow activists and readers that 'this technology should be complimentary [sic] and a logistical support for whatever we do ON THE GROUND'. El-Hamalawy argues that 'the general strike is coming, but from below' ."[68] This evolutionary context illustrates that images were part of a wider process of subversion that sought to "demonstrate the inherent instability of seemingly hegemonic structures, that power is diffused throughout society, and that there are multiple possibilities for resistance by oppressed people."[69]

Images in the revolution

Social media images

"Facebook Revolution" is one of the names that have been given to the January 25 Revolution in Egypt, in recognition of the role that the social media played in this monumental event. While it is reductionist to tag the revolution as such, the online media did indeed play several roles, as Khamis and Vaughn summarize:

> The role of new media before, during, and after the Egyptian revolution was especially important in three intertwined ways, namely: enabling cyberactivism, which was a major trigger for street activism; encouraging civic engagement, through aiding the mobilization and organization of protests and other forms of political expression; and promoting a new form of citizen journalism, which provides a platform for ordinary citizens to express themselves and document their own versions of reality.[70]

Cyberactivism mainly took place before 25 January. The "We Are All Khaled Said" Facebook group was seminal in rallying online support for gathering in the street on 25 January, and a YouTube video by a young activist called Asmaa Mahfouz was not just disseminated online but also covered by the mass media. The video was a simple to-camera statement by Mahfouz, asking Egyptians to join her on 25 January in Tahrir Square, using colloquial language that invoked patriotism, chivalry and women's honor as reasons to join in the protest – another example of the reliance on very local cultural and linguistic references as methods of mobilization. This localization was important as it bridged the gap between "elitist" online activism and the experience of the ordinary Egyptian. The cyberactivism messages looked and sounded familiar, intimate and "from within."

Civic engagement and mobilization through the social media took both practical and symbolic forms. On the practical front, the social media were used "to transmit information on medical requirements, essential telephone numbers and the satellite frequencies of Al Jazeera" when the channel was being disrupted by the Egyptian government.[71] Crowdmapping, the use of online interactive maps to document crisis events through open-source software like Ushahidi, was also used to document incidents of abuse as well as to create a visual online history of protests.[72] On the symbolic front, the social media were rife with anti-Mubarak images and self-reflexive pictures supporting the revolution. A popular photo circulated through several online platforms was that of three policemen in riot gear that was photoshopped so that the placards that originally said "Central Security" on their shields now said "Facebook" and "Twitter" instead.

Citizen journalism was an important factor in the revolution, especially as the Egyptian government tried to block journalists from reporting on the protests. Citizen journalism takes the symbiosis between activists and the media[73] to a higher level as ordinary people themselves "become" the media when they record and disseminate images of public action through mobile phones and the internet. Strömbäck argues that "it is possible to reach out to wider audiences through the Internet, but in the absence of coverage in the traditional news media, this possibility is seldom realized."[74] Citizen journalism during the Egyptian revolution recognized the importance of "metacoverage,"[75] as footage recorded by protesters in Tahrir Square became a primary form of recorded images of the revolution broadcast on television.

The importance of images generated through citizen journalism is that they were visual records of the subjectivity of the protesters. As Susan Sontag argues, a photograph is an "objective record and personal testimony, both a faithful copy or transcription of an actual moment of reality and an interpretation of that reality."[76] Citizen videos and photos communicated the individual and collective experience of "being" in the revolution. They were visual records of the revolution as an experience mediated through the body, both through the fact that it was the body of the individual protester being present in the space of protest that allowed those images to be created, and also through the recorded images being visual testimonies of the performance of the body in public action. This duality lent the recordings a sense of intimacy that, along with the synergy between protesters, mobile phones and the social media, not only allowed the transmission of news that otherwise would not have made it to broadcast media, but that was also "instrumental in garnering the attention of the citizens of the world who expressed solidarity with those suppressed individuals."[77] Particularly touching were the images of protesters carrying signs with humorous slogans, such as "Leave already, my arm hurts," and of those who had improvised helmets from everyday objects like plastic bottles, cardboard boxes and even loaves of bread, to protect their heads from the assault of police bullets. Those earthy methods stood in strong contrast to the shields carried by the police, or the F16 fighter jets sent by the Egyptian government to terrorize the protesters through flying at low altitude over Tahrir Square (to which the protesters reportedly responded by spontaneously chanting "Mubarak has gone mad!"[78]). The images of victimized, unarmed, yet high spirited Egyptians resorting to "primitive" non-violent methods of self-preservation spoke of resistance to the state's attempt at reducing the human being to bare life[79], and made the experiences of the Egyptians emotionally closer, more subjective and thus more open to identification.

Fig. 38. A demonstrator protects his head with a kitchen pot carrying the Arabic slogan "Down with Mubarak" at a barricade in Cairo's Tahrir Square on 4 February 2011. Photo by AFP–Patrick Baz.

The social media and mobile phones allowed the political voice of protesters to have a wider reach, and thus acted as tools of political agency. They were "both *agents* of change, shaping their contexts of use, and *objects* of change, which [were] shaped and redesigned by users."[80] Mobile phones, specifically, became an essential tool of documenting protests, and when the Egyptian government shut down access to the internet and mobile phone networks and tried to impose a media blackout, mobile phone photos and videos were the only evidence that certain events during the protests happened.[81] Gergen writes that "the cell phone is virtually unique in its capacity to link otherwise absent worlds to the immediate circumstance"[82]; the Egyptian revolution illustrated this, so that, as Beaumont says, the defining image of the Arab Spring became that of a man or a woman using his or her mobile phone to capture footage of an uprising.[83]

The aesthetic of mobile phone videos also became the new aesthetic of authenticity for television. The screening of jerky, blurry mobile phone videos communicated an aesthetic of intimacy that changed the way spectacle is conceived. Unlike the high-resolution drama of the collapse of the Twin Towers on September 11, 2001, mobile phone video recordings from Tahrir Square were low resolution, changing the way a "mind bomb"[84] (an image event that changes people's worldview) is visualized or imagined. The ultimate example of this low-resolution mind bomb is the Battle of the Camel, when the Egyptian government sent thugs on camel and horseback to attack protesters in Tahrir Square. The medieval aesthetic of this violent incident was aptly captured through jerky video images, with the style of the attack and the low-resolution images making the incident more spectacular than if it had been captured and disseminated through polished, high-resolution images, which, one could argue, would have had a distancing effect on the viewer as they would have resembled fictional cinematic clips.

The image as a revolutionary tactical aid

The online media were not the primary method of rallying the masses during the revolution. A report by the Dubai School of Government argues that, during the Egyptian revolution, "for many protestors these tools were not central. It can also be argued that Facebook was an instrumental tool for a core number of activists who then mobilized wider networks through other platforms or through traditional real-life networks of strong ties."[85] It is important to note that the biggest demonstration in Tahrir Square, on Friday 28 January 2011, took place during a period when the Egyptian government had shut down the internet and mobile phone communication. The shutdown started on 25 January, with partial blocking of mobile phone networks and of Twitter and then Facebook, and had become a full blockage by 27 January. Tahrir Square protesters reacted by starting to hold up signs detailing the time and location of the next day's protests.[86]

It is therefore important to examine the ways in which offline methods were used for this purpose. Mohammad Mustafa, an Egyptian political activist and coordinator of the National Coalition for Change campaign, is quoted by Khamis and Vaughn explaining one such method:

> Because not everyone in Egypt has Internet access, we had to also make sure through street activism that those who do not have Internet access could also be reached and that their sentiments are in support of the revolution. That was secured in previous campaigns through collecting signatures from lay people to document their support of the "Change Declaration" that was drafted by Dr. ElBaradei; knocking on peoples' doors and rallying their support; and even rehearsing for this major event through sporadic, mini-protests to guarantee public support.[87]

The "rehearsal" that Mustafa refers to is an important visual act, an example of the role of the visual as a tactic in offline mobilization. De Certeau argues that tactics are the strategy of the weak. He says:

> A *tactic* is a calculated action determined by the absence of a proper locus...The space of a tactic is the space of the other...It is a maneuver "within the enemy's field of vision"... and within enemy territory...It operates in isolated actions, blow by blow. It takes advantage of "opportunities" and depends on them...It must vigilantly make use of the cracks that particular conjunctions open in the surveillance of the proprietary powers...It creates surprises in them. It can be where it is least expected...In short, a tactic is an art of the weak.[88]

Images were used as tactics in two ways just before and during the revolution. First, images were used to provide offline logistical help. "On Twitter, images were posted showing satellite maps marked with arrows indicating where protesters could go to avoid pro-government thugs."[89] Images were also used in a manual that advised people on how to protest that was distributed both online and offline, making the Egyptian revolution the first in recorded history that saw the distribution of such a manual. The manual, "How to Protest Intelligently," contained both a list of protester demands and tactical advice on how to act during the revolution. The manual began with a list of political demands, and then a list of tactical aims: taking over government buildings; attempting to win over the police; and the protection of fellow protesters. This was followed by tactical advice on the mechanism for gathering, which told people to first gather in small streets and then head to main areas.

The manual was unique in its use of images to illustrate its points. A hand-drawn image of a neighborhood had arrows in red directing people on how to move from small streets to main roads, and this was followed by a satellite image of the area of the Radio and Television building in Cairo with arrows showing precise entrance points that would allow the protesters to surround the building. Other similar satellite images with directions followed, targeting the presidential palace and various police stations. The next section listed the necessary attire for protesters, along with hand drawings of clothing items and accessories: a hooded sweater, protective eyeglasses, rubber gloves and a scarf, all to protect from tear gas; a rose to indicate peacefulness; a pot cover to be used as a shield against rubber bullets; spray paint to be sprayed on the visors of police helmets and on the windshields of their vehicles to block their vision; and tennis shoes. The manual then had a drawn illustration of how the accessories like the spray paint and the shield could be used. Potential scenarios for how to deal with police attacks were also presented, such as on page 17, where an illustration showed the throwing of a tear gas canister back at the police (the instructions stated that it would be best if this was done while wearing rubber gloves).

The manual indicated a high awareness of the visual message sent by the style of the protests, and the power of symbolism. It emphasized presenting a peaceful and organized image. On page 14, the manual showed a drawing of people carrying roses and standing in rows with their heads bowed as if in prayer. The written instructions declared: "Group tactics: After Friday prayers, go out to the streets in organized rows carrying roses and flowers, without chants or slogans. Walk in organized lines (as if in prayer), and continue till we reach our targets (the most important government building in your area)." It also gave examples of the kind of protest banners that could be created. This was illustrated in a drawing depicting a policeman standing between a veiled woman and an unveiled woman (making the drawing itself a symbolic message about the inclusiveness of the protest action), holding a sign declaring "The police and the people are together against injustice! Long live Egypt!" and another showing Gamal Mubarak with his name changed to "Gaban [Coward] Mubarak," with the caption "Where is pappy now?" The manual's use of local humor as well as Egyptian slang in the language it was written in is another example of the cultivation of intimacy that aimed to make this activism call accessible to the ordinary Egyptian.

This effort at cultivating intimacy and accessibility was also demonstrated in the second tactical role that the visual played, and which was highlighted by the April 6 movement as its members sought to gather large numbers of people in the street. Ahmed Salah, one of the founders of the movement, explained that the movement went door-to-door to survey people and to find out what would encourage them to take part in a demonstration. The answer that was given by most of those who were surveyed was "I would go if everybody was going." Salah came up with a strategy to achieve this. On 25 January, he and his fellow activists organized mini-protests in narrow alleys in Cairo, thereby creating the illusion that "everybody was going." The alley protests encouraged those in the neighborhoods to join in, after which the protesters headed to Tahrir Square.[90] In this sense, the spectacle itself became a mobilization tool.

Reversing the image of Mubarak

One of the main visual acts during the revolution was the deliberate reversal of the image of Mubarak. An effigy of Mubarak was hung directly over Tahrir Square. Images with both local and global historical references were used by protesters in the square, projecting a self-knowing acknowledgement of the multiple audiences their protest was targeting. Protesters carried photos of Mubarak that were photoshopped to make him dressed up as Egypt's deposed monarch King Farouk, while other placards displayed the image of Mubarak with a Hitler moustache and hairdo, dressed in a football outfit spelling "30 years of corruption" on its front, alongside a referee holding up the red card.

Images in the street reversed the visual references that had been used by Mubarak in his image management campaign. Graffiti appeared on the streets which targeted Mubarak and his family, with satirical depictions of his sons as well as his wife Suzanne, the latter referred to as a "spoilt duck" in one roadside caricature. Mubarak was painted as a grimacing King of Spades in one graffito in Zamalek, and as a pharaoh in another. During one demonstration, a protester carried a sign that spelt the word "Leave" in Arabic and hieroglyphics, along with the Arabic caption "It's in hieroglyphics so that maybe you understand it, you pharaoh." After Mubarak's departure, a graffito on a street near Tahrir Square was of a large chess board with the king knocked out. All those visual depictions carried symbolic statements about Mubarak's authoritarian regime being absolutely monarchic in all senses but the name.

Humorous images of Mubarak quickly permeated pan-Arab popular culture. On al-Jazeera's website, one cartoon showed Mubarak holding on tight to the leg of a chair as a man tagged "The Egyptian Street" pulled him away, dragging Mubarak's trousers down and exposing his underwear, while another had a sweating Mubarak's palm being read by a clairvoyant predicting "Ahead of you is a travel path." Blogs and social media sites also disseminated humorous images, such as a fake ad for "Mubarak Super Glue, guaranteed for 30 years." The Jordanian online cartoon company Kharabeesh added humorous videos of Mubarak to its repertoire, eventually creating a series titled "Arab leaders" that poked fun at dictators in the Arab Spring like Ben Ali, Mubarak, Qaddafi and Bashar al-Assad. Through this variety of roles, the image in the revolution became a central method of expressing political dissent.

The ultimate reversal of Mubarak's image happened when he was finally brought to trial in the summer of 2011. Gone was the image of the "modern" president, the "hero" of 1973, and the father of the Egyptian people. In its place was that of a frail man lying down on a stretcher in a cage, who was at one point caught off-guard, picking his nose, by the television cameras broadcasting the trial live, sending thousands of Egyptians into roars of laughter as they witnessed this scene.

The creation of images reversing those established by Mubarak was coupled with another visual act, the tearing down and shredding of the images of Mubarak that had dominated public space. This was not the first time that protesters in Egypt had done this. A landmark incident took place during a workers' strike in Mahalla al-Kubra in April 2008, when protesters tore down a large billboard of Mubarak and stampeded on it. The photograph of the event, taken by Nasser Nouri, became an iconic, widely circulated image. While this attack could be read as a symbolic one, with the image of Mubarak used as a substitute for the man himself because of the inability of protesters to actually oust him[91], similar attacks during the revolution were not acts of sublimation; they were political moves driven by a sense of citizen empowerment. The visual acts were articulations of presence by Egyptian citizens, replacing the image of Mubarak with the physicality of the citizen. In this, the acts, as visual events meant for being witnessed, were also an articulation of what Horst Bredekamp calls *"bildakt,"* the "picture act."[92] The picture act is a way of understanding the power of the image. This power does not derive from the meaning that an image imposes – after all, all images have multiple meanings for the beholders – but from the act of being seen. Bredekamp argues that once an image has been seen, it captures the viewer, making it impossible for the viewer "to see the world in any way other than through this medium ... it becomes impossible for the beholder to return to the status quo" before the image was seen.[93] As such, those visual acts of destruction, as images in themselves, can be read as deliberate efforts to permanently change the political status quo in Egypt, and as changing the way Egyptian citizens are perceived by the regime, the world and themselves.

The image of the revolution: the spectacle of Tahrir Square

Tahrir Square was the physical and symbolic heart of the Egyptian revolution, and the world's gaze was turned to this locale throughout the revolution, with al-Jazeera's cameras relaying live footage from the square 24 hours a day (when its transmission was not interrupted or its journalists prevented from reporting), and the mass media and social media relaying photographs and videos taken by citizen journalists in the square to the globe. The revolution was itself a spectacle, a drama with highs and lows, expressing the full range of human emotion, from joy to fear to rage, emotions felt by protesters in Tahrir Square and shared by those watching the revolution unfold from afar.

The image of Tahrir Square itself has come to define that of the revolution. The importance of Tahrir Square, Liberation Square, is that, first, it is a symbolic national space in Egyptian territory, signifying national liberation (from colonial rule), and thus is a space where "the nation's history [is] written in soil."[94] Second, as Mills argues, "[e]ach society's 'moral order' is reflected in its particular spatial order and in the language and imagery by which that spatial order is represented. Conversely, the social is spatially constituted, and people make sense of their social identity in terms of their environment."[95] Tahrir Square is the largest public square in Cairo, and as such, it is a mini cosmos of the country's moral order as expressed in spatial order, a space that was controlled by the state and which had seen many protests crushed by the Egyptian police since the days of the Kifaya movement. This quelling of public dissent served to control citizens' social identities by restricting their freedom of action in space. Dasgupta says that space is constructed as a "complex product of physical, affective, and social space where aesthetic representation, discursive spatial practice, and the spatial practice of the social all form a complex ensemble of productive practices."[96] During the revolution, Tahrir Square became an example of this complex space. The revolution highlighted the visual dimension of spatialization, the processes through which space is represented and experienced.[97]

The revolution changed the way Tahrir Square was represented. Jaworski and Thurlow argue that the way space is seen is often mediated through its visual representation. Sörlin calls this the "articulation of territory,"[98] the way landscape features are reproduced and represented in art and other visual and literary forms. The January 25 Revolution created a new way of seeing Tahrir Square. The square became a "symbolic system of signifiers" that changed its representation in people's spatial imagination.[99] One element of this change is the visual products representing the square itself. The image of thousands of people gathering in the circular surroundings of Tahrir Square has become one of the iconic images of Egypt, reproduced in memorabilia commemorating the revolution, becoming a national icon akin to the image of the pyramids. It was also reproduced in art, like the posthumous installation by Ahmed Basiony who was killed in the 27 January protest, and which was selected as Egypt's contribution to the 2011 Venice Biennale. The installation featured footage of protests in Tahrir Square during the first three days of the revolution which were shot by the artist, presenting a new way in which Tahrir Square is articulated; Tahrir Square, as an iconic national space, now narrates the history of the nation as one harboring empowered citizens. Another way in which this change of representation of space manifested itself was through the "nation's collective gaze"; Jaworski and Thurlow say that "our sense of national or regional identity is closely linked to the nation's collective gaze at the physical attributes of landscape... iconic images of the urban... have themselves been... incorporated into popular and official imaginings of national identity."[100] The square's image in the eyes of the Egyptians, a space transformed into the hub of political action, changed the imaginings of national identity as it became about a people reclaiming their freedom and dignity. "Lift your head, you are Egyptian" became one of the most prevalent slogans of the revolution.

The revolution also changed the way the space of Tahrir Square was experienced. De Certeau argues that "space is a practiced place," meaning that it is people's acts and interactions with the place that transform it into a space.[101] Tahrir Square became a national hub, the site of community action that linked together the online and offline worlds as people rallied for a common cause and communicated their messages to the world at large. In this sense, the revolution transformed Tahrir Square into what Castells calls a "space of flows," a space that allows "for simultaneity of social practices without territorial contiguity."[102] Castells characterizes the space of flows as being made of networks of interaction, hubs of activity and "habitats for the social actors who operate the networks."[103] The habitats of Tahrir Square were both the physical tents in which the protesters "lived" in the square, and the virtual locations they carved for themselves on YouTube, Twitter and other social media. The interactions and activities in the square were not limited to chants and the holding of placards but also included international interactions as protesters communicated with the world outside Egypt through citizen journalism and symbolic performances.

Lefebvre argues that "a revolution, whether violent or nonviolent... acquires the new significance of a liberation from the quotidian and the resurrection of the Festival."[104] Tahrir Square liberated Egyptians from the routine of quotidian life that had become a metaphor for political stagnation, and became a festive space, with music and theatre performances, vendors selling food and paraphernalia and communities of citizens getting together in a shared experience. This joyful shared experience was important as a protest strategy. As Ehrenreich argues, "[p]eople must find, in their movement, the immediate joy of solidarity, if only because, in the face of overwhelming state or corporate power, solidarity is their sole source of strength."[105] At the same, time, as Shepard, Bogad and Duncombe put it, politics must engage in the seemingly more ephemeral realms of desire and fantasy, spectacle and performance, if they are to take on meaning for people. A politics without meaning is a politics that mobilizes no one. But political meaning is empty, unrealized, unless expressed in policies and politics with material results. We need to think of political performance as...moving forward as part of an overall plan to change...the shape of material reality itself.[106]

The presence of protest communities in the space of Tahrir Square was symbolically important, for, as Castells argues, communities of resistance act in the space defined by the state.[107] "Resistance, then, not only takes place in place, but also seeks to appropriate space, to make new spaces."[108] The protesters of Tahrir Square sought to reclaim space as their own. Tahrir Square became the space where they "lived" – ate, slept, sang, protested, even got married – and they treated it like their home, mopping and collecting garbage from the square in an action that spoke of pride of belonging to this space. Tahrir Square also harbored new symbolic actions by the protesters. It was where they carried defecting policemen on their shoulders, and hugged soldiers perched on their tanks, giving some of those soldiers roses and posing with their children next to the tanks in family snapshots. It was also where thousands of people prayed in unison, with Christians forming a circle to protect the Muslims while they prayed, and vice versa. The act of prayer in the square linked experience with representation. Dramatic high-angle images of the thousands of Egyptians moving rhythmically in prayer in Tahrir Square sent a strong symbolic message about citizen solidarity and was an example of the symbolic political power of "the aestheticization of everyday life...the project of turning life into a work of art."[109] Tahrir Square was also a space of defiance and ability to overcome hardship. Like the nearby 6 October Bridge, it was where people continued kneeling in prayer despite being sprayed with water by the military, forcing the water cannon tanks to retreat in defeat. The images of those actions have themselves become iconic, sealing the transformation of Tahrir Square into what bell hooks calls a "homeplace,"[110] a space that itself acts as a source of dignity and agency, and a site of "solidarity in which and from which, resistance can be organized and conceptualized."[111]

What the above also highlights is the way the image of the bodies of protesters and the space of Tahrir Square came to seamlessly merge. The protest in the square became an embodied performance of patriotism, and a declaration of belonging to the land. Political agency was expressed through being in the square, through public visibility. The body and the space defined one another as they shared a common experience and representation. Nowhere was this process symbolized more than through the breaking down of pieces of pavement from Tahrir Square into stones that protesters hurled at the police and thugs as they attempted to defend themselves from attack. This physical act was also a symbolic one, speaking of the body of the city sacrificing itself to protect the bodies of the people. This symbolic act was itself commemorated after the revolution, with one corner of Tahrir Square displaying some of the broken pavement stones that had been used in the revolution, which were arranged on the ground above the words "Egypt is my heart." The self-referential display acted as a visual reminder of the sacrifices and goals of the revolution, and of the importance of carrying on its legacy.

Fig. 39. Demonstrators break a pavement at Cairo's Tahrir Square to use it as projectiles against pro-regime opponents on 2 February 2011. Photo by AFP–Mohammed Abed.

Images by the revolution: graffiti and community art

De Certeau argues that "there has never been cultural innovation without social conflicts and political victories."[112] The January 25 Revolution is an example of this dynamic, producing new forms of visual expression in public space in Egypt: community art, graffiti and murals.[113] Those forms of visual expression can be understood as a way through which citizens have reclaimed public space, and have freely expressed sentiments that before could only be expressed obliquely or fleetingly.

The revolution saw the rise of the Revolution Artists Union, a collection of artists who roped off an area of Tahrir Square to be used as an open-air space where people could create and display art. This democratization of art space challenges the traditional authority of the curator and opens up artistic practice as an equal right. In this space, pencil drawings on notebook paper hung side by side next to water colors, satire was displayed next to documentary and the secular and the religious shared equal representational potential. On one day, the simple line drawing of a snake above the slogan "No to ideology" was displayed just beneath that of a Muslim sheikh and a Christian priest holding their hands together and raising them as the former carried a Quran and the latter a cross. Handler argues that "[l]anguage is an act of power, a form of social action. 'To acquire and exercise a language is to engage in the most profound of political acts . . .'." It is through democratic dialogue that the powerless become engaged. Democratic dialogue denies closure."[114] The image is also an act of power. The visual art created and displayed in Tahrir Square acted as a means of democratic dialogue as well as of the expression of power: Everybody could participate, everybody was empowered. The square became a new creative space that dissolved the barrier between the viewer and the art and united diverse communities in art.

Another art form produced by the revolution that also created "a more immediate, direct form of engagement with the viewer" is graffiti.[115] Before the January 25 Revolution, graffiti and murals were virtually non-existent in the public areas of Cairo, as control over visual representation in public space was firmly in the hands of the government, which had erased any such visual expressions almost as soon as they appeared. The revolution saw a rapid rise in graffiti that ranged from the simple to the elaborate. At first, simple stencils

153

depicting light bulbs appeared, symbolizing the shining light of the revolution, as were those of a clenched fist, the symbol of the April 6 movement (in turn symbolizing the power of the people). The stencils quickly grew into the more elaborate form of murals.

The graffiti artist Banksy says that graffiti is a form of "answering back."[116] During and after the January 25 Revolution, graffiti and murals were another way for Egyptian citizens to answer back through reclaiming space as well as sending messages countering those of the regime. It is this duality of roles that Neil Jarman highlights in his argument that murals should be understood as both art and artifacts. Murals are art because of their symbolic content, and they are artifacts because of their fixed location in space.[117]

Graffiti and murals as art

Graffiti and murals as works of art performed two key roles. First, they were used to reclaim the notion of agency for citizens. Stencils of revolution martyrs started appearing early on, depicting the faces of martyrs along with slogans such as "Glory to the martyr" and "Glory to freedom." Martyr depictions then evolved into large murals giving an individual identity to each martyr through depicting his or her image along with the person's name, age and profession. The murals later evolved beyond individualization. A graffiti image that has been repeated in Cairo shows the stencil of a young man, with an aura around his head, along with the slogan "I am the people." The use of the aura is an appropriation of its visual use by authoritarian rulers in the Middle East like Khomeini, Qaddafi and Hafez al-Assad, which relies on its connotation with eternity.[118] In doing so, the image is presenting a new discourse for the Egyptian nation, based on the endurance of the people, not the leader, which in turn responds to Mubarak's appropriation of pharaohnic symbols associated with eternity.

Second, they were used to reclaim the notion of community-based nationalism. This was shown through depicting the people as diverse while erasing the previous chaperoning of this diversity by a ruler or a ruling party (as in the Mubarak and NDP billboards of Egyptians from different walks of life discussed earlier). An example is a drawing on a wall that showed a woman and a child standing under the protective arm of a man carrying the Egyptian flag. Community-based nationalism was also connected with alluding to the people's defiance of the regime. One graffito had two panels: On the right panel, the drawing of a traditional Egyptian man wearing a turban on his head, an indication of being a peasant, is shown above the word "subjected." The man is outlined in black and white, but is shown to be crying red blood. The panel on the left simply depicts the word "No" written in red, signaling the defiance of the disenfranchised individual as written in blood.

Graffiti and murals as artifacts

Graffiti and murals as artifacts performed a political role that went beyond symbolism. This role was produced by their interaction with the space in which they existed. As Jarman argues, location infuses murals with meaning, while murals' presence in a location also lends meaning to that particular site. In other words, murals interact with their social and physical environment, and can act as boundary markers or identity definers.[119] Murals were used as such boundary markers in Tahrir Square. Jaworski and Thurlow describe signs marking physical boundaries as experiential spaces that identify place as a perceptual space.[120] The revolution saw a manifestation of this after the government's violent attacks on protesters resulted in the death of several martyrs. The northern entrance of Tahrir Square became an experiential space. It displayed a large painting with the words "Martyrs' Square" on it, in acknowledgement of the role of those who died during the revolution. The government was no longer the power in charge of directing the perception of public space; the people possessed this power.

Graffiti and murals also became a relatively established way of sending direct political messages, with a number of artist activists becoming known as they continued to create murals to comment on political developments after Mubarak's departure. Ganzeer is one such artist whose work is an attempt at overt intervention in the political trajectory in post-Mubarak Egypt. In particular, he achieved acclaim for his work against the rule of Egypt's Supreme Council of the Armed Forces (SCAF) in the summer of 2011, as the SCAF sought to retain its political power. Ganzeer created a graffito showing the pillars of the SCAF who were still in power, under the slogan "The people want the fall of those loved by the regime." Another huge graffito he created showed, on the right, a traditional bread vendor, peddling the streets on his bike, standing off against a tank on the left, a sharp departure from the rosy picture of the military that protesters in Tahrir Square had painted through handing the Egyptian army roses and proclaiming that the army and the people were one; with the SCAF holding on to power, the military was no longer seen as being on the side of the people. The importance of location for

Ganzeer's work is that it appears in the same space where protesters succeeded in overthrowing Mubarak, thereby calling attention to the need for sustaining protest in this space.

Another artist whose murals "work" through interacting with space is Sad Panda, who is known for adding the stencil of a hunched, pot-bellied, sad-looking panda to existing graffiti like Ganzeer's vendor vs. tank piece. This visual addition appends another layer of experience to the original graffito; the addition, happening at a later time than that of the creation of the original graffito, signals the persistence of the problem critiqued in the original graffito, while the panda's stare symbolizes the people's witnessing and awareness of this problem. Sad Panda's panda can be read as a floating image in itself. This floating image sometimes comments on other floating images. An example of this dynamic can be found in the addition of the panda to one of the stencils of Amr Beheiry. The stencil of Amr Beheiry is an example of the translation of the online banners that had been used before the revolution by bloggers to call for the freeing of detained fellow bloggers and activists (which itself was derived from the use of such banners in physical space in the first place) into the graffiti world. It is one of a number of stencils calling for the freeing of detained activists that appeared in Cairo after the revolution. Amr Beheiry's stencil depicts his picture under the slogan "Freedom for Amr Beheiry," and features the added explanation "I am in military jail because I participated in the revolution." Sad Panda's panda was added to the left of this graffito, staring directly at the image of Beheiry. The latency of the panda's appearance lends the original graffito an added layer of time. On its own, the original graffito could be seen as frozen in time. With the appearance of the panda, a sense of elapsed time is conveyed, implicitly highlighting the necessity of action to stop an ongoing transgression on freedom.

In this way, graffiti and murals quickly evolved from simple comments on and commemorations of the revolution to political weapons in the revolution's aftermath. Political groups like the April 6 movement have used this method in a more explicit way, such as through the stencil of a young man who is covering his mouth with a scarf, a reference to tear gas bombs, which was painted in the summer of 2011 to advertise the movement's website and its mission against the SCAF. "We are continuing," the stencil's caption said. Graffiti was also used as a call to action. An example is the embrace of the floating image of Khaled Said. On the first anniversary of the killing of Khaled Said, in June 2011, stencils of his face were painted all over the exterior of the Ministry of Interior after protesters stormed the military line surrounding the building. The stencils bore the writing: "Will my blood become water, in your eyes? Will you forget my clothes that are stained with blood?" The floating image of Khaled Said, then, became both a "physical" political weapon (due to its being painted on the wall of the Ministry of Interior) as well as a symbolic one.

This stencil of Khaled Said was part of a larger set of anti-SCAF graffiti. Some of this graffiti was created to announce planned anti-SCAF demonstrations. One graffito image appeared calling for a demonstration on 27 May through simply depicting the date and the image of a Molotov bomb. Another graffito announced the anti-SCAF demonstration of 8 July through depicting handcuffs under a red beret and the date of the protest. Supporting the call was a stencil of Mubarak with a red "No" sign over his face along with the date of the protest and the caption "He has not yet been tried."[121] Another mural showed Field Marshal Mohammad Hussein Tantawi in military uniform wearing a Salafist-style beard, in criticism of his perceived support of the fundamentalist group, which protesters regarded as an anti-democratic stance. Just before the protest itself, a large mural of a man throwing a gas canister back in the direction of

Fig. 40. A mural in Cairo in July 2011 showing Mubarak pulling the strings of the SCAF. Photo by Kay Dickinson.

where the police line had been during the revolution appeared in Tahrir Square, not only referencing real photographs of protesters who had engaged in this act during the revolution, but also symbolically indicating the people's refusal of a police state, as well as warning of a repeat of revolutionary tactics. Another graffito sending this message had the words "The People" under the computer icon for "Standby," indicating that the people are in a state of temporary stillness, prepared to reactivate popular protest at any moment. This use of a computer world reference is part of a larger symbiosis between graffiti and computer iconography, which includes the social media. Street art frequently referenced the role that the social media played in the revolution, extending the media's experience into physical space. An example is a mural in Zamalek that showed the head of a screaming young man, his neck emerging from a broken chain as three arms extend to him carrying a mobile phone, the Facebook logo and a crescent. The power of the digital media was thus presented as a pillar on par with religious belief, and the interaction between street art, physical space and the social media lent all those communication tropes further power.

Fig. 41. A mural in Cairo in August 2011 highlighting the role of the social media in the Egyptian Revolution. Photo by Ben Rowswell.

In addition to graffiti's derivation of power from interacting with physical space and referencing the social media, this art form has also claimed further clout from its remediation through the mass media and the social media.[122] The online graffiti map of Cairo set up by Ganzeer, Cairo Street Art[123], is an example of this process put into practice. The map documents new pieces of graffiti and murals appearing in Cairo through adding their images to their precise locations on a Google map. Clicking on the map's place markers opens windows showing photos of the street art pieces with the dates the photos were taken. The photo entries are updated if a piece of art is defaced. "The lovers of the regime" mural by Ganzeer, for example, had such a fate, which led to the uploading of a new photo of it after its defacing that was added to the original entry, with an explanation by Ganzeer that the new photo showed the mural "after it was defaced by stupid people." In this way, the social media reverse the ephemeral nature of graffiti and murals, granting them a "permanent" place in (virtual) space. In doing so, not only do they extend the experience of those murals, they also create a digital visual archive of the revolution and its aftermath. The notable political role of graffiti and murals is that they transform space from mundane to politicized, extending the message of resistance into an everyday experience.[124] Moreover, different graffiti spaces "interact with one another . . . and with the social actors inhabiting these spaces in creating complex networks of meaning, or 'semiotic aggregates'."[125] The remediation of street art aids both processes: It allows this art form to send its messages to a wider public while also addressing the local one[126], and it in turn extends the scope of semiotic aggregates, as remediation is itself based on the virtual presence of images that become part of people's networks of meaning.[127]

The traveling revolutionary image

The images in, of and by the Egyptian revolution travelled into other locations in the Arab world as protests calling for reform started in Bahrain, Yemen, Algeria, Oman, Jordan, Syria and Libya. Videos documenting regime brutality as well as citizen defiance have become a standard visual output of uprisings across the Arab world, as have images acting as a tactic or a symbol. Protest performances like holding regular demonstrations on Fridays after prayers have also become rituals. In Syria, the killing of 13-year old Hamza al-Khatib gave the Syrian uprising its own symbolic martyr. A video of the boy's mutilated body was shot by his family, in direct defiance of orders by the Syrian security services to not reveal the circumstances of Hamza's death. The video was distributed online and screened on al-Jazeera, becoming a deliberately produced piece of visual evidence that Hamza's family created to prove to the world the brutality of the Assad regime. The circulation of the video led to the creation of a Facebook page referencing "We Are All Khaled Said," titled "We Are All Hamza Al-Khatib," while the "We Are All Khaled Said" page carried an image showing the photos of Mohamed Bouazizi, Hamza al-Khatib and Khaled Said side by side under the Tunisian, Syrian and Egyptian flags.

One factor behind this "travel" is the transnational character of protest communities that share similar cultural expressions across borders. Simon Cottle writes that

> [t]he way images of political dissent and protest spill over national borders or leapfrog across entire countries or even regions, to impact upon political struggles waged elsewhere around the world, points once again to the transnational-izing nature of global protest communications as well as their capacity to help build and sustain feelings of political affinity and solidarity.[128]

Fig. 42. An online banner featuring Khaled Said, Hamza al-Khatib and Mohamed Bouazizi on the "We Are All Khaled Said" website.

This argument is presented by Hjarvard as being an inevitable consequence of the age of networks. He says:

> In the era of globalization the media not only provide channels of communication between nations and peoples, but also establish networks across all manner of geographical areas and actors. This development leads in turn to a greater cultural reflexivity. As influxes of media products and communication cross more and more frontiers, virtually no culture will be able to develop in isolation from others.[129]

Jansson says that this global experience is about the establishment of deterritorialized expressive communities:

> [W]hile the media, in general, support the development of deterritorialized *cultural communities*, the visual media play a crucial role in the development of *expressive communities*...These are communities that are not merely based on invisible denominators like values, interests, demographic characteristics, etc., but also, and sometimes exclusively, on semiotic expressions of a shared interpretative framework.[130]

What those three arguments have in common is the sense that communication technologies have the potential to facilitate the creation of a global civil society.[131] However, the Arab Spring complicates those arguments. The arguments can be critiqued for their inattention to the importance of geography in directing the process of cultural expression and political solidarity. The Arab Spring was a process very firmly grounded in geographical location; the fact that the domino effect of uprisings was limited to the *Arab world* is important. It illustrates the rise of a *regional* (not global) civil society that is also grounded in time and space. But the notion of "regional" itself has been challenged by the Arab Spring, for it now not only refers to those present in a neighboring location, but also those in the diaspora in physically far-away places. The Syrian and Libyan diasporas, for example, played a key role in circulating factual information, photographs and videos as well as lobbying during the Arab Spring.[132] This expanded notion of the "regional" entails an expansion and redefinition of political space: It is at once local, national, regional and global. Tahrir Square becomes the symbolic locus of this much wider, fluid "terrain of resistance."[133] Its boundaries go beyond its physical dimensions. The uprisings' domino effect is an indicator of the presence of an Arab imagined community and unity of cause that is nevertheless *rooted in particular national contexts*.[134] The images may be similar but the underlying challenges in each country are articulated and dealt with according to the particularities of each location.

The image, in this context, acted as a catalyst that ignited the surfacing of issues that authoritarian ruling had buried deep, like oppression and inequality, and which had manifested themselves differently in each country. Azza El-Hassan calls this catalysis "image hysteria." She argues that Arab viewers have been awed by the non-stop spectacle of revolutions, which not only captured the viewers' imagination but also caused them to subconsciously internalize the "character" of revolutionaries fighting against authoritarianism.[135] This role of the image as an activator goes against the characterization of "looking" as substituting "doing," as presented by de Certeau.[136] On the contrary, the traveling image of the revolution was a narrative that operated as a framework fostering collective action, aligning personal and collective identities and strengthening the protests' appeal to the mainstream.[137]

Representing ourselves

One of the key visual dynamics of the Arab Spring has been the creation of visual products, from memorabilia to pictures to exhibitions and museums, that capture the stories of the uprisings from the peoples' point of view. In Libya, an exhibition opened in Benghazi in August 2011 titled "The Tyrant's Crimes," and it was housed in al-Manar palace, a former government headquarter. The exhibition showed 250 pieces by Libyan artists that depicted different kinds of crimes inflicted by Qaddafi's regime, like a painting of dead bodies laid out on the ground; anti-Qaddafi images, like posters depicting the face of Qaddafi as a mask behind which can be seen the face of Satan, and Qaddafi holding a rat, with the caption "Those are Satan's rats, al-Sa'idi, Saif, and Khamis" (Qaddafi's sons); and paintings supporting the rebels, with the resurrected multicolored Libyan flag featuring prominently in a number of works.[138] The exhibition followed an earlier one set up in June 2011 in Misrata that displayed weapons used by Qaddafi's troops against the Libyan people in the crackdown on the rebellion.[139] Although the art on display at the exhibitions was crude, it was an important visual indicator of "answering back" after 42 years of silence under Qaddafi's rule, when the only visual depictions in public space were those sanctioned by the leader.

In Egypt, a large range of memorabilia commemorating the revolution and its martyrs has been created, from postcards to stickers to baseball caps and t-shirts. Some ridicule Mubarak and the NDP, such as a sticker that transforms the Egyptian flag into a takeaway flyer advertising "January 25 Combo: Thieves Kebab," which features the image of Mubarak and NDP members on a skewer being grilled on an open fire. Others honor the Egyptian people, utilizing the colors of the Egyptian flag and featuring the slogan "The Egyptian people's revolution." A museum of the revolution is also being planned, to be housed in the building that used to be the NDP headquarter in Cairo[140], in addition to another museum with the same theme at the American University in Cairo. Both museum projects are characterized by their focus on commemorating the martyrs who died for the Egyptian revolution. In addition, different forms of art, from murals to cartoons to temporary sculptures, have emerged, which all narrate the story of the revolution. A colorful mural on one wall in Tahrir Square depicted the Egyptian security forces attacking civilians. Another mural in Zamalek displayed the Egyptian flag into which depictions of protesters were inserted, with the caption "The martyrs wrote it [the story of the revolution] with their blood, and we drew it with our colors." Images recognized the iconic status of other images. A cartoon circulated on the internet showed protesters carrying placards declaring "Down with Mubarak" juxtaposed with the image of Mubarak carrying a placard declaring "Down with al-Jazeera." After Mubarak's departure, a cartoon appearing online depicted the sign that stated "Leave already, my arm hurts," which was carried during one of the demonstrations in Cairo, as abandoned on the ground by its owner as he runs, carrying the Egyptian flag and singing, to the tune of the Egyptian national anthem, "My country, the arms have now been freed." In July 2011, a Styrofoam model of the events in Tahrir Square on the day of the Battle of the Camel was temporarily on display in the square itself. The model, with a diameter of eight feet, had a toy police car and tanks and two wooden camels of the kind normally sold in souvenir shops, surrounding a roundabout upon which tents and a large Egyptian flag were placed, along with a placard stating "The story of the revolution."

Fig. 43. Egyptian Revolution merchandise on sale in Cairo in July 2011. Photo by Kay Dickinson.

The creation of such quotidian products signals the reclaiming of the practice and performance of nationalism in everyday life from the state, while the urge to document and narrate the revolutions speaks back to the authoritarian regimes' denial of the power to represent to their citizens. This speaking back is driven also by the need, and opportunity, to exert power over one's history. As Kavanagh argues, history exhibitions are a form of history writing.[141] Museums and memorabilia also have symbolic power, signifying nations' shared cultures, territories and histories. The physicality of museums and their location in geographical space point to those projects' being further attempts at reclaiming the national (imagined and physical) space. As Archard says, the nation binds its people, dead, alive and unborn, becoming a narrative that tells their story, and constituting "identity simultaneously as a past, present and future"; in this way, the nation is both "an inheritance and a project."[142] The creation of those visual objects signifies the intention to create a new national project in Libya and Egypt that aims to redirect sovereignty into the hands of the people for generations to come.

Image lessons from the Arab Spring

Chelkowski and Dabashi have argued: "A revolution sees itself in the mirror of the images it creates. A revolution is the images it creates."[143] This statement echoes the Egyptian revolution in particular and the Arab Spring in general, recognizing the visual productivity of revolution as well as the centrality of the image in the way revolution is understood. The multiple ways in which the image has "worked" during the Arab Spring generate a number of lessons about the political role of the image during this period in the history of the Middle East.

First, images should be understood as "vectors of dissent." Routledge uses this notion to refer to "voices" that

> articulate the symbolic creativity enmeshed in everyday life, from which people shape and articulate their struggles. They are what I would term "vectors of dissent" in that they "travel" within and between civil and political societies, and potentially relay messages to a variety of audiences (including movement supporters and opponents), across a variety of scales (from the local to the global). They may remain despite defeat, bring to life other resistances, or relate to the repression if not the uprisings.[144]

This calls for a change in the way politics in the Arab world is perceived. Protest is where hard politics and soft politics meet, and images are one way in which this conjuncture is articulated. The image is one of "the often unstated processes by which struggles over power occur in everyday life."[145] Paying attention to the image, then, is one way of acknowledging the importance of the diffused politics of the everyday. As the revolutions demonstrated, this informal, subversive politics has a real potential to translate into formal political change.

Second, protests as visual performances necessitate acknowledging a change in the way politics is practiced in the Arab world. Politics is now an intentionally visual act performed on a global public stage, where political agents are acutely aware of the resonance of the image projected by this performance. A statement by a Yemeni political activist summarizes this dynamic. Speaking in May 2011, three months after the start of peaceful anti-regime protests in Yemen, a country where almost every household is armed, he said, "We have *performed* peacefully for three months now; it is time for the international community to support us."[146]

Third, the Arab Spring has effected a change in the way the Arab world is perceived. The peaceful protests in Egypt and Tunisia were an exemplary performance in a region characterized by turmoil. But more importantly, the mass protests by Arab citizens erased the perception of the Arab world as politically dormant. This new perception of the Arab world as a politically active space is not just held by those "outside" the region, but also by Arab citizens themselves who now see their region differently.

And this leads to the fourth lesson, which is that the Arab Spring is about a change in Arab citizens' relationship with power and representation. They are no longer subjected; they are empowered political agents. In particular, the Arab Spring is witness to the rise of the *individual* as a political agent. Individual dignity – for Imad al-Kabir, Mohamed Bouazizi – and the individual's right to life – Khaled Said, Hamza al-Khatib – are at the forefront of political life. The face of the nation is no longer that claimed by the leader. It is that of the citizen. The Egyptian revolution recognized this through displaying on the "We Are All Khaled Said" Facebook page an image of Khaled Said's face, painted with the colors of the Egyptian flag and captioned: "I am Egypt." The citizen as an empowered agent is the producer and disseminator of images, claiming back from the ruler the power to represent as an individual right. Citizens have reclaimed the notion of nationalism back from the authoritarian state through the production of images, both on the official level (through the creation of museums for example) and the banal level (through the production of revolution memorabilia and the performance of nationalist acts in everyday life).[147] Through those two modes, Arab citizens are laying claim over their present and future.

The reclamation of the notion of nationalism is also related to the reclamation of national space and the articulation of the power of presence. The fifth lesson is that unlike arguments like Meyrowitz's[148], Featherstone's[149] and Thompson's[150], who all say that identities in the media age have become deterritorialized as social interaction takes place through a "shared national realm of experience,"[151] the Arab Spring has demonstrated a return to the importance of national space. The identities expressed through the new and old media during the Arab Spring are firmly grounded in territory even as they use transnational frameworks to disseminate their messages, and even as they constitute an Arab imagined community.

Finally, the Arab Spring demands acknowledging the image as "alive." Images are not just created objects, they are also beings whose physicality and presence capture the viewer. They are political weapons that act and activate.[152] Understanding the political dynamics of the Arab world, and the Middle East in general, demands a new way of conceptualizing images as central agents in those dynamics. As Mitchell puts it, what is needed is "[n]ot just a history of images as human productions (the traditional task of iconology and art history), but a new, critical history of images that emphasizes their role as 'living' historical agents at turning points in human affairs and human understanding."[153] This chapter – and the two that follow – has been a modest attempt at contributing to the writing of such a critical history of images in relation to a seminal period in the political life of the Arab world.

5

Television Images and Political Struggle

A popular joke that circulated in the Arab world and beyond in 2011 was, "What are Arab dictators most scared of? Al-Jazeera, Facebook and Fridays." The joke is pertinent because al-Jazeera's prominence during the Arab Spring has necessitated paying further attention to the role of television, particularly satellite television, in political struggle in the Arab world. The uprisings of 2011 were television events that transformed street protests into a global spectacle. The eyes of the world were turned to the Arab region, as the global media chronicled the political transformations in Tunisia, Egypt, Libya, Yemen and Syria on a regular basis. The uprisings also expanded the "al-Jazeera effect"[1] and affirmed a change in the image of al-Jazeera. The channel moved from being regarded by some in the West as an al-Qaeda mouthpiece to being seen as telling the story of the Arab Spring with a level of detail, timeliness and accessibility that endeared it to a global audience – in the case of al-Jazeera English – and resonated closely with Arab audiences – in the case of al-Jazeera Arabic. But the joke also hints that al-Jazeera was not a mere detached reporter of the uprisings. Al-Jazeera's political position often directly challenged those of Arab state television channels in Tunisia, Egypt, Syria, Libya and elsewhere, but in doing so, it shared a characteristic with those channels: They were all participants in political struggle. This kind of participation is an established phenomenon for television in the Arab world. As such, one can argue that al-Jazeera's prominent role was both new and old: new in transforming the global image of the channel, but old in the channel's acting as a political player. The aim of this chapter is to examine al-Jazeera's as well Arab state television's roles as political players during the Arab Spring.

The rise of satellite television as a political actor[2]

Since the mid-1990s, satellite television has affirmed its place as the primary news medium in the Middle East. The establishment of al-Jazeera in 1996 was the region's first attempt at entering the world of 24-hour news channels. However, although al-Jazeera was a respected and relatively well-known channel in the Arab world at the time, it did not enjoy a primary position in people's homes. It was the second Palestinian Intifada in 2000 that made al-Jazeera a recognized brand in the region. Al-Jazeera devoted much of its broadcasting time to coverage of the Intifada, presenting a clear pro-Palestinian stance towards the issue.[3] Zayani argues that in doing so, al-Jazeera set itself a political role in the Arab world:

> Al Jazeera's intense coverage of the intifada has not only fed Arab fury but also fostered anti-government behavior in the Arab world, making Arab governments vulnerable to charges and open to criticism that they have not sufficiently supported the Palestinians or decisively acted on the Palestinian cause. In this sense, Al Jazeera places itself as a counter-force to the official indifference towards the plight of the Palestinian people.[4]

At the same time, al-Jazeera's coverage of the Intifada marked a significant change in the Arab television landscape: the assertion of the primacy of the image as a means of political communication. Ayish notes that al-Jazeera "went one step further by showing live footage of clashes in Jerusalem between Palestinian stone throwers and heavily armed Israeli soldiers."[5]

Less than a year later, the events of 11 September 2001 consolidated the transformation of Arab satellite television into a visually saturated medium. September 11 was a television landmark, dominating the screens of television channels in the Arab world and beyond. Jean Baudrillard famously said that the September 11 attacks were the "absolute event, the 'mother event', the pure event."[6] The attacks gave birth to images that have carved a permanent space in the visual memory of people across the globe. Notable among those images were the video tapes sent by al-Qaeda to al-Jazeera following the attacks. The channel's decision to air Osama bin Laden's video messages gave the station worldwide notoriety while transforming it into a household name across the globe. Through the "war on terror," satellite television in the Arab world grew in presence and impact, establishing itself as one of the most widely consumed media in the region.

In the decade and a half since the "war on terror" started, satellite television in the Arab world witnessed much contestation and competition, the most notable of which being the rivalry between al-Jazeera and al-Arabiya, which is part of the Qatari-Saudi power struggle in the region.[7] This period also saw a proliferation of channels, including non-Arab channels like al-Hurra, that formed part of competing international public diplomacy efforts in the Arab world, and which aimed at disseminating messages countering those of al-Jazeera.[8] Within this context, satellite television moved from a medium seen as providing a space for political dialogue in the Arab world, to a challenger to this very space. Satellite television in the region has not been only a tool of communication. It has also been a symptom and sometimes even a cause of power struggles in the Arab word.

The various overlapping power struggles in the Arab world play an important role in shaping the visual and political television landscape in the region. Satellite television is firmly and actively embedded within this complex structure. On one hand, some non-state television channels attempt to challenge the state's political points of view. This is mostly seen in al-Jazeera's coverage of the uprisings in Tunisia, Egypt, Libya, Yemen and Syria during the Arab Spring, which challenged the regimes' versions of the events, and earlier, of the Iraq war, which challenged the American version of the war and its aftermath. On the other hand, satellite television also engages in processes of political struggle by proxy, becoming a platform for rivalries between Arab countries, clashing political groups and international political agents. When doing so, satellite television acts as a mouthpiece for warring political factions. Both roles that satellite television plays in the Arab world indicate that satellite television itself has become a political actor in the Middle East.

The Arab Spring and satellite television's promise of democracy

Despite the political factors governing satellite television, the medium does possess the potential for supporting the creation of a dialogic political sphere, in which audiences get together in sharing a democratic space of expression. In the 1990s, when satellite television in the Arab world was still in its early stages, this development was hailed as a catalyst of social and political change in the region. Subsequently, much was written about the role of satellite television in countering Western narratives about the region, and, with the rise of al-Jazeera, about the potential of this one television station to transform the Arab political sphere.[9] This romanticism is understandable when considered in context of the many constraints on freedom of speech in the Arab world, and the fact that the majority of Arab countries at the time previously had access only to the television stations owned by the states governing them. The image of the leader on television was an indirect domination tool by the state, serving to "enforce obedience and induce complicity" among the people, and producing "belief in the regime's appropriateness."[10]

Scholarly debate on satellite television in the Arab world has since become concerned with television's potential as a democratizing tool. Al-Hail[11] and Amin[12] have written that television strengthened civil society in the Arab world, while Marc Lynch has argued that al-Jazeera is opening up a space for competing voices that encourages questioning the status quo in the region.[13] In this, Lynch shares Jon Alterman's stance that Arab satellite television has created a sense of a shared Arab destiny[14], and that satellite television "has dramatically affected conceptions of Arab and Muslim identity, linking together geographically distant issues and placing them within a common Arab 'story'."[15]

The Arab Spring was the ultimate product of this ongoing process, a landmark in the Arab satellite television landscape that transformed this landscape into a dynamic political stage with global reach. Media scholars who had been arguing about al-Jazeera's potential to effect democratic change saw their visions come to pass. Al-Jazeera was unique among Arab channels in its coverage of the Tunisian uprising and in its taking an anti-regime stance early on. It also played a prominent role in the Egyptian uprising, in which the channel triumphed as the premier satellite television station in the Middle East. This prominence continued as the uprisings spread to other Arab countries, with al-Jazeera's cameras hot in pursuit.

The Arab Spring saw the interplay of important dynamics in the Arab satellite television landscape, particularly in relation to al-Jazeera. First, it presented the most direct confrontation between al-Jazeera and state television. In Egypt, this confrontation also was extended to private television stations affiliated with the National Democratic Party, both in terms of content and in terms of lasting images. Not only did al-Jazeera dispel the myths that Egyptian state television was trying to propagate about the revolution (for example, that the revolution was very limited in scope, or that the police was being attacked by the people), it also took on private Egyptian satellite channels that were attempting to spread rumors. On 2 February 2011, al-Mihwar television broadcast a video of a young woman whose face was blurred, in which the woman claimed that she and others had received Israeli-backed anti-regime training in Washington and Qatar and that her group was the party responsible for the Egyptian uprising. It was later discovered that the woman was a journalist who worked for a newspaper called *24 Hours* that was close to the regime.[16] This discrediting broadcast by al-Mihwar came as an attempt to divert attention away from extraordinary events that had taken place earlier that day, when the Egyptian government sent plain-clothed thugs on camel and horseback to attack protesters in Tahrir Square, as well as military vehicles to run over demonstrators. Al-Jazeera's broadcasts were firmly fixed on the square, transmitting footage of the attacks to the globe, and making history as the day came to be known as the day of the Battle of the Camel. The broadcasts became visual evidence of the falsity of state images, and sealed the image of the Mubarak regime as brutal, evil and medieval, and of the protesters as legitimate in their cause as they strived to topple a rotten regime that killed its own people.

Second, the Arab Spring saw television facilitating direct confrontation by pro-democracy activists of state tactics. As the Egyptian government first shut down Twitter and then Facebook, al-Jazeera featured Egyptian activists such as Nawwara Nagm ridiculing this measure by stating that one could always resort to proxies to access banned sites. Al-Jazeera also gave a voice to ordinary citizens to express their anger at then president Mubarak's offering of cosmetic concessions in an attempt at quelling the revolution, through dedicating several hours on its Live channel to phone-ins from Egypt and from Arab audiences worldwide, who were united in expressing their rejection of Mubarak's concessions.

Third, this television arena fostered a sense of pan-Arab solidarity in revolution. This solidarity could be seen as having spurred on the protesters, as they saw that their revolutionary zeal was supported by fellow Arabs everywhere. It also was a confidence booster; as Strömbäck argues, "the depictions of reality as conveyed by the media...have an impact on how people perceive reality, and these perceptions...matter when people form their opinions."[17] Al-Jazeera played a role in changing Arab perceptions about the potential success of revolution as a democratic mechanism, and thus, in catalyzing further uprisings in the Arab world.

Fourth, this catalysis can be additionally attributed to the success of two consecutive revolutions, in Tunisia and Egypt, that al-Jazeera presented not just as victorious achievements but also as entitlements for all Arabs. In this sense, Al-Jazeera's coverage of the Arab Spring is important both on agenda setting and framing levels – the first in terms of highlighting what topics the audience should think about, and the second in terms of how those topics should be thought about.[18] Al-Jazeera carried this process both through its satellite television channel and its website. Al-Jazeera's website displayed a banner carrying the slogan "Egypt: The Revolution of a People," imposed on a collage of images from the January 25 Revolution: From right to left, the images were of people carrying a banner with the slogan "The people demand the fall of the regime"; protesters sitting on the ground in Tahrir Square; the pointed finger of a protester in the face of a policeman wearing a gas mask; and a child participating in one of the demonstrations. As such, the banner narrated the story of the revolution in four simple frames, starting with collective action, moving to the theme of steadfastness and ending with the revolution as shaping the future of Egypt and its people. This "story" can be read as an example of the shared "Arab story" that, as Alterman argued, al-Jazeera has helped weave.

Fifth, by featuring personal stories, al-Jazeera helped give the protests an individualized, human face that brought the experiences of protesters closer to the viewer. As Simon Cottle writes:

> Mass uprising on the streets of Egypt now appeared less distanced, less humanly remote. Visceral scenes and emotional testimonies elicited on the street brought home to watching millions something of the protestors' everyday despair and democratic aspirations as well as their extraordinary courage in confronting, by non-violent means, repressive state violence.[19]

Sixth, the uprisings demonstrated the existence of a new media matrix in which the digital media and the mass media adapt to one another.[20] Al-Jazeera did not only rely on its own reporting; it also gave a space for people to become citizen journalists through encouraging them to send their own user-generated video footage to the channel for broadcast.[21] This was particularly the case in places like Libya and Syria where the state imposed media shutdowns that prevented al-Jazeera and other television reporters from operating on the ground.

Finally, the Arab Spring illustrated the firm role of al-Jazeera as a political actor. Al-Jazeera's images had deliberate anti-regime messages in places like Egypt and Syria. The channel did not only grant generous air time to dissidents, it also created special promos praising the uprisings. It ran short videos featuring scenes of police brutality, reminding viewers of the regimes' actions towards their citizens. It commemorated the martyrs of the revolutions, weaving a unified narrative of Mohammed Bouazizi, Khaled Said, Hamza al-Khatib and others as Arab martyrs. It broadcast user-generated videos displaying the large numbers of protesters in places like Syria. This gave a feeling of empowerment to Syrian citizens not only because they saw their own taped footage screened on al-Jazeera[22], but also because the footage acted as an affirming visual indicator for the protesters on the ground who did not have other means of finding out what trajectory the uprising was taking in the rest of the country. As Lemert et al. and Voltmer argue, when the media commit to a cause, they offer "mobilizing information"[23] that "has the potential to strengthen political identities and encourages participation."[24] This also had a positive impact on the way al-Jazeera has been perceived, as it became the "voice of the voiceless," a slogan it had adopted many years before the Arab Spring and which came to be affirmed. Al-Jazeera has attempted to capitalize on this positive image by drawing attention to people's recognition of its role. On 11 February 2011, following the departure of Mubarak, al-Jazeera's website displayed the photograph of an Egyptian man carrying a banner thanking al-Jazeera for its role in the revolution.

Yet despite its commitment to the uprisings, al-Jazeera's politics remains closely tied to that of the Qatari state. Al-Jazeera's passionate coverage of the Egyptian revolution did not start immediately. Following political rapprochement between Qatar and Egypt in late 2010, al-Jazeera had started granting "soft" coverage to the Mubarak regime, even glossing over the many transgressions in Egypt's most fraudulent parliamentary election in November 2010. This trend continued when the Egyptian revolution began, as al-Jazeera did not report live from Cairo during the first three days of demonstrations. However, following a change in Qatari policy towards Egypt on the fourth day, al-Jazeera threw its weight behind the revolution, and from

Friday 28 January 2011, suspended its normal schedule to focus on covering the revolution's development, and dedicated its al-Jazeera Live channel to 24-hour coverage from Tahrir Square. What helped bolster al-Jazeera's role was that 28 January saw the Egyptian government completely shutting down both the internet and phone lines in Egypt. As Egyptian state television tried to ignore the revolution or distort it, al-Jazeera became the main source of information for Egyptians on what was going on on the ground.

Al-Jazeera also initially took a cautious approach to covering the uprising in Syria, and, like al-Arabiya, granted scant coverage to the uprising in Bahrain. This inattention to Bahrain, which in the case of al-Arabiya was more pronounced as the channel actively defended the regime by broadcasting a stream of positive stories about it, was due to Saudi-dominated Gulf politics that drew a red line at political instability reaching the region. Qatar and Saudi Arabia had reached their own rapprochement in 2009, and Qatari and other GCC states, led by Saudi Arabia, sent troops to Bahrain in March 2011 to help quell the uprising there. In this context, al-Jazeera's role as a political actor undermines its "supporter of the Arab people" image, and it is a reminder of the concealing role of television frames. As Entman argues, frames "call attention to some aspects of reality while obscuring other elements."[25] The celebration of al-Jazeera's coverage of the Arab Spring conceals the story of the uprising in Bahrain.

State television and regime image management[26]

Al-Jazeera's backing of protests during the Arab Spring brought a new need by those Arab states which were facing internal popular challenges to present their regimes in a positive way to the outside world. Before the uprisings, Arab authoritarian regimes, for the most part, had managed to maintain good ties with the West that were based on mutual interests. One result was that authoritarianism in the Arab region was an enduring feature of governance, and effectively normalized as a characteristic of the region.[27] Regimes that were friendly towards the West managed to maintain a positive image abroad, an attractive feat coveted by other regimes aspiring to a similar relationship. As one Syrian political analyst put it in 2007,

> "Tunisia is our model. Just look at them! They are much more repressive than we are, yet the West loves them. We need to figure out how they do it."[28]

Authoritarian regimes rely on both persuasion and coercion in relaying their messages to the public. The Arab Spring presented a challenge to those regimes as it shattered the images they had cultivated to target the West. Consequently, the Arab Spring saw a rise in attempts at cultivating attraction by regimes facing protests. Those strategies were in response to the uprisings' being worldwide events, watched closely by international audiences and governments alike. It was important for the Arab regimes whose existence was under threat to perform in an appealing way to those audiences. The strategies also aimed to convince both citizens and outsiders of the legitimacy of the regimes. Information about developments in the Arab Spring was packaged by regimes in a way that presented them as friendly, or as victims of conspiracy. This effort at persuasion involved "manipulating the discursive field, managing the producers of knowledge, and carefully creating images of state and society for popular consumption."[29] It was motivated by the need to keep international condemnation at bay, maintain good relations with foreign allies and prevent a change in international perceptions from affecting "the domestic discursive space in unpredictable and unmanageable ways, thus creating new challenges for domestic control."[30] Coercion, on the other hand, was squarely directed at citizens within. Both coercion and persuasion messages were played out on the public stage, as they were mainly performed through the medium of state satellite television. The Arab Spring, then, saw a televised struggle over the social construction of reality.[31]

The defining feature of the image management efforts by despotic Arab regimes during the Arab Spring is that they engaged in authoritarian learning. "Authoritarian learning" refers to how regimes adopt strategies used by other regimes to quell democracy, especially when those strategies are deemed to be successful.[32] During the Arab Spring, authoritarian learning went beyond governance as it also applied to how despotic regimes publicly handled the threat the uprisings caused their image. The regimes followed a curiously uniform pattern in their individual attempts at presenting an attractive image to the West and at quelling internal dissent.

One of the first regime reactions to budding protests in the Arab world was to simply ignore them and their potential. In Tunisia, state television did not grant the initial protests much coverage. While the pace of the protests was picking up, Tunisian state television broadcast non-political programs, such as a documentary about the Seven Wonders of the World. President Zine El-Abidine Ben Ali, accompanied by the television cameras, also visited Mohammed Bouazizi in hospital, using Bouazizi as an opportunity to present himself as a "caring" leader to the world. It later emerged that Bouazizi was most probably already dead during Ben Ali's visit, and that this was not disclosed to ensure a positive photo opportunity for the despotic president. In Egypt and Syria, state television used the tactic of streaming "live" images from places like Cairo and Homs which were accompanied by the screen captions "Cairo now" and "Homs now," respectively, and which showed empty streets in those locations, as visual "evidence" that no demonstrations were taking place, when the reality testified to the opposite.[33] In Libya, state television went even further in the early days of the rebellion by actually broadcasting footage of Muammar Qaddafi joining the protests himself. This move was an attempt at cementing Qaddafi's self-proclaimed image as the "Brother Leader" as well as protecting Libya's newly established "friend of the West" status by belittling the seriousness of the rebellion.

As the pace of protests picked up, Arab regimes realized that they could no longer dismiss the uprisings, especially with worldwide attention by the media and by (largely Western) allies who were calling for those regimes to engage in a degree of political reform. The regimes' response was to offer their people a range of largely

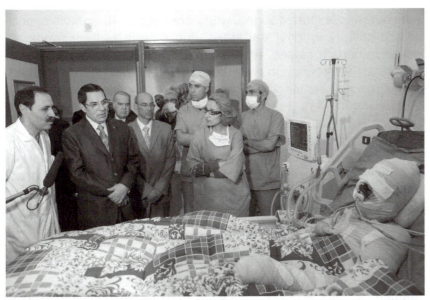

Fig. 44. A handout picture released by the Tunisian Presidency showing Ben Ali visiting Mohamed Bouazizi at a hospital in Ben Arous near Tunis on 28 December 2010. Photo by AFP.

cosmetic concessions, and state television became the platform through which this was disseminated. The rulers of Bahrain, Oman and Saudi Arabia announced that they were offering their citizens monetary support; those of Jordan and Yemen declared that they were dissolving their governments; and those of Egypt, Tunisia and Yemen promised that they were not going to run for re-election. The image presented to the world was supposed to be one of leaders "listening to their people." Indeed, this did generate praise from allies at times. US Secretary of State Hillary Clinton's early reaction to Hosni Mubarak's promise, following the start of the January 25 Revolution, of not running for re-election was to paint him as one such leader.

But while Western allies, driven by enduring shared interests, did not take a tough line on Arab despots as a first course of action, the uprisings continued as Arab citizens refused to buy the image their regimes were trying to sell them. One by one, the regimes began to characterize their situations in exceptional terms. "Egypt is not Tunisia." "Syria is not Egypt." "Yemen is not Tunisia or Egypt." Those statements by Arab rulers, mainly disseminated through state television, were attempts at whitewashing themselves, and at both convincing and warning their people that the regime change that happened "over there" would not happen "over here." This strategy succeeded to a certain degree, as the architecture of power in different Arab countries is indeed varied, with different social, economic, political and military dynamics at stake. Public protests were eventually quelled in certain places, mostly through varying levels of violence (limited, as in Jordan, and more severe, as in Bahrain). But in Egypt, Syria, Libya and Yemen, the strategy failed as protests continued.

State television's reaction was to disseminate coercive messages. In Syria, president Bashar al-Assad gave a televised speech in which he referred to protesters as "germs" that Syria needs to be immunized against (leading to hilarity among online commentators about the inaccuracy of this medical analogy, especially that Bashar al-Assad is a doctor himself), while in Libya, Muammar Qaddafi had several television appearances in which he called the rebels "rats," the most important of which was a rambling speech on 22 February 2011 whereby he vowed that "we will march in our millions, to purify Libya inch by inch, house by house, home by home, alleyway by alleyway, person by person, until the country is purified from dirt and impurities." The speech is notable for directly addressing the role of the pan-Arab media, especially al-Jazeera, in sending anti-Qaddafi messages. As Qaddafi denied that he had fled Libya for Venezuela, the camera cut to a left-to-right pan of the outside of his pockmarked Bab Al-Aziziya complex, where Qaddafi could be seen behind the glass giving the speech. Qaddafi angrily proclaimed, "These Arabic channels are the biggest enemy, and they are on to you. They want you to destroy the oil, the freedom, public authority and Libya, because they are jealous of you. Our brothers in Qatar, is this the end of it? Is this the friendship we had between us?" Libyan state television also had a landmark broadcast in August 2011, when a male presenter brandished a rifle on air, declaring that he would fight "till the last drop of blood," which was followed by another broadcast a few days later, in which female presenter Hala al-Misrati waved a handgun at the camera as she sat behind her desk, declaring "kill or be killed." Perhaps those broadcasts are not too surprising, having come from a regime that had regularly relied on the live broadcasting on state television of public executions, themselves spectacles of coercion, as a means of quelling political opposition.

As the pressure on those regimes increased, they responded through invoking victimization, blaming the protests on "foreign" elements and "criminal gangs." The state media, particularly television, became tools through which the regimes tried to frame public discourse. Gitlin defines media frames as "persistent patterns of cognition, interpretations, and presentation, of selection, emphasis, and exclusion, by which symbol-handlers routinely organize discourse."[34] The Egyptian, Syrian, Libyan and Bahraini governments (and others) framed the protesters as "disturbers of order" by "ignoring and undercounting, favoring counterdemonstrators, scanting of content, and trivialization and marginalization," and by labeling "even activists who are victims of terrorist activities (death threats, physical violence)...terrorists."[35] This framing gave those regimes a "legitimate" reason to engage in violence to quell the demonstrations, under the pretext of protecting national security and maintaining national unity. The Syrian regime announced that it was fighting Salafis and gangs, providing visual "proof" of this through manufactured videos of "captured thugs" broadcast on Syrian state television, while the regime in Bahrain blamed the protests on Iran, and cited Iranian Arabic-language satellite channel al-Alam and Hizbullah's pro-Iranian channel al-Manar as being a factor behind the protests. In Yemen, the protests were also partly blamed on Islamist groups like al-Qaeda. In all three cases, it is clear that those regimes were trying to invoke the fear of Islamists (and Iran) shared in the West, and consequently to present themselves as the only credible alternative.

The regimes also engaged in disseminating "noise," which Jervis defines as "statements and actions not designed to provide the listener with information."[36] The regimes in Egypt, Syria, Yemen and Jordan pretended that their violence was "spontaneous" and performed by "criminal gangs" and thus not orchestrated by the government as they relied on plain-clothed thugs to attack protesters in the streets. In Libya and Bahrain, mercenary armies were used to quell the protests by force. In the latter's case, the country appealed to the GCC, which sent troops to Manama to halt the uprising under the pretext of maintaining security in the Gulf region. The GCC intervention was sold as a legitimate case of regional allies helping one another at a time of crisis. To further emphasize the need for averting this "crisis," some regimes like those in Yemen and Libya warned that civil war would break out if they were to crumble. Regimes manufactured fake images to support their claims. In Libya, following international military action against the Qaddafi regime, it has been reported that dead bodies were brought by the Libyan government into sites bombed by NATO to show the world media that the bombings killed civilians, and in Syria, videos shot via mobile phones – to visually indicate "authenticity" – were circulated online and broadcast on television, allegedly showing "gangs" attacking civilians. The response by Syrian protesters was to start displaying the date on a daily newspaper at the start of protest footage they were shooting to guarantee its credibility.[37] Blaming the violence on vague gangs failed to convince the protesters who had already viewed all government communication with suspicion. If anything, it strengthened people's conviction in their own power. As Jervis argues, "people interpret incoming information in the light of their pre-existing views…the greater the ambiguity of the information, the greater the impact of the established belief."[38]

The Arab people involved in the uprisings were not deterred from rallying for their cause at any of the stages above, yet Arab regimes continued to engage in similar actions, reactions and strategies. Taken in isolation, such image management strategies, when used by an individual country alone, may be effective: Weaving a plausible image of a country while undercutting the plausibility of alternative narratives may be a useful combination to resist internal unrest.[39] Yet, the case of the Arab Spring was unique because it was a regional, rather than a national, phenomenon. The more Arab regimes engaged in similar behavior, the less credible their repetitive image management strategies became. Regimes were astonishing in their choice of actions, which only served to undermine them further. After Libyan rebels overtook Tripoli in August 2011, the Syrian regime granted Qaddafi access to pro-regime, Syrian-based satellite television channel al-Rai, which became a shared mouthpiece for both despotic regimes. This tactic became a sign of the despair of both regimes as their end was looming. Having lost most of their international political, military and popular support, all the regimes had to appeal to the outside world were empty images.

Politics as consumption

The importance of the diverse voices presented by al-Jazeera during the Arab Spring cannot be denied, as those voices were a challenge to state television propaganda. This performance by al-Jazeera consolidated the positive contributions that satellite television channels have made to the pan-Arab media landscape. The Arab Spring was an occasion for al-Jazeera to play a constructive role in the process of democratic transition in the region. However, whether the Arab Spring marks the start of a new era for the Arab media landscape characterized by real political dialogue through television remains uncertain. Satellite television stations continue to present different versions of the same events that are indicative of their political stances. Competing stations closely monitor and respond to each other, but often do so to discredit the other, rather than engage with them, as seen in the television battles that erupted following the opening up of the media space in Tunisia and Egypt after the revolutions. News coverage has therefore become an exercise in political strategy, and it has confirmed television's role as a participant in political struggle. The result is that satellite television in the Arab world transmits images of contention.[40]

This contentious landscape is a symptom of power struggles within the Arab world. As long as satellite television stations engaged in political reporting act as mouthpieces for clashing political actors whose primary motive is the propagation of messages favorable to the self while discrediting "others," real engagement in political dialogue through television in the Arab world will be difficult. Instead, and despite the remarkable contribution of channels like al-Jazeera to the empowerment of the Arab citizen, what we get is the transformation of politics into a commodity, where viewers are no longer citizens, but "are turned into consumers."[41]

6

From Images of Dictators to Images of Citizens

"Big Brother" is looking out for you. He never sleeps. He is always there. When he isn't making a speech or heading a parade, he is keeping an eye on you. Don't let him down![1]

Until the Arab Spring of 2011, if one walked around most cities in the Middle East, one would have been under the watchful eye of the leader. Whether he was a president, a monarch or a local *za'im*, the face of the leader in the Middle East was a prominent feature in public space and in the media. The Middle East is a region well-versed in the *language* of leadership. But leaders in the Middle East are also increasingly seen, not just heard. Leaders dead and alive are known or remembered as much for their words as their images. Who can think about Yasser Arafat without imagining his kaffiya? Or Hafez al-Assad without his posters populating Syria and neighboring Lebanon? Or Muammar Qaddafi without his flamboyant outfits and female bodyguards? From personal style to public representations to public performance, the image has become a key element in the personas of Middle Eastern leaders.

And it is this key element that was a focus of much street action during the uprisings in Egypt, Syria and Libya. For the first time in Syria and Libya, protesters tore down the posters of Bashar al-Assad and Muammar Qaddafi, and in the latter, went further by replacing the murals venerating Qaddafi with ones ridiculing him and his family. In Egypt and Libya, effigies of Hosni Mubarak and Qaddafi were burnt in the streets. The contrast between the images that those leaders had created for themselves and those projected by the protesters could not have been bigger; the protesters were reclaiming their countries as belonging to them, the people. The leaders, on the other hand, had always conceived of the states they ruled not just as personal possessions but also as being a product of their own greatness.

The Egyptian, Syrian and Libyan regimes were both centralized and personalized. The leader was the system, and even if he (and it was always a he) was a president, he acted like a monarch.[2] Particularly, Muammar Qaddafi and Bashar al-Assad embodied Lacoutre's definition of the personification of politics:

> the system leading from the acquisition of power to the individual interpretation of it, to the "stage setting" for the hero, to the preparation of the crowd through propaganda, to the weaving of the myth, to the incarnation of the individual, and to the gradual merging of the sign-given group with the sign-giving demigod.[3]

The Arab Spring changed this dynamic, forcing a permanent re-imaging of those Arab dictators.

Gamal Abdel Nasser: the original modern Arab leader

To understand the image that Arab autocrats have weaved for themselves, one cannot but refer to the original modern Arab leader, Gamal Abdel Nasser, for no Arab leader has commanded the degree of loyalty across the Arab world that Nasser had. Nasser was a master of public speaking, a charismatic figure par excellence, and an inspiration for generations of leaders to come.

If there is one quality that is attributed to Nasser without contestation, it is charisma. Weber defines charisma as

> a certain quality of an individual personality by virtue of which he is considered extraordinary and treated as endowed with supernatural, superhuman, or at least specifically exceptional powers or qualities. These are such as are not accessible to the ordinary person, but are regarded as of divine origin or as exemplary, and on the basis of them the individual concerned is treated as a "leader."[4]

As such, Weber sees charisma as a trait inherent to the leader in question, rather than as a set of behaviors. What makes Nasser an interesting case for the application of Weber's theory is not just his personality, but also the enduring belief in his exemplary status by people across the Arab world. Extraordinary qualities are attributed to Nasser that are framed as forming an inherent part of his identity.

But Nasser was also a masterful manager of his image, and thus, it is worth examining some of the characteristics of his public persona. One characteristic was creating a symbiotic relationship with the people. Nasser had a natural style when engaging with his audience, often resorting to improvisation in his speeches. After his assassination attempt in 1954 while he was giving a speech, Nasser addressed the audience by improvising, "If Abdel Nasser dies then every one of you is Abdel Nasser...Each of you is Gamal Abdel Nasser. Gamal Abdel Nasser is of you and from you and he is willing to sacrifice his life for the nation."[5] Through this statement, not only did Nasser appeal to his people by stressing that he is one of them, he also infused the audience with his divine qualities, empowering them and thus lifting them up to his status – a mixture of humbleness and superiority. This was a masterful way of getting around the "exemplifier paradox" of charismatic leadership: being "one of us, but not one of us."[6] Nasser knew how to tailor his language to his audience, often using *baladi* rhetoric when addressing Egyptians – he used colloquial banter and local Egyptian jokes in his Alexandria speech when the Suez Canal was nationalized[7] – and a more classical style when, for instance, addressing the citizens of the United Arab Republic after the union of Egypt and Syria.[8]

The second characteristic was the power of the deed. Nasser was the first modern Arab leader to openly challenge the West as he announced plans to build the High Dam in July 1956, and then nationalized the Suez Canal. The ability to promise and deliver sealed the belief in his extraordinary qualities. This led to a third characteristic: Nasser's nationalization of the Suez Canal made him personify the state. As such, Nasser became the father of the Egyptian republic, and potentially, the Arab nation. A further characteristic was his active use of the media. Nasser utilized the media masterfully, often using Voice of the Arabs to announce his policies. Later, he would use film to transmit his speeches to cinema audiences, and the press to distribute his photographs.[9] After the nationalization of the Suez Canal, photos of Nasser could be found across the Arab world. Nasser therefore displayed an awareness of the role of the image in the political process at a time when the visual media were starting to increase in presence in the Arab world. The Arab world has not known a leader like Nasser since his death; however, Nasser's imprint on modern leadership can be found in the styles adopted by subsequent leaders in the region, like Hassan Nasrallah, as presented in Chapter 2 in this book, or aspired to, like in the case of Muammar Qaddafi.

Qaddafi: from the father of the nation to "zenga zenga"

Muammar Qaddafi spent his youth listening to Nasser's speeches on the radio, regarding him as a personal and national hero and a model to be emulated, and it is reported that he fainted twice during Nasser's funeral.[10] Qaddafi grew up to become a revolutionary leader himself, and a self-styled father of the Libyan nation, after he led a coup d'état in 1969 that transformed Libya from a monarchy into a state of the masses, although this state quickly became one of the most oppressive in the world. Qaddafi acquired the title "Brother Leader and Guide of the Revolution," and regarded himself the inheritor of pan-Arabism after Nasser. He tried to create a Libyan-Sudanese union in 1969, and another with Egypt, Syria and Tunisia in 1971, but those attempts failed, and Egypt's signing of a disengagement agreement with Israel in 1974 thwarted his ambition for a pan-Arab federation. After the flying of the Egyptian flag in Israel during Sadat's visit in 1977, Qaddafi declared his rejection of Egypt's stance through changing the Libyan flag from one identical to the Egyptian flag to a plain green one, symbolizing the color of Islam. In the 1980s, having given up on pan-Arabism, Qaddafi changed his position into one promoting pan-Africanism. He arranged a special meeting of the Organization of African Unity in Sirte on 9 September 1999, coinciding with the thirtieth anniversary of the establishment of the Libyan Jamahiriyya, when he announced his design for a United States of Africa.[11] From the 1970s till his death, Qaddafi's image has been one of controversy, moving from that of a sponsor of international terrorism to a friend of the West, with countless occasions of bizarre outbursts and behaviors along the way, to an enemy of his own people following the rebellion against him in 2011.

Throughout the period of oscillating ideological declarations that marked Qaddafi's rule, Qaddafi personified the system he had created in Libya. His image was a classic authoritarian one of a self-obsessed leader who blurred the line between himself and the state. Ronen writes that the popular equation in Libya was "Qaddafi is Libya and Libya is Qaddafi," an equation based on a cult of personality that painted Qaddafi as the spiritual father of the nation.[12] There was no distinction between "Qaddafi's hegemonic leadership and [the] country's political life."[13] Leadership for Qaddafi was a performance in which he became "an actor vested with a symbolic role, the nation's mouthpiece and the projection of its image."[14] Qaddafi's public image, as Yehudit Ronen wrote in 2008, was part of a set of

> suppressive measures to block any deviation from his self-styled revolutionary principles and political norms. He has employed a wide variety of means to achieve the objective of popular identification with his leadership and unique ideology. His colorful, larger-than-life portrait gazes down from billboards and tall buildings all over Libya, radiating fatherly love, determination, and self-assurance and projecting an image of Qaddafi as two sides of the same coin. Qaddafi exudes confidence in the system he has created and the benefits it can bestow on the Libyan state and its people.[15]

Qaddafi relied on visual techniques to achieve three key aims: disseminating ideology; legitimating himself as a leader; and demobilizing his people.[16] One way in which he sent ideological and self-legitimizing messages was through fashion. Gaddafi's reliance on attire can be seen as an exaggerated version of the strategy that had been used by Palestinian leader Yasser Arafat to merge his personal image with that of the Palestinian nation. Arafat had begun wearing a kaffiya as a sign of Palestinianness early on, with his first public appearance in one for this purpose being during the International Students' Congress in Prague in 1956.[17] After the Karameh battle in 1968, which Fatah packaged as a victory against an Israeli attack on its headquarters, Arafat became "the courageous leader with a human touch," and started placing his kaffiya in the shape of the map of Palestine, a painstaking task that reportedly took almost one hour of his time to perfect every morning.[18] However, unlike Arafat, Qaddafi's fashion eccentricity and excess served to cement his reputation as "that mad guy in Libya," in the words of late Egyptian president Anwar Sadat. Qaddafi's attire reflected his support for pan-Arabism and/or pan-Africanism. He became known for wearing cloaks that blended the styles of traditional Arab abayas and African robes. When he arrived in Mozambique in July 2003 for the African Heads of State summit, he was wearing a shirt decorated with the map of Africa and black and white photos of African freedom fighters. At a press conference in 2008, he wore a military uniform imprinted with the photos of iconic Arab leaders, the most prominent of which was that of Nasser.[19] When he declared himself the King of Kings of Africa the same year, he took to wearing shirts printed with motifs of the map of Africa, and golden-hued outfits in pan-African meetings to signify his "royal" status.

Fashion was also a way of displaying Qaddafi's appropriation of Libya's national symbols. On his visit to Italy on 11 June 2009, Qaddafi descended from his airplane having pinned to his chest a photo of a chained Omar al-Mokhtar, the Libyan anti-colonial activist who was executed by the Italian colonialists in 1931 – a message of defiance that served to temper his new "friend of the West" status which he had acquired after Libya's reconciliation with the United States and Europe. Qaddafi used Mukhtar as a method of legitimizing himself. The date of his first speech on 16 September 1969 was chosen to coincide with the anniversary of Mukhtar's death, and in 1981, Qaddafi sponsored a film epic about Mukhtar's life, titled *Lion of the Desert*.[20] Another established technique deployed by Qaddafi to achieve his three aims was the use of state television as his personal channel. Like many Arab state televisions (in Iraq during Saddam Hussein's rule, for example), Libyan television dedicated much air time to covering Qaddafi's whereabouts. Television's focus on reporting the minute details of the public life of Qaddafi served to cultivate a cult of leadership for him.[21]

A third visual technique was the total control of visual representations in public space. This technique, used by other Arab leaders but more pronounced in the cases of Qaddafi and Saddam Hussein, served to infuse daily life in Libya with reminders of the eminence of the leader. Qaddafi was consistent in using public campaigns to present himself as a legitimate ruler. After the American raid on Tripoli in 1986, which targeted his Bab Al-Aziziya compound, Qaddafi deliberately did not renovate the exterior of the compound, leaving it as a "visual evidence" of the righteousness of his anti-American ideology. He also sponsored the dissemination of pictures in public space. Every year, on the anniversary of the establishment of the Libyan Jamahiriyya (2 March), billboards commemorating the event would appear all over Libya, installed by the government's Popular Public Committee for Culture and Media (*Al-lajna al-sha'biya al-'amma li al-thaqafa wa al-i'lam*). Sometimes, the same billboards from previous years would be reused. The following discussion presents examples of those billboards, taken from the Jamahiriyya's 38th anniversary campaign in 2008.

Billboards were used for legitimation and demobilization through depicting Qaddafi as being in partnership with his people. A billboard in Tripoli carried, on the right, a painting of Qaddafi smiling, with his hands clasped and held high in a congratulating salute, and the number 38 engulfed in sun rays on the left, along with the slogan: "Hand in hand, for yesterday, today and tomorrow," placing Qaddafi as a partner with the Libyan people. Yet achieving legitimacy as a leader and ensuring people's demobilization also required Qaddafi to be on a higher level than that of the people. No citizen should aspire to play Qaddafi's role, for he saw himself as being of an elevated status not attainable by others. Therefore, another visual technique was the elevation of Qaddafi to an almost divine status. A painting of him on the side of a building in Tripoli, commemorating the anniversary, showed him posing with raised clasped hands and with sun rays painted behind him, as if emanating from his body. Qaddafi was thus likened to the sun, bringing enlightenment and guidance. Another painting, on a billboard, further emphasized this. It depicted the map of Africa, in green, on the left, with the picture of the sun and its long rays emanating from Libya and the number 38 floating above, with the words "Al-fateh is freedom's sun" written in huge letters. Another billboard coupled the clasped-hands image of Qaddafi with the slogan "Wherever you go, happiness prevails and life is embellished." Non-anniversary billboards echoed the same message. One such billboard carried the slogan: "Glory for the maker of glory." Another depicted a painting of men and women from different backgrounds and occupations[22] (one is a soldier, another wears a construction helmet, one woman wears a veil, another does not and a child carrying a school bag on his back also can be seen on the left) coming together to raise the Libyan flag, with the sun in the background disseminating its rays – signifying Qaddafi – and the slogan "With the great conqueror [al-fateh] we liberated the land and embraced the stars." A side of a building had a photo of a giant, smiling, sunglasses-wearing Qaddafi, his arm extended in front of him in a greeting gesture, looming large over a crowd of people of ant-like dimensions. The caption stated: "O Muammar: You have strived, so you liberated and you gained." Other images were more symbolic. On the side of a building, a green space was dominated by the drawing of a giant forearm extending from the earth, the fist clenched, with small, green stick figures of people with their arms up in the air in salutation and exaltation in the

foreground. The difference in scale between the arm and the people figures suggested the exalted status of the leader compared
with his people.

This visual technique was also used to disseminate ideological
appeals, such as pan-Africanism. A billboard commemorating the Sirte
Declaration of 9 September 1999 depicted a green ship with the flags
of African countries as sails (the Libyan flag occupied the very top position), along with the slogan: "September 9, 1999: A historic day in the
life of Africa." Another billboard simply presented a green map of Africa
with the words "We are no longer slaves to any body (sic)" written in
Arabic, English and French. Another promoted pan-Africanism through
depicting the black and white photographs of ten African leaders (that
of Nasser occupied the top left corner) under the title "The African
Founding Leaders," with the map of Africa drawn to the right of the
photographs, the sun emanating from Libya on the map and illuminating the continent with a green hue. A further one credited Qaddafi with
liberating Africa. The same slogan mentioned above, "O Muammar:
You strived, so you liberated and you gained," could be found on a
banner hung on the side of a building depicting a green map of Africa,
with Libya as the illuminating sun, and a photo of Qaddafi standing in
front of the map with his arm extended forward as the hands of black

Fig. 45. A pro-Qaddafi billboard in Libya proclaiming "Wherever you go, happiness prevails and life is embellished." Photo taken on 27 July 2008.

Africans reach out to him. The billboards also depicted Qaddafi's global outlook. One showed the map of the world with the Green Book emanating from Libya and circulating around the earth. At the bottom, the text said: "The Green Book promises the age of the masses."

Neotraditionalism, which refers to the focus on carefully selected traditions of the past, was another method used by Qaddafi to achieve his triple aims. As Crystal argued about Arab leaders, "[r]ulers throughout the region invoke tradition selectively, using whatever construction suits their present political needs (and often such constructions bear little resemblance to any actual historical experience)."[23] This invention of tradition was therefore an ongoing process for leaders like Qaddafi.[24] Qaddafi's use of neotraditionalism was centered on his construction of a narrative of the history of the revolution that was led by himself. A set of revolving billboards in Tripoli presented this narrative. In the first one, a young Qaddafi leads a demonstration challenging French soldiers who are shown as standing helplessly. The caption stated: "The student Qaddafi leads a demonstration protesting and denouncing the crime of the arrest of five Algerians by the French colonizers." The second one showed a slightly older Qaddafi in military uniform, crouching on the ground with three other young men in traditional garb, examining a map.

Fig. 46. A pro-Qaddafi billboard in Libya in 2008 proclaiming "O Muammar: You have strived, so you liberated, and you gained."

The caption below read "Captain Qaddafi meets with some of his colleagues in the city of Zawiya," in reference to Qaddafi's pre-revolution military rank, before he promoted himself to colonel. The third one depicted Qaddafi as he recited the revolution's first statement on the radio, his clenched fist held up in the air in defiance, and flanked by two officers with their rifles and hands held high. The caption read: "Captain Qaddafi gives the revolution's first statement, on the morning of the great fateh, 1969." The final billboard showed Qaddafi as the established father of the nation.

A final method used by Qaddafi is the appeal to developmentalism.[25] This method revolves around the dissemination of promises about the future that would improve life for the people. In addition to his ideological promises, Qaddafi utilized this method through the focus on the Great Man-Made River project which he initiated (ignoring the non-viability of the river in the long term). This accomplishment was commemorated in several billboards in Libya, such as one showing the map of the river along with the slogan "The great river for the great people."

While there are some parallels between the story of Qaddafi the revolutionary and that of Nasser, the major difference between the two leaders is that while Nasser was publicly associated with the 1952 Revolution, he did not present the self-obsessed, narcissistic image

Fig. 47. A revolving billboard showing Qaddafi giving the first speech after taking over the leadership of Libya in 1969. Photo taken on 27 July 2008.

that Qaddafi continued to present after more than four decades of rule. Nasser was also a man of deeds, and although Egypt suffered a defeat in 1967 under his leadership, the people demanded that he return to power after stepping down following the *naksa*. As such, he is an example of the charismatic military leader described by Bensman and Givant, who explain that this kind of leader is not elected but selects himself "if he can evoke and direct an immediate belief among a band of followers that he possesses divine power."[26] In contrast, Qaddafi's constant return to the glories of the past spoke of stasis. In *The Wretched of the Earth*, Franz Fanon[27] argues that when a leader fails to involve his people in the future of a state, he recourses to the past, beckoning "the people to look backward, plying them with epic memories of the days of resistance."[28] Qaddafi's legacy was fraught with problems and was characterized by oppression, possessing few honorable deeds. Therefore, it does not become surprising that Qaddafi relied on the glories of the past in celebrating the anniversary of the Libyan state. In this, Qaddafi symbolized a stale leadership that, despite later attempts at opening up Libya to the international community, lacked a real vision for the development of a viable, modern state that can exist independently from the persona of the leader.

Qaddafi's image was of a leader who saw himself as an emblem of identity for his people, infusing them with his own glory; his presence symbolized their own existence.[29] This extreme personification of the regime led to a similarly personified process of visual reversal with the Libyan rebellion of 2011. Visual reversal applied to different arenas: the national flag; national symbols; the image of Qaddafi; and the presence of non-regime images in public space. One of the first acts of visual reversal was the reinstating of the old Libyan red, black and green flag that had been used as the national flag between 1951 and 1969 when Libya was a monarchy. Another was the adoption of Omar al-Mukhtar as an idol for the rebels. Qaddafi had mentioned al-Mukhtar in one of his anti-revolt speeches in February 2011 as a reminder of his own appropriation of this figure. The rebels responded not only through displaying images of al-Mukhtar, but also through calling themselves "the people of Omar Mukhtar."[30]

On 21 February 2011, four days after the start of the Libyan rebellion, which had been quickly embraced by pan-Arab satellite channels like al-Jazeera, Libyan state television transmitted Qaddafi's shortest speech. Wearing a ushanka hat and sitting in a "tuk-tuk" while carrying a huge white umbrella, Qaddafi spoke for just 20 seconds to denounce rumors that he had fled the country to Venezuela: "I am satisfied, because I was speaking in front of the youth in the Green Square tonight, but the rain came, praise to God it bears well. I want to clarify for them that I am in Tripoli not in Venezuela. Do not believe these channels they are dogs. Goodbye." This short television appearance created an iconic image of Qaddafi that inspired Libyan rebels and Arab satirists to create subversive images of him standing with his umbrella in the rain. Ibtisam Barakat created a caricature of the event that featured the text: *"Now for Qaddafi's speech titled 'Song of the Rain'. And if you, the Libyans who are revolting, are not cleansed by the rain from your misconceptions about needing freedom, then you're asking for the Umbrella Special Forces and they shall be deployed to handle all of you . . ."*[31] Libyan rebels created a more serious image in a mural in Benghazi that showed Qaddafi standing under his umbrella as the sky rained blood, covering the umbrella and his extended arm.

Qaddafi followed up this speech with another on 22 February in which he presented himself in megalomaniac terms: "Muammar Qaddafi is history, resistance, liberty, glory, revolution."[32] He called the rebels "cockroaches" and "rats" and declared that he would hunt them down "alleyway to alleyway." The speech triggered a spoof by Israeli journalist and musician Noy Alooshe, who sampled the speech, particularly the words for "alleyway to alleyway" – *"zenga zenga"* – in a hip-hop music video titled "Zenga Zenga" that he posted on YouTube. The video featured footage of Qaddafi giving the speech edited so that its beats resembled a rhythmic hip-hop track. The Jordanian cartoon company Kharabeesh referenced the video in one of its Qaddafi spoofs. The spoof was created in the form of an advert for a nightclub. The "advert" starts with pictures of protests against Qaddafi and a voiceover announcing: "Would you like an evening out with the best sounds of bullets, with a wonderful view of a pool of blood, in the best bloody night out with the king of world kings Muammar Qaddafi?" A cartoon of Qaddafi then appears, showing him behind a lectern that displays the sign "The chief, the struggler leader, the colonel, the prince of believers, king of kings of Africa." The clip then presents fragments from Qaddafi's earliest speech during the revolt, when he asked Libyans to go to the streets and rejoice as a way of dismissing the rebellion: "Youth of Libya! Take hallucinogenic pills, dance, be merry, stay up, go to the squares, dance, dance, dance!" The voiceover returns: "All this and more, in Zenga-Zenga nightclub." The "advert" ends with an audio clip from Alooshe's video to which Qaddafi's cartoon is shown dancing in a nightclub. Kharabeesh followed this spoof with a series of others, such as one cartoon depicting Qaddafi as a contestant on the talent contest "Arabs Got Talent" in the stand-up comedy genre, in which real audio clips of Qaddafi making nonsensical declarations like "People, without electricity, we would be watching television in the dark" were reproduced. The speech was also referenced in demonstrations in Libya, where people carried placards showing a drawing of Qaddafi with a noose around his neck and the words "the end, murderer," in reference to his threat to eliminate the opposition. The appropriated image of the speech then, is an example of the "floating image" that has become prevalent in the visual discourse of the Arab Spring.

Another example of this visual reversal is the murals created by Libyan rebels, which grabbed worldwide attention, particularly through photographs taken by Rory Mulholland which appeared in several news outlets and online. "Go to Hell," said one mural depicting Gaddafi, wearing sunglasses and standing against his trademark green background. "I'll either rule you or I'll kill you," said another showing Qaddafi in a white military uniform flanked by bombs falling from the sky, a reference to his air raids over Libyan cities. A caricature depicted Qaddafi and his son, Saif, as monkeys, with the father picking lice off his son. Ridicule was coupled with depictions of rebel defiance. One mural showed a

Fig. 48. An anti-Qaddafi caricature exhibition in Benghazi on 1 April 2011. Photo by AFP–Aris Messinis.

rebel emerging from the head of Qaddafi that he split into two with his bare hands, under the slogan "It's Enough," and a second showed a helpless, barefoot Qaddafi tied to a rocket about to be launched by a rebel into space.[33] Mulholland cites other caricatures of Qaddafi that he witnessed on the walls of Benghazi during the rebellion:

> There are posters of Gaddafi pumping petrol into a winged camel, Gaddafi with the tail of a snake and a forked tongue, Gaddafi as Dracula, Gaddafi as a clown, Gaddafi being bitten by a dog, Gaddafi getting a boot in the head. The variations are countless. Another popular theme is an often bloodstained Gaddafi terrorising or slaughtering his people or plundering the oil-rich nation's wealth.[34]

Like the Egyptian murals, the Libyan murals are an example of subversion and the effort to reclaim public space by citizens, testifying to the eagerness to reclaim the right to representation which the Libyan

Fig. 49. An anti-Qaddafi mural in Benghazi on 12 April 2011 proclaiming "The people have said their word." Photo by AFP–Odd Andersen.

people had been denied. They are also tools of symbolic revenge. After the taking over of Tripoli by the rebels in August 2011, some of the first visual acts by the rebels were to remove any green objects that Qaddafi had installed, chop the heads off his statues, erase his murals from the walls and deliberately tear posters bearing his image in front of the cameras of the international media. Rebels also looted his Bab Al-Aziziya compound, whereby they destroyed the sculpture of a hand crushing an American fighter jet that used to take pride of place at the compound's entrance, after hanging Qaddafi's underwear (which had been looted from his home) on it. They also photographed the objects found in Qaddafi's and his daughter's residences to display the images as a sign of the fallen dictator's opulence, which, despite not being as crass as that of Saddam Hussein, still marked a great departure from the standard of living of ordinary Libyans. Of particular note is the image of a golden sofa in Aisha Qaddafi's mansion that bore a sculpture of a mermaid with Aisha's head cast in gold. The intentionality of those visual acts of erasure and display can be seen as an example of the recognition of the power of the image as a political tool by a new generation of Libyans who were working towards political recognition in their own country and outside.

But the final method of visual reversal came with the arrest and death of Qaddafi. In October 2011, Qaddafi was found hiding in a sewer by Libyan rebels. The irony of this location was not lost on the rebels who had been branded "rats" by Qaddafi himself. Shortly after his arrest, footage shot on mobile phones was circulated online and in the media, showing Qaddafi being subjected to violence by his captors. This was soon followed with news announcing his death. The exact circumstances surrounding Qaddafi's death were unknown at the time of writing this book, but there is a strong indication that he died as a result of violence at the hands of his captors. It certainly is disturbing to see that those who had taken up arms to fight against Qaddafi's injustice and state violence themselves acted in a manner far removed from a justice framework. But beyond ethics, international law, and morality, how can we understand the images of Qaddafi's arrest and death? Why were those problematic images created and circulated in the first place? The answer is threefold. First, the mobile phone footage can be seen as part of image hysteria driven by decades of denial of the right to represent, which was heightened when Qaddafi was found. Second, they were driven by an unexpected physical proximity to the body of the leader who had cast himself as an unreachable demigod. Third, they were (very raw) ways to assert the power of the rebels over the now-powerless dictator. Disseminating the images to the world was a crude way to signal this power shift. After Qaddafi's death, image hysteria went further as Qaddafi's body was put on display in a warehouse freezer in Misrata, to be visited by scores of fighters and civilians who took photographs of themselves as they posed with the half-naked, decomposing body. The display erased the subjectivity of Qaddafi, whose image, as discussed earlier, had gazed at Libyans in public and private space, casting them in the role of objects – now Qaddafi was transformed into the object of the gaze of the citizen. The display also went further in asserting a reversal in image and power. Qaddafi had persistently cast the bodies of the Libyans as objects: From public hangings to the torture of prisoners to reported cases of sexual attacks on women, the Libyan people under Qaddafi's rule had no control over the fate of their own bodies. With Qaddafi himself having been personally responsible for many of those physical acts, the display of Qaddafi's dead body, in as bare a condition as possible, minus the adornments and the flair, marked a radical change in the relationship between the bodies of Libyan citizens and the body of Qaddafi. It also transformed Qaddafi from a "superior being" into a literal object, from someone who imbued himself with superhuman qualities to a non-human. Image reversal, in the case of Qaddafi's death, is an indicator of the destructive legacy of dictatorship. Not only does dictatorship destroy human essence while dictatorship prevails, it also has the ability to leave a disturbing legacy in its wake, where the direction of mercilessness is simply reversed, rather than it being erased.

Bashar al-Assad: "legacy," "legitimacy" and "love"

Like Libya, Syria saw the creation of a new regime when Hafez al-Assad led a bloodless coup in 1970. The Baath regime led by Hafez al-Assad created an "authoritarian-populist state"[35] that relied on a " 'mass base' of society to mobilize participation and support for its rule and its goals."[36] Lisa Wedeen argues that Hafez al-Assad's strategy of domination was "based on compliance rather than legitimacy."[37] It was a strategy reliant on spectacle and performance "operating as a disciplinary device, generating a politics of public dissimulation in which citizens act *as if* they revere their leader."[38] A Syrian official is quoted by Wedeen in reference to Hafez al-Assad as saying: "Lack of inner conviction is acceptable as long as every single party member and official is prepared to demonstrate publicly his/her commitment to party and President."[39] In her book about Hafez al-Assad's regime, Wedeen illustrates how people from all ranks of Syrian society, especially the youth, artists and intellectuals, were periodically called upon to engage in public spectacles in support of the president. The spectacles were part of a wider visual strategy that saw Assad immortalized in posters, statues and media representations. Like Qaddafi, Hafez al-Assad established a cult of leadership, yet the two differed in style, as Qaddafi's was flamboyant and relied on mythologization while Assad's was stern.[40]

Hafez al-Assad's images still permeated public space in Syria after his death and the overtaking of the presidency by his son, Bashar, "as if even in death he is still at least in spirit guiding and overseeing the country, and by implication, his son."[41] "Our leader forever" was the slogan that often accompanied images of Hafez al-Assad. The slogan was modified in posters of Bashar: "With you forever, following the legacy of the leader [Hafez] al-Assad." Those posters were joined by photos of Bashar with the image of Hafez placed in the top right corner, with both men looking in the same direction, implying a sense of continuity. "Yes, leader of the course," announced a poster bearing the photo of Bashar, with the Syrian flag superimposed on the Syrian landscape, in a message confirming the natural continuity of the course set by Hafez.

Bashar was initially not groomed for the presidency, and only assumed that role after the death of his elder brother, Basil – who was due to take over after his father – in a car accident in 1994. Basil's death created public mythologization. As Ghadbian documents,

> The heir was lavishly lamented in the official media with a train of epithets: he was Basil the doctor, Basil the engineer, the major, the knight, and the parachutist – referring respectively to the fact that he had written a doctoral thesis in military sciences, had completed a degree in engineering, died as a ranking officer in the military, had been an accomplished equestrian, and had trained in parachute-jumping. What better qualifications could a people have hoped for in a leader?[42]

This mythologization presented an idealized type of leadership that Bashar was presented as following. Photos of Hafez al-Assad with his two eldest sons could be seen around Syria, captioned "the Leader, the Example and the Hope" (the latter two referring to Basil and Bashar, respectively).[43] The posters served as a visual clue preparing the people of Syria for their next leader. Lesch reports that some pictures at the time "had Bashar look much more muscular than his current trim physique; [while] some had him look older, and thus wiser, than his youth indicated."[44]

Although mindful of maintaining Hafez al-Assad's legacy, Bashar al-Assad wanted to present a different image to the Syrian people from that of his father, one of a more moderate leader. He engaged in a limited liberalization effort through releasing some political prisoners and allowing the establishment of Syria's first private newspaper in 2000.[45] As Hinnebusch puts it, Bashar al-Assad "positioned himself as a 'modernizer'. Educated in Britain, an advocate of information technology and economic modernization, leader of an anti-corruption campaign under his father, and seemingly representative of the educated younger generation, he had acquired a certain legitimacy among those who longed for orderly change."[46] His regime circulated the buzzwords "*infitah* (openness) in politics and *islah* (reform) of the economy" in public discourse to cultivate this modern, moderate image.[47] Yet Bashar al-Assad only engaged in symbolic statements about commitment to reform and political openness, not in concrete practical measures.[48] By the end of the short-lived "Damascus Spring" the Bashar regime had started rivaling Qaddafi's in political oppression.

Bashar's marriage to Asma al-Akhras less than six months after taking over the presidency was a useful step in the direction of disseminating a modern image. Born and educated in London and a former Wall Street employee, with a high sense of fashion, Asma projected the image of a modern first lady with flair. Her celebrity status was consolidated in a badly timed article in Vogue published in February 2011 that described her as "The Rose of the Desert." For more than a decade, Asma al-Assad was seen as lending credibility to her husband's image as a modern president.[49] The couple thrived on the image of a liberalized Syria that was active in the international community. The first lady supervised cultural events in Syria, and the president relaxed laws on internet access and supported tourism and art. In 2009, Syria had its first art pavilion at the Venice Biennale, and the year before Damascus was named Arab Capital of Culture. "I believe in Syria," declared an official billboard in English and Arabic displaying the photo of a smiling, waving Bashar in a sharp suit.

"Legacy" and "legitimacy" were not the only values invoked by Bashar's choreographed image – the third "l" was "love." On the one hand, Bashar al-Assad wanted to show that he loved his people, and thus projected the image of a caring president. A billboard in Damascus displayed his photo on the right and that of two children carrying the Syrian flag on the left, with the slogan "Syria is our country, Bashar is our hope." Another depicted Bashar flanked by balloons in the colors of the Syrian flag, with the photo of a child carrying a giant flag on the left, under the words "The grandchildren of civilization. Bashar is our leader." The sign for the Public Board of the Children's Hospital in Damascus included a photograph of Bashar attending to a sick child on the left side of the sign. On the other hand, Assad wanted to appear as a leader loved by his people, while trying not to extend the cult surrounding his father to himself. In 2008, he announced that he would ban people from displaying his image in public space, a ban that was "defied" by the Syrians as they "insisted" on doing so in an ultimate expression of their "love" for the president. Writing about people's display of posters of Hafez al-Assad, Wedeen quotes a Syrian saying, "People post the signs not because they love him, but because the system is self-enforcing and people are accustomed to it. People have internalized the control."[50] Václav Havel called this "auto-totality," whereby the people's participation creates new norms that sustain the status quo.[51] This auto-totality seems to have been passed down from the father's era to the son's.

Prior to the uprising of 2011, posters of Bashar al-Assad could be found all over Syria, and they were centered on this theme of love. "The most precious of men," one declared, carrying the photo of a smiling, waving Assad. "We love you," another poster said, superimposing a photo of Bashar on the map of Syria. The entrance of the building of the Public Board of the Solace Hospital in Damascus displayed a billboard with Bashar's photo and the image of an ink stamp carrying the slogan "We love you," which was repeated in the background of the billboard. This expression of love was presented as a result of concrete mass popular support. Assad orchestrated a referendum in 2007 whereby he "won" 97.62% of the vote to serve a second presidential term. More posters of him appeared all over Syria, declaring "Yes to the leader Bashar al-Assad, a voice for the benefit of society and the elevation of the nation," "Your young men are with you," "The people of Syria know better about its Bashar," "We are all with you, Bashar al-Assad," "Yes to the symbol of the nation," "Yes to who proved to the whole world that he and his people would not kneel except in front of God," "The people are with you: yes and a thousand yeses, for a strong country, for a prosperous country, for a better life, for a civilized country, for a just peace, for a bright future, for safety and stability." The last slogan, displayed in a poster by the ruling Baath Party, referenced Assad's economic liberalization, his "resistant" stance towards Israel and the United States and his national security measures – celebrating the country's "stability" that was in fact based on an extended declared state of emergency and on curbs on political action and freedom of expression.

Fig. 50. Pro-Assad fridge magnets on sale in Damascus in 2008.

Those slogans neatly summarize the official line that Assad presented to his people to cultivate the senses of legacy, legitimacy and love. When the Syrian uprising of 2011 started, out of the three qualities, it was the latter – love – that Assad chose to focus on the most in the messages disseminated by the regime in response to the anti-Assad demonstrations around Syria. Syrian state television saw persistent displays of large crowds of Syrians pledging allegiance to Assad, and the online media were flooded with similar images and declarations that were carefully orchestrated by Assad and his public relations team. An example of this is the televised speech in parliament that Bashar al-Assad gave in May 2011, in which he announced cosmetic reforms. The speech was notable for the synchronized clapping by members of parliament who cheered for Bashar and told him that he deserved to be the "leader of the world," as the president beamed in delight. A later speech was staged at Damascus University, leading commentators to point out the large number of middle-aged men in suits in what was supposed to be a student audience. In a response that echoed the Green Movement's reaction to the Iranian government's "spontaneous-ed" rallies, Syrian anti-regime activists created a new term for the followers of Assad who declared their love for the president in public: "*minhibbakjiyyeh*," meaning the "we love you's." But despite the prioritization of love over legacy, and the subsequent differences in image between Assad the father and Assad the son, their style of authoritarianism was the same. Both styles were "populist, inclusionary, and participatory."[52]

The 2011 uprising in Syria revealed that Bashar al-Assad indeed did not depart greatly from the path set by his father, as he responded to public protests with severe crackdowns that recalled Hafez's genocide in Hama in 1982, albeit on a different scale. Bashar al-Assad's bloody response marked the failure of the mask of a Western-educated, young, reformist leader (as had been the case of Saif al-Islam Qaddafi). Even the mask of a "modern" first lady fell after hacked emails obtained by the international media revealed Asma al-Assad as spending her time shopping for luxury items online while the Syrian people were being slaughtered by the Baath regime, and as being a fierce defender of her husband's actions.

As with Mubarak and Qaddafi, Syrian protesters projected their rejection of Bashar through visual symbolism. On 25 March 2011, demonstrators in Daraa toppled a statue of Hafez al-Assad, in a scene that recalled the toppling of the statue of Saddam Hussein in 2003, except that this one was not staged. The toppling of this statue was a powerful statement about pulling the regime from its roots. This triggered further acts of visual reversal. As Caldwell writes:

> Many Syrian activists christened this action as the beginning of *"Hamlat al-Tathir"* or the "cleansing campaign" [purification campaign is a more accurate translation] against visual symbols of the Asad regime. Dozens of "cleansing campaign" videos have since appeared on YouTube. Most of the clips were shot on cell phone cameras in Homs, Hama, and Deraa. They capture scenes that range from two-man operations setting fire to what they call the largest poster of Bashar in Homs or crowds of people cheering on as a poster of Bashar is ripped from a government building in Hama.[53]

The choice of the word "purification" to describe this campaign was a direct reference to Bashar's speech about immunizing Syria against "germs." The internet became a hub for the circulation of videos documenting the erasure of Baath symbols. Videos on several sites showed posters of Assad being pelted with shoes and stones or burnt, and Facebook carried the photo of a soldier urinating on a poster of Bashar. The internet was also full of satirical and self-reflexive representations of Bashar, from cartoons to digital posters that superimposed the image of Bashar on other photographs, such as one showing Bashar as a soldier pointing a rifle at a little girl (the caption reads, reflecting the words of the girl: "I am not hiding from you because I am afraid of you, but because I am ashamed of the way you are killing me"), and another that presented Bashar as the face of a bull named "the regime" that was being confronted in a ring by a matador carrying a cloth displaying the Facebook logo. Following the release of a number of hacked emails by Bashar al-Assad and his family and associates in the Spring of 2012, in which flirtation between Assad and one of his communication advisers led to her affectionately calling him a "duck," the internet became full of cartoons and edited images depicting Assad as a duck, taking the animal references to Assad (whose name means "lion" but who was often mocked by activists as a "giraffe" due to his physical appearance) to a new level of power reversal.

Protesters against Bashar al-Assad in public space also engaged in a process of visual reversal similar to the one witnessed in Libya. One of the Fridays in August 2011 was named "We don't kneel in

Fig. 51. Still from a Youtube video depicting the tearing down of an Assad poster in Syria, distributed by the Sham News Network in 2011.

front of anyone but God," an appropriation of one of Bashar al-Assad's slogans (as presented above), but also a response to a statement issued by the pro-regime Mufti of Damascus saying that it is halal for Muslims to pray on a rug that bears the image of Bashar, and to several videos of Syrian soldiers and *shabbeeha* (government thugs) asking detained protesters, "Who is your God?" to which the detainees were forced to answer, "Bashar al-Assad." During a demonstration in Daraa, protesters carried a drawing of Bashar with a noose around his neck that was very similar in style to the one of Qaddafi that was carried by Libyan rebels. In a direct rejection of the cult of *minhibbakji-yyeh*, the placard had the caption "Run away. We don't love you."

"Asadescu," read the graffiti on Damascus walls "when the Rumanian regime of Nicolae Ceaucescu, ostensibly similar to Hafiz al-Asad's Syria, succumbed to revolution at the end of 1989."[54] The contagion of revolution did not reach Syria for another 22 years, but when it did, there was no turning back for the Syrians. We can refer to the words written by Ray Hinnebusch shortly after Bashar al-Assad's ascent to the presidency for a sign of what was to come: "It remains to be seen whether Bashar can overcome the legitimacy deficit inherent in the seeming transforming of a radical republic into a new monarchy."[55] A decade after Hinnebusch's words, Bashar's legitimacy deficit finally exploded into popular revolt, changing the image of Bashar al-Assad forever as he joined the ranks of disgraced Arab dictators. After the fall of Qaddafi, the renowned Syrian cartoonist

Ali Ferzat drew a cartoon depicting Bashar al-Assad hitching a ride with Qaddafi. Recalling Iran's imprisonment of Jafar Panahi, Ferzat was subsequently severely beaten up and his hands broken. But this violent attack on an image maker did not deter the Syrian protesters. At one demonstration, they referenced Qaddafi's fall through carrying a banner showing Bashar looking over his shoulder towards Ben Ali, Qaddafi and Mubarak, who are all sitting behind a table as judges on the talent show Arabs Got Talent. Using the familiar terminology that the show's judges use when a contestant is picked to proceed to the next stage, the banner had the ousted dictators beckoning Bashar al-Assad: "You are certainly with us."

But the Syrian uprising differs from the rest of the uprisings in the Arab Spring through adding a new role for the image as a political tool. A significant movement engaging in nonviolent resistance spread across Syria, even in places witnessing military crackdown by the regime like Daraa and Idlib. In those places, citizens took to the streets to engage in what can only be characterized as visual acts of the absurd as a means of resistance. In Damascus in 2011, as Wendell Steavenson documents,

> Activists have tried to confound the authorities by singing the national anthem or throwing roses into the fountain in Marjeh Square. They have tied messages of defiance to balloons, and tucked them inside packages of dates given out at mosques, and taped them to Ping-Pong balls thrown into the street from high buildings. In one ingenious scheme [replicating a tactic that was used by the Green Movement in Iran], they wrote "freedom" on banknotes...One day...dozens of people simply wore white and walked around a block in an upscale neighborhood [in Damascus]. Several were arrested.[56]

One protest in Idlib in 2011 saw citizens simply taping their mouths while carrying blank placards. The same year in Homs, young men launched small fireworks in the direction of the Syrian army, which duly retaliated with live fire, while the young protesters recorded the exchange on video and later disseminated it through the online media. Such methods of resistance through the absurd pushed nonviolent protest to the fore, to literally stand in the face of state violence. This resistance possesses two powerful characteristics. First, it appropriates the state's oppression. In 2012, the Chinese artist and activist Ai Weiwei installed cameras all over his home, relaying online live 24-hour footage of his daily life, in protest against the state's surveillance over him. The Syrian protesters' appropriation of state violence is a similar case of "choosing the margin as a space of radical openness," in the words of bell hooks.[57] Occupying the margin, then, becomes a case of asserting a position of power. The oppression of the state, in turn, is transformed into an assertion of its weakness. Second, it resists the state's relegation of the citizen into "bare life" by assuming a position of "bare life" and speaking back from that position.[58] For we must remember that the acts of resistance-through-the-absurd did not take place online – they took place on the street and in the midst of ongoing assault by the regime, exposing the human body in all its vulnerability, and in doing so, transcending this vulnerability. Although the Syrian uprising eventually became an armed struggle against the regime, putting the bare human body on the frontline sent a powerful message against the state's dehumanization of its citizens. It was the ultimate expression of the breakdown of the wall of fear. By engaging in these visual acts of the absurd as a means of resistance, Syrians challenged the regime narrative that was trying to render them silent and invisible (we should not forget that this narrative denied the existence of an uprising in the first place, instead insisting that protesters were "armed criminal gangs").

Visual acts of the absurd also took street protest beyond the utilization of presence and visibility, which had characterized public acts in the Egyptian revolution, for example. Protest through visual acts of the absurd transformed the image of the Syrian citizen itself into a floating image haunting the regime. The citizen's image as a floating image changed the original context in which "citizenship" was conceived by the Syrian state, imbuing it with a new meaning focused on empowerment. The image of the new empowered citizen engaging in acts of the absurd acknowledged and referenced other images of citizens in protest (as seen in the blank placards protest mentioned above, for example). This floating image, with its reliance on fantasy (in the acts of the absurd), also blurred the lines between the real and the represented. This image is also at once a mediated image (recorded through cameras) and a physical representation in offline space. It is an image with inherent agency that, as I argued in the introduction to this book, "imposes its identity by the sheer fact of its presence." The dynamic presented here goes beyond identifying with the floating image of an individual, like in the case of Khaled Said or even Hamza al-Khatib. This is more than "We Are All Khaled Said" or "We Are All Hamza Al-Khatib." This time, the intrinsic meaning of being Syrian has changed: In the face of Bashar al-Assad's dictatorship, the floating image of the empowered people could be simply declared as: "We Are All Syrian."

The new Big Brother

In both Libya and Syria, the uprisings signalled the end of the era of personification. One can reflect on several reasons for the prominence of personification of politics in the Arab world for so many decades. First, personification can become established in societies because "it is easier to understand a man than a program."[59] Taking over not long after the Arab world was emerging from colonialism and exploitative European mandates, leaders like Qaddafi made politics more easily digestible. They associated politics with their personas, which summarized a set of attractive values like freedom and national pride. Even when it later became clear that such leaders were delivering mere rhetoric, this pattern of governance had become too rooted to be done away with through gradual reform alone. Second, this long history of autocratic governance created a political milieu in which such governance was expected and even admired in certain instances (such as in the context of defying the West). This in turn created an environment favorable to sustaining this kind of leadership.[60] Third, as Lacoutre argues, when people are struggling and have few resources, they can offset their weakness through strong leadership personified in an individual.[61] Bensman and Givant argue that charismatic leadership often arises in "times of crises in which the basic values, institutions, and legitimacy of the society are at least in question."[62] The Arab world was in a state of ongoing hardship that was nurtured by authoritarian leaders who benefited from the broken spirit of their people, and who in turn nurtured this broken spirit to sustain their dominance.

Yet, what the Arab Spring has demonstrated is that even broken spirits can rise again. The Arab Spring has not just re-imaged Arab dictators. It has clearly announced that the age of demigods is approaching its end. Perhaps the most notable characteristic of all the uprisings in the Arab world in 2011 is that they were leaderless. Unlike Nasser's, Qaddafi's, Hafez al-Assad's and Saddam Hussein's revolutions, the Arab Spring revolutions were not led by a single man. They were people's revolutions, in which the image of the singular leader was erased, to be replaced with the image of the multitude. It is the people who are now the political agents of the Arab world. The people are the ones keeping their leaders in check. The power equation has changed. As Mark Crispin Miller once put it, "there is no Big Brother out there watching you – not because there isn't a Big Brother, but because Big Brother is you, watching."[63]

Notes

Introduction

1. Groys, Boris (2008). *Art Power*. Cambridge, MA: The MIT Press, p. 9.
2. Newman, Bruce I. (1994). *The Marketing of the President: Political Marketing as Campaign Strategy*. London: Sage.
3. Shyles, Leonard (1984). "Defining 'Images' of Presidential Candidates from Televised Political Spot Advertisements." *Political Behavior* 6(2): 171–181.
4. Morgan, David (2005). *The Sacred Gaze: Religious Visual Culture in Theory and Practice*. Berkeley: University of California Press, p. 33.
5. Street, John (1997). *Politic and Popular Culture*. Philadelphia: Temple University Press; Dahlgren, Peter (2009). *Media and Political Engagement: Citizens, Communication, and Democracy*. Cambridge: Cambridge University Press.
6. Wedeen, Lisa (1999). *Ambiguities of Domination: Politics, Rhetoric, and Symbols in Contemporary Syria*. Chicago: University of Chicago Press, p. 30.
7. Parry-Giles, Shawn J. and Trevor Parry-Giles (2007). "The Man from Hope: Hyperreal Intimacy and the Invention of Bill Clinton," in Negrine, Ralph and James Stanyer (eds.), *The Political Communication Reader*. London: Routledge, p. 251.
8. Cottle, Simon (2011). "Media and the Arab Spring." *Journalism* 12(5), p. 652.
9. Lundby, Knut (2009). "Introduction: 'Mediatization' as Key," in Lundby, Knut (ed.), *Mediatization: Concept, Changes, Consequences*. New York: Peter Lang, p. 13.
10. Kraidy, Marwan. (2007). "Saudi Arabia, Lebanon and the Changing Arab Information Order." *International Journal of Communication*. 1, p. 140.
11. Ibid.
12. Etling, Bruce et al. (2009). *Mapping the Arabic Blogosphere: Politics, Culture, and Dissent*: Internet & Democracy Case Study Series, Berkman Center Research Publication number 2009–06. Berkman Center for Internet & Society. Available: http://www.alhaqqsociety.org/research/MappingTheArabicBlogosphere.pdf, p. 7.
13. Livingstone, Sonia (2009). "On the Mediation of Everything." *Journal of Communication* 59, p. 1.
14. Silverstone, Roger (2005). "The Sociology of Mediation and Communication," in Craig J. Calhoun, Chris Rojek, and Bryan S. Turner (eds.), *The Handbook of Sociology*. London: Sage, pp. 190–1.
15. Amin, Hussein (2002). "Freedom as Value in Arab Media: Perceptions and Attitudes among Journalists." *Political Communication* 19(2), pp. 127–8.
16. Jansson, André (2002). "The Mediatization of Consumption: Towards an Analytical Framework of Image Culture." *Journal of Consumer Culture* 2(1), pp. 14–15.
17. Hepp, Andreas, Stig Hjarvard, and Knut Lundby (2010). "Mediatization, Empirical Perspectives: An Introduction to a Special Issue." *Communications* 35, p. 224.
18. Schickel, Richard (2000). *Intimate Strangers: The Culture of Celebrity in America*. Chicago: Ivan R. Dee.
19. Evans, Jessica (2005). "Celebrity, Media and History," in Evans, Jessica and David Hesmondhalgh (eds.), *Understanding Media: Inside Celebrity*, pp. 11–56. Maidenhead: Open University Press.

209

20. Bergmann, Knut and Wolfram Wickert (1999). "Selected Aspects of Communication in German Election Campaigns." In Newman, Bruce I. (ed.), *Handbook of Political Marketing*, pp. 455–84. London: Sage.
21. Voltmer, Katrin (2006). "The Mass Media and the Dynamics of Political Communication in Processes of Democratization: An Introduction," in Voltmer, Katrin (ed.), *Mass Media and Political Communication in New Democracies*, pp. 1–20. New York: Routledge.
22. Khouri, Rami G. (2011). "Middle East Awakening." *The Cairo Review of Global Affairs* 1: 126–134.
23. Manheim, Jarol B. (1994). *Strategic Public Diplomacy and American Foreign Policy: The Evolution of Influence*. Oxford: Oxford University Press.
24. Hansen, Lene (2006). *Images, Identity and Security: Bringing Together International Politics and Media Research*. Nordicom conference paper. Available: http://www.nordicom.gu.se/common/publ_pdf/269_hansen.pdf.
25. Sussman, Gerald (2005). *Global Electioneering: Campaign Consulting, Communications, and Corporate Financing*. Oxford: Rowman and Littlefield, p. 207.
26. Lefebvre, Henri (1971). *Everyday Life in the Modern World*. London: Allen Lane, p. 146.
27. Lefebvre, *Everyday Life in the Modern World*, p. 147.
28. Foucault, Michel (1995). *Discipline and Punish: The Birth of the Prison*. New York: Vintage Books.
29. Wedeen, *Ambiguities of Domination*, p. 5.
30. Benjamin, Walter (2008). *The Work of Art in the Age of Mechanical Reproduction*. London: Penguin.
31. Wedeen, *Ambiguities of Domination*.
32. Benjamin, *The Work of Art in the Age of Mechanical Reproduction*.
33. Lefebvre, *Everyday Life in the Modern World*, p. 62.
34. Sontag, Susan (2003). *Regarding the Pain of Others*. New York: Picador, p. 52.
35. Ibid.
36. Gamson, William et al. (1992). "Media Images and the Social Construction of Reality." *Annual Review of Sociology* 18, p. 385.
37. Nimmo, Dan and Robert L. Savage (1976). *Candidates and their Images: Concepts, Methods, and Findings*. Santa Monica, CA: Goodyear.
38. Barthes, Roland (1977). *Image, Music, Text*. New York: Hill and Wang, p. 47.
39. Lefebvre, Henri (1971). *Everyday Life in the Modern World*, p. 148.
40. Castells, Manuel (2000). "Materials for an Exploratory Theory of the Network Society." *British Journal of Sociology* 51(1), p. 24.
41. Schweiger, Günter and Gertraud Schrattenecker (1995). *Werbung*. Stuttgart: Gustav Fischer Verlag.
42. Handler, Joel F. (1992). "Postmodernism, Protest, and the New Social Movements." *Law and Society Review* 26(4), p. 727.
43. Sontag, *Regarding the Pain of Others*.
44. Sontag, *Regarding the Pain of Others*, p. 20.
45. Ibid.
46. Hepp, Hjarvard, and Lundby, Mediatization, Empirical Perspectives.
47. Bayat, Asef (2010). *Life as Politics: How Ordinary People Change the Middle East*. Stanford, CA: Stanford University Press, p. 11.
48. Groys, *Art Power*, p. 14.
49. Welsh, Madeline B. (2011). Oriental Hall, etc. *The Cairo Review of Global Affairs* 1: 9.
50. Groys, *Art Power*, p. 27.
51. Sontag, *Regarding the Pain of Others*.
52. Sontag, *Regarding the Pain of Others*, p. 22.

53. Hemphill, David F. (2001). "Incorporating Postmodernist Perspectives into Adult Education," in Sheared, Peggy and Vanessa Sissel (eds.), *Making Space: Merging Theory and Practice in Adult Education*. Westport, CT: Greenwood, p, 24.
54. Parry-Giles, Shawn J. and Trevor Parry-Giles (1999). "Meta-Imaging, *The War Room*, and the Hyperreality of U.S. Politics." *Journal of Communication* 49(1): 28–45.
55. Kraidy, Saudi Arabia, Lebanon and the Changing Arab Information Order.
56. Groys, *Art Power*, p. 83.

I

1. Maasri, Zeina (2009). *Off the Wall: Political Posters of the Lebanese Civil War*. London: I.B. Tauris.
2. Haugbolle, Sune (2010). *War and Memory in Lebanon*. Cambridge: Cambridge University Press.
3. Maasri, *Off the Wall*, p. 16.
4. Van Bakel, Martin, Renée Hagesteijn and Pieter van de Velde (1986). "Introduction," in Van Bakel, Martin, Renée Hagesteijn and Pieter van de Velde (eds.), *Private Politics: A Multi-Disciplinary Approach to "Big Man" Systems*. Leiden: Brill, p. 1.
5. Betsky, Aaron et al. (1997). *Icons: Magnets of Meaning*. San Francisco: Chronicle Books.
6. Butler, Patrick and Neil Collins (1999). "A Conceptual Framework for Political Marketing," in Newman, Bruce I. (ed.), *Handbook of Political Marketing*, pp. 55–72. Thousand Oaks, CA: Sage.
7. Nasr, Assem (2010). "Imagining Identities: Television Advertising and the Reconciliation of the Lebanese Conflict." *Arab Media and Society*, issue 10, p. 13.
8. Khalaf, Samir (2006). *Heart of Beirut: Reclaiming the Burj*. London: Saqi Books.
9. Nasr, Imagining Identities.
10. Barak, Oren (2007). "'Don't mention the war?': The Politics of Remembrance and Forgetfulness in Postwar Lebanon." *Middle East Journal* 61(1), p. 66.
11. Perloff, Richard M. (1999). "Elite, Popular, and Merchandised Politics: Historical Origins of Presidential Campaign Marketing," in Newman, Bruce I. (ed.), *Handbook of Political Marketing*, pp. 19–40. Thousand Oaks, CA: Sage.
12. Nasr, Imagining Identities.
13. Lefebvre, Henri (1971). *Everyday Life in the Modern World*. London: Allen Lane The Penguin Press, p. 90.
14. Jain, Dipak and Suvit Maesincee (2002). *Marketing Moves: A New Approach to Profits, Growth and Renewal*. Boston: Harvard Business School Press.
15. Baudrillard, Jean (1999). *Simulacra and Simulation*. Ann Arbor: The University of Michigan Press.
16. Bhabha, Homi (1994). *The Location of Culture*. London: Routledge.
17. Roka, Jolan (1999). "Do the Media Reflect or Shape Public Opinion?" in Newman, Bruce I. (ed.), *Handbook of Political Marketing*, pp. 505–518. Thousand Oaks, CA: Sage.
18. De Certeau, Michel (1997). *Culture in the Plural*. Minneapolis: University of Minnesota Press, p. 119.
19. Butler and Collins, A Conceptual Framework for Political Marketing.
20. Featherstone, Mike (1991). *Consumer Culture and Postmodernism*. London: Sage, pp. 89–90.
21. Sontag, Susan (2003). *Regarding the Pain of Others*. New York: Picador, p. 85.
22. Barak, Don't Mention the War?
23. Sontag, *Regarding the Pain of Others*, p. 85.

24. Haugbolle, Sune (2007). "Memory as Representation and Memory as Idiom," in Choueiri, Youssef (ed.), *Breaking the Cycle: Civil Wars in Lebanon*. London: Stacey International, p. 121.
25. Ibid.
26. Barak, Don't Mention the War?
27. Stack, Megan (2005). "Lebanon Finally Facing Its War." *Los Angeles Times*, 14 April.
28. Haugbolle, Memory as Representation and Memory as Idiom, p. 130, emphasis added.
29. Hacker, Kenneth L. (1995). "Introduction: The Importance of Candidate Images in Presidential Elections," in Hacker, Kenneth L. (ed.), *Candidate Images in Presidential Elections*. London: Praeger, p. xii.
30. Scammell, Margaret (1999). "Political Marketing: Issues for Political Science." *Political Studies*, XLVII: 718–39; Lees-Marshmant, Jennifer (2001). *Political Marketing and British Political Parties: The Party's Just Begun*. Manchester: Manchester University Press.
31. Blumler, Jay G. and Dennis Kavanagh (1999). "The Third Age of Political Communication: Influences and Features." *Political Communication* 16(3): 209–30.
32. Plasser, Fritz with Gunda Plasser (2007). "Global Political Campaigning: A Worldwide Analysis of Campaigning Professionals and Their Practices," in Negrine, Ralph and James Stanyer (eds.), *The Political Communication Reader*. London: Routledge, p. 140.
33. Bennett, W. Lance (2003). "Lifestyle Politics and Citizen-Consumers: Identity, Communication and Political Action in Late Modern Society," in Corner, John and Dick Pels (eds.), *Media and the Restyling of Politics*. London: Sage, p. 143.
34. Negrine, Ralph and Stylianos Papathanassopoulos (1996). "The 'Americanization' of Political Communication: A Critique." *Press/Politics* 1(2): 45–62.
35. Plasser and Plasser, Global Political Campaigning.
36. Lees-Marshmant, Political Marketing and British Political Parties, p. 28.
37. Lees-Marshmant, Political Marketing and British Political Parties, p. 29.
38. Sussman, Gerald (2005). *Global Electioneering: Campaign Consulting, Communications, and Corporate Financing*. Oxford: Rowman and Littlefield, p. 219.
39. Kotler, Philip and Neil Kotler (1999). "Political Marketing: Generating Effective Candidates, Campaigns, and Causes," in Newman, Bruce I. (ed.), *Handbook of Political Marketing*. Thousand Oaks, CA: Sage, p. 5.
40. Sontag, *Regarding the Pain of Others*, p. 109.
41. Corner, John and Dick Pels (2003). "Introduction: The Re-styling of Politics," in Corner, John and Dick Pels (eds.), *Media and the Restyling of Politics*. London: Sage, p. 7.
42. Debord, Guy (1994). *The Society of the Spectacle*. New York: Zone Books.
43. Jansson, André (2002). "The Mediatization of Consumption: Towards an Analytical Framework of Image Culture." *Journal of Consumer Culture* 2(1): 5–31, p. 17.
44. Sontag, *Regarding the Pain of Others*, p. 109.
45. Lacoutre, Jean (1970). *The Demigods: Charismatic Leadership in the Third World*. New York: Alfred A. Knopf, p. 33.
46. Glassman, Ronald M. and William H. Swatos, Jr. (1986). "Introduction," in Glassman, Ronald M. and William H. Swatos, Jr. (eds.), *Charisma, History, and Social Structure*. New York: Greenwood Press, p. 6.
47. Glassman and Swatos, Introduction.
48. Gibbins, John R. and Bo Reimer (1999). *The Politics of Postmodernity: An Introduction to Contemporary Politics and Culture*. London: Sage, p. 146.
49. Glassman, Ronald M. (1986). "Manufactured Charisma and Legitimacy," in Glassman, Ronald M. and William H. Swatos, Jr. (eds.), *Charisma, History, and Social Structure*, pp. 115–128. New York: Greenwood Press.
50. Mazzoleni, Gianpietro and Winfried Schulz (1999). "'Mediatization' of Politics: A Challenge for Democracy?" *Political Communication* 16(3), p. 249f.
51. Stanyer, James (2007). *Modern Political Communication*. Cambridge: Polity Press.
52. Corner and Pels, Introduction, p. 4.

53. See Chapter 2.
54. For a fuller analysis of this topic, see: Khatib, Lina (2007). "Television and Public Action in the Beirut Spring," in Sakr, Naomi (ed.), *Arab Media and Political Renewal: Community, Legitimacy and Public Life*, pp. 28–43. London: I.B.Tauris.
55. Shaw, Michael (2006). "Cracking The Cedar: How Hezbollah Re-Envisioned The Democracy Movement (And The West Hardly Noticed)." *Bag News*, 16 December. Available: http://www.bagnewsnotes.com/2006/12/cracking-the-cedar-how-hezbollah-re-envisioned-the-democracy-movement-and-the-west-hardly-noticed/.
56. www.lebanon-ilovelife.com, *emphasis in original*.

2

1. Kaid, Linda Lee and Mike Chanslor (1995). "Changing Candidate Images: The Effects of Political Advertising," in Hacker, Kenneth L. (ed.), *Candidate Images in Presidential Elections*, pp. 83–97. Westport, CT: Praeger Publishers; King, Pu-Tsung (1997). "The Press, Candidate Images, and Voter Perceptions," in, McCombs, Maxwell E., Donald L. Shaw, and David H. Weaver (eds.), *Communication and Democracy: Exploring the Intellectual Frontiers in Agenda-setting Theory*, pp. 29–40. Mahwah, NJ: Lawrence Erlbaum Associates; Miller, Mark M., Julie L. Andsager, and Bonnie P. Reichert (1998). "Framing the Candidates in Presidential Primaries: Issues and Images in Press Releases and News Coverage." *Journalism and Mass Communication Quarterly* 75 (2): 312–24.
2. van Ham, Peter (2001). "The Rise of the Brand State: The Postmodern Politics of Image and Reputation." *Foreign Affairs*, 10 October.
3. Leonard, Mark (2002). "Diplomacy by Other Means." *Foreign Policy* 132 (Sep.–Oct.): 48–56.
4. Which is not a political actor in the pure sense, but whose actions are driven by political developments.
5. Glasser, Susan B. and Steve Coll (2005). "[The Web as Weapon." *The Washington Post*, 9 August, p. A01; Conway, Maura (2006). "Terrorism and the Internet. New Media – New Threat?" *Parliamentary Affairs* 59(2): 283–98; Lynch, Marc (2006). "Al-Qaeda's Media Strategies." *The National Interest* 83: 50–56; Qin, Jialun (2007). "Analyzing Terror Campaigns on the Internet: Technical Sophistication, Content Richness, and Web Interactivity." *Human-Computer Studies* 65: 71–84; Weimann, Gabriel (2008b). "The Psychology of Mass Mediated Terrorism." *American Behavioral Scientist* 52(1): 69–86.
6. Dalacoura, Katerina (2001) "Islamist Movements as Non-state Actors and their Relevance to International Relations," in Josselin, Daphné and William Wallace, (eds.), *Non-state Actors in World Politics*. London: Palgrave Macmillan, pp. 235–50.
7. McLaughlin, W. Sean (2003). "The Use of the Internet for Political Action by Non-state Dissident Actors in the Middle East." *First Monday* 8(11, 3 November). Available: http://firstmonday.org/htbin/cgiwrap/bin/ojs/index.php/fm/article/view/1096/1016.
8. Harb, Zahera (2011). *Channels of Resistance in Lebanon: Liberation Propaganda, Hezbollah and the Media*. London: I.B.Tauris.
9. Plasser, Fritz with Gunda Plasser (2002). *Global Political Campaigning: A Worldwide Analysis of Campaign Professionals and Their Practices*. London: Praeger, p. 16.
10. Plasser and Plasser, Global Political Campaigning.
11. Scammell, Margaret (1995). *Designer Politics: How Elections are Won*. New York: St Martin's Press, p. 9.
12. Khatib, Lina (2011). "Hizbullah's Political Strategy." *Survival: Global Politics and Strategy* 53(2): 61–76.
13. Harnden, Toby (2004) "Video Games Attract Young to Hizbollah." *The Telegraph*, 21 February.
14. Leonard, Diplomacy by Other Means, p. 51.

15. Blumenthal, Sidney (1980). *The Permanent Campaign: Inside the World of Elite Political Operatives*. Boston: Beacon, p. 8.
16. Blumenthal, *The Permanent Campaign*, p. 7.
17. Harb, *Channels of Resistance in Lebanon*.
18. Dutton, Jane E. and Janet M. Dukerich (1991). "Keeping an Eye on the Mirror: Image and Identity in Organizational Adaptation." *The Academy of Management Journal* 34(3): 517–54.
19. Khatib, Hizbullah's Political Strategy.
20. El Houri, Walid and Dima Saber (2010). "Filming Resistance: A Hezbollah Strategy." *Radical History Review* 106: 70–85.
21. Solanas, Fernando and Octavio Getino (1970). "Towards a Third Cinema." *Cineaste* IV(3): 1–10.
22. Groys, Boris (2008). *Art Power*. Cambridge, MA: The MIT Press.
23. See *al-Ahd/al-Intiqad* special spreads of the parades for examples.
24. Saad-Ghorayeb, Amal (2002). *Hizbu'llah: Politics and Religion*. London: Pluto Press.
25. Atrissi, Talal (2010). Matha yourid al-shia min dawlatihim? *An-Nahar*, Wednesday 25 August. Available: http://www.annahar.com/content.php?priority=6&table=main&type=main&day=Wed.
26. Al-Agha, Joseph Elie (2006). *The Shifts in Hizbullah's Ideology: Religious Ideology, Political Ideology, and Political Program*. Amsterdam: Amsterdam University Press.
27. Jorisch, Avi (2004). "Al-Manar: Hizbullah TV, 24/7." *Middle East Quarterly* XI(1): 17–31. Available: http://www.meforum.org/583/al-manar-hizbullah-tv-24-7.
28. Norton, Augustus Richard (2000). "Hizballah and the Israeli Withdrawal from Southern Lebanon." *Journal of Palestine Studies* 30(1): 22–35; Norton, Augustus Richard (2009). *Hezbollah: A Short History*. Princeton, NJ: Princeton University Press.
29. Baylouny, Anne Marie (2006). *Al-Manar and Alhurra: Competing Satellite Stations and Ideologies*. DTIC Document. Available: http://www.dtic.mil/cgibin/GetTRDoc?AD=ADA478865&Location=U2&doc=GetTRDoc.pdf.
30. Khatib, Lina (2007). "Television and Public Action in the Beirut Spring," in Sakr, Naomi (ed.), *Arab Media and Political Renewal: Community, Legitimacy and Public Life*, pp. 28–43. London: I.B.Tauris.
31. Safa, Osama (2006). "Lebanon Springs Forward." *Journal of Democracy* 17(1): 22–37.
32. Wedeen, Lisa (1999). *Ambiguities of Domination: Politics, Rhetoric, and Symbols in Contemporary Syria*. Chicago: University of Chicago Press, p. 13.
33. Ibid.
34. Ibid.
35. Ibid.
36. Matar, Dina (2008). "The Power of Conviction: Nassrallah's Rhetoric and Mediated Charisma in the Context of the 2006 July War." *Middle East Journal of Culture and Communication* 1(2): 122–37.
37. Baylouny, Al-Manar and Alhurra.
38. Norton, Augustus Richard (2006). *Lebanon: Securing a Lasting Cease-Fire*. Opening statement (updated) of testimony for a hearing of the US Senate Foreign Relations Committee 13. Available: http://www.globalsecurity.org/military/library/congress/2006_hr/060913- norton.pdf.
39. Kalb, Marvin and Carol Saivetz (2007). "The Israeli-Hezbollah War of 2006: The Media as a Weapon in Asymmetrical Conflict." *The Harvard International Journal of Press/Politics* 12(3): 43–66.
40. Ajemian, Peter (2008). "Resistance Beyond Time and Space: Hezbollah's Media Campaigns." *Arab Media & Society*, issue 5, Spring, pp. 1–17.
41. Rosen, David M. (1984). "Leadership in World Cultures," in Kellerman, Barbara (ed.), *Leadership: Multidisciplinary Perspectives*, pp. 39–62. Englewood Cliffs, New Jersey: Prentice-Hall.

42. Ajemian, Resistance Beyond Time and Space.
43. Weimann, Gabriel (2008). "Hezbollah Dot Com: Hezbollah's Online Campaign," in Caspi, Dan and Tal Samuel-Azran (eds.), *New Media and Innovative Technologies*, pp. 17–38. Beer-Sheva, Israel: Ben-Gurion University Press.
44. Quoted in Aaker, David (1995). *Building Strong Brands*. New York: The Free Press., p. 303.
45. van Ham, The Rise of the Brand State.
46. Weimann, Hezbollah Dot Com.
47. Tayyar.org (2007). "Hezbollah Launches Another Anti-Israel Computer Game." *Free Patriotic Movement* website, 15 August. Available: http://www.tayyar.org/tayyar/articles.php?type=news&article_id=32018.
48. Falkowski, Andrzej and Wojciech Cwalina (1999). "Methodology of Constructing Effective Political Advertising: An Empirical Study of the Polish Presidential Election in 1995," in Newman, Bruce I. (ed.), *Handbook of Political Marketing*. Thousand Oaks, CA: Sage, p. 286.
49. Ibid.
50. Aaker, Building Strong Brands.
51. Quilty, Jim and Lysanda Ohrstrom (2007). "The Second Time as Farce: Stories of Another Lebanese Reconstruction." *Middle East Report* 243: 31–48.
52. Hunt, Sonja M. (1984). "The Role of Leadership in the Construction of Reality," in Kellerman, Barbara (ed.), *Leadership: Multidisciplinary Perspectives*, pp. 157–78. Englewood Cliffs, New Jersey: Prentice-Hall.
53. Kellerman, Barbara (1984). "Leadership as a Political Act," in Kellerman, Barbara (ed.), *Leadership: Multidisciplinary Perspectives*, pp. 63–90. Englewood Cliffs, New Jersey: Prentice-Hall.
54. Mueller, Claus (1973). *The Politics of Communication: A Study in the Political Sociology of Language, Socialization, and Legitimation*. New York: Oxford University Press, p. 129.
55. Kalb and Saivetz, The Israeli-Hezbollah War of 2006.
56. Shadid, Anthony (2006). "Israel, Hizbollah Vow Wider War." *The Washington Post*, Saturday 15 July, p. A01. Available: http://www.washingtonpost.com/wp-dyn/content/article/2006/07/14/AR2006071400385.html.
57. Newman, Bruce I. (1999). "A Predictive Model of Voter Behavior: The Repositioning of Bill Clinton," in Newman, Bruce I. (ed.), *Handbook of Political Marketing*. Thousand Oaks, CA: Sage, p. 261.
58. Newman: A Predictive Model of Voter Behavior, p. 278.
59. Arkin, William M. (2007). "Divining Victory: Airpower in the 2006 Israel-Hezbollah War." *Strategic Studies Quarterly* 1(2): 98–141.
60. Peraino, Kevin (2006). "Winning Hearts and Minds." *Newsweek*, 2 October. Available: http://www.newsweek.com/2006/10/01/winning-hearts-and-minds.html.
61. Ibid.
62. Ibid.
63. Ibid, emphasis added.
64. White, Hayden (1980). "The Value of Narrativity in the Representation of Reality." *Critical Inquiry* 7(1, Autumn): 5–27.
65. Hegel, Georg Wilhelm Friedrich (1956). *The Philosophy of History*. New York: Dover, p. 61.
66. White, The Value of Narrativity in the Representation of Reality, p. 23.
67. Ibid.
68. McCloud, Scott (1993). *Understanding Comics: The Invisible Art*. New York: Harper Paperbacks.
69. Bergmann, Knut and Wolfram Wickert (1999). "Selected Aspects of Communication in German Election Campaigns." In Newman, Bruce I. (ed.), *Handbook of Political Marketing*, pp. 455–84. London: Sage, p. 458.

70. Radunski Peter (1980). *Wahlkämpfe: Moderne wahlkampfführung als politische Kommunikation.* Munich: Olzog, p. 9.
71. Grafe, Peter (1994). *Wahlkampf: Die Olympiade der Demokratie.* Frankfurt: Eichborn, p. 155.
72. Weber, Max (1978). *Economy and Society.* Berkley: University of California Press.
73. Corner, John and Dick Pels (2003). "Introduction: The Re-styling of Politics," in Corner, John and Dick Pels (eds.), *Media and the Restyling of Politics.* London: Sage, pp 1–18.
74. Hackman, Michael Z. and Craig E. Johnson (2004). *Leadership: A Communication Perspective.* Long Grove, Illinois: Waveland Press, p. 115.
75. Nasrallah, Hassan (1997). "Speech about the martyrdom of Hadi Nasrallah." *Al-Manar,* 13 September. Available: http://www.youtube.com/watch?v=I3AOlwDL_M0.
76. Nasrallah, Hassan (2000b). "Speech about the liberation of South Lebanon." *Al-Manar,* 25 May. Available: http://www.youtube.com/watch?v=V_EAmIzqtu8.
77. Nasrallah, Hassan (2000a). "Speech about the liberation of South Lebanon." *Al-Manar,* 25 May. Available: http://www.youtube.com/watch?v=oeIBWvE5vNA&feature=related.
78. Pels, Dick (2003). "Aesthetic Representation and Political Style: Re-balancing Identity and Difference in Media Democracy," in Corner, John and Dick Pels (eds.), *Media and the Restyling of Politics.* London: Sage, p. 59.
79. Schweitzer, Arthur (1984). *The Age of Charisma.* Chicago: Nelson-Hall.
80. Hackman and Johnson, *Leadership,* p. 113.
81. Belt, David Douglas (2006). "Global Islamism: Understanding and Strategy." *Connections* 4, p. 47.
82. Pintak, Lawrence (2008). *The Role of the Media as Watchdogs, Agenda-setters and Gate-keepers in Arab States.* Paper 5.3, The Role of the News Media in the Governance Reform Agenda. World Bank/Harvard Kennedy School.
83. *Al-Abaya* (2006). Dir. Reda Qashmar. Produced and broadcast on Al-Manar.
84. Ajemian, Resistance Beyond Time and Space.
85. Pels, Aesthetic Representation and Political Style, p. 59.
86. Ibid.
87. Weber, *Economy and Society.*
88. Groys, *Art Power,* p. 131.
89. Stanyer, James (2007). *Modern Political Communications: National Political Communication Systems in an Uncertain, Fragmented and Unequal Age.* Cambridge: Polity Press.
90. Khalili, Laleh (2007). *Heroes and Martyrs of Palestine: The Politics of National Commemoration.* Cambridge: Cambridge University Press.
91. Fuery, Patrick and Kelli Fuery (2003). *Visual Cultures and Critical Theory.* London: Arnold, p. 121.
92. Fuery and Fuery, *Visual Cultures and Critical Theory,* p. 122.
93. Baudrillard, Jean (1999). *Simulacra and Simulation.* Ann Arbor: The University of Michigan Press.
94. Baudrillard, *Simulacra and Simulation,* p. 3.
95. Ajemian, Resistance Beyond Time and Space, p. 6.
96. Benjamin, Walter (2008). *The Work of Art in the Age of Mechanical Reproduction.* London: Penguin, p. 12.
97. Mowlana, Hamid (1997). *Global Information and World Communication.* London: Sage.
98. Foucault, Michel (1980). *Power/Knowledge: Selected Interviews and Other Writings.* New York: Pantheon Books.
99. Groys, *Art Power,* p. 127.
100. Burke, Edmund (1756). *A Philosophical Enquiry into the Origin of Our Ideas of the Sublime and Beautiful.* London: J. Dodsley.
101. Quoted in Benjamin, *The Work of Art in the Age of Mechanical Reproduction,* pp. 36–7
102. Mowlana, *Global Information and World Communication.*

103. Jervis, Robert (1970). *The Logic of Image in International Relations*. Princeton, NJ: Princeton University Press, p. 8.
104. Suchman, Mark C. (1995). "Managing Legitimacy: Strategic and Institutional Approaches." *The Academy of Management Review* 20(3), p. 574.
105. Al-Amin, Ibrahim (2008). Speech on 15 May. *Al-Manar*. Available: http://www.almanar.com.lb/NewsSite/NewsDetails.aspx?id= 43820&language=ar
106. McLaughlin, The Use of the Internet for Political Action by Non-state Dissident Actors in the Middle East.
107. Suchman, Managing Legitimacy, p. 574.
108. van Ham, Peter (2001). The Rise of the Brand State, p. 2.
109. Schweitzer, *The Age of Charisma*.
110. Hackman and Johnson, *Leadership*.
111. Nasrallah, Hassan (2010). Speech accusing Israel of assassinating Rafic Hariri. Press TV, 9 August. Available: http://www.youtube.com/watch?v=5odeTwU2zjw.
112. Khatib, Lina (2010). "Hezbollah's Mobilization of Multitudes." *Foreign Policy Middle East Channel*, 29 October. Available: http://mideast.foreignpolicy.com/posts/2010/10/29/hizbullah_ s_mobilization_of_the_multitudes? showcomments=yes.
113. Nasrallah, Hassan (2011). "Speech on the Lesson of the Tunisia Revolution." *Orange TV*, 16 January. Available: http://mrzine.monthlyreview.org/2011/nasrallah170111.html.
114. Press TV (2011). "Hezbollah Hails Egypt Revolution," 11 February. *Press TV* website. Available: http://www.presstv.ir/detail/164799.html.
115. BBC (2009). "Hezbollah Confirms Egypt Arrest." *BBC* website, 10 April. Available: http://news.bbc.co.uk/2/hi/7994304.stm.
116. Al-Intiqad (2011). "MP Moussawi Condemns Ugly Massacres Conducted by Qaddafi against the Libyan People." *Al-Intiqad* website, 23 February (Arabic). Available: http://www.alintiqad.com/essaydetails.php?eid=41095&cid=75&st=%E1%ED%C8%ED%C7.
117. Saleh, Naziha (2011). "Will Syria be the Key of the 'New Middle East' Map?" *Moqawama.org*, 28 June. Available: http://www.english.moqawama.org/essaydetails.php?eid=14367&cid=269.
118. Majed, Ziad (2012). "The Hizbullah Regime." *Ziad Majed blog*, 28 February. Available: www.ziadmajed.net.
119. Ghaddar, Hanin (2012). "Adieu, Hezbollah." *Now Lebanon*, 19 March. Available: http://www.nowlebanon.com/NewsArticleDetails.aspx?ID= 377701.
120. Staten, Cliff (2008). "From Terrorism to Legitimacy: Political Opportunity Structures and the Case of Hezbollah." *The Online Journal of Peace and Conflict Resolution* 8(1): 32–49.
121. Arzheimer, Kai and Elisabeth Carter (2006). "Political Opportunity Structures and the Extreme Right." *European Journal of Political Research* 45(3), p. 422.

3

1. Milani, Abbas (2005). "U.S. Foreign Policy and the Future of Democracy in Iran." *The Washington Quarterly* 28(3), p. 46.
2. Poulson, Stephen C. (2009). "Nested Institutions, Political Opportunity and the Decline of the Iranian Reform Movement Post 9/11." *American Behavioral Scientist* 53(1): 27–43.
3. Khaniki, Hadi (2008). Interview with the author. Tehran, March.
4. Ibid.
5. Ibid.
6. Ibid.
7. Motamedarya, Simin (2008). Interview with the author. Tehran, March.
8. Bayat, Asef (1997). *Street Politics: Poor People's Movements in Iran*. New York: Columbia University Press, p. 159.

9. Naji, Kasra (2008). *Ahmadinejad: The Secret History of Iran's Radical Leader*. London: I.B. Tauris.
10. Ansari, Ali (2008). "Iran under Ahmadinejad: Populism and its Malcontents." *International Affairs* 84(4): 683–700.
11. Ansari, Iran under Ahmadinejad; Naji, *Ahmadinejad*.
12. Groys, Boris (2008). *Art Power*. Cambridge, MA: The MIT Press.
13. Ram, Haggai (2002). "Multiple Iconographies: Political Posters in the Iranian Revolution," in Balaghi, Shiva and Lynn Gumpert (eds.), *Picturing Iran: Art, Society and Revolution*. London: I.B.Tauris, p. 90.
14. Flaskerud, Ingvild (2010). *Visualizing Belief and Piety in Iranian Shiism*. London: Continuum, pp. 253–4.
15. Chelkowski, Peter (2002). "The Art of Revolution and War: The Role of the Graphic Arts in Iran," in Balaghi, Shiva and Lynn Gumpert (eds.), *Picturing Iran: Art, Society and Revolution*. London: I.B.Tauris, p. 128.
16. Hobsbawm, Eric (1993). "Mass Producing Traditions: Europe, 1870–1914," in Hobsbawm, Eric and Terence O. Ranger (eds.), *The Invention of Tradition*. Cambridge: Cambridge University Press, p. 303.
17. Gershoni, Israel and James Jankowski (2004). *Commemorating the Nation: Collective Memory, Public Commemoration, and National Identity in Twentieth-Century Egypt*. Chicago: Middle East Documentation Center, pp. 238–9.
18. Chelkowski, Peter and Hamid Dabashi (2000). *Staging a Revolution: The Art of Persuasion in the Islamic Republic*. London: Booth-Clibborn Editions, p. 34.
19. Groys, *Art Power*, p. 139.
20. Foucault, Michel (1980). *Power/Knowledge: Selected Interviews and Other Writings*. New York: Pantheon Books.
21. Comaroff, Jean and John Comaroff (1991). *Of Revelation and Revolution: Christianity, Colonialism, and Consciousness in South Africa*, volume 1. Chicago: University of Chicago Press, p. 23.
22. Chelkowski and Dabashi, *Staging a Revolution*.
23. Gruber, Christiane (2008). "The Message is on the Wall: Mural Arts in Post-Revolutionary Iran." *Persica* 22, p. 16.
24. Chelkowski, The Art of Revolution and War.
25. Gruber, The Message is on the Wall, p. 24.
26. Evans, Harriet and Stephanie Donald (1999). "Introducing Posters of China's Cultural Revolution," in Evans, Harriet and Stephanie Donald (eds.), *Picturing Power in the People's Republic of China: Posters of the Cultural Revolution*. Oxford: Rowman and Littlefield, p. 5.
27. Maasri, Zeina (2009). *Off the Wall: Political Posters of the Lebanese Civil War*. London: I.B.Tauris.
28. Fluck, Winfried (2003). "Aesthetic Experience of the Image," in Haselstein, Ulla, Berndt Ostendorf, and Peter Schneck (eds.), *Iconographies of Power: The Politics and Poetics of Visual Representation*, pp. 11–41. Heidelberg: Winter.
29. Eiesenstein, Elizabeth (1991). "The Rise of the Reading Public," in Crowley, David and Paul Heyer (eds.), *Communication in History: Technology, Culture, and Society*, pp. 94–102. New York: Longman.
30. Ansari, Iran under Ahmadinejad, p. 689.
31. Ansari, Iran under Ahmadinejad, p. 690.
32. Rajaee, Farhang (1993). *The Iran-Iraq War: The Politics of Aggression*. Gainesville: University Press of Florida.
33. Gruber, The Message is on the Wall, p. 36.
34. Groys, *Art Power*, p. 2.
35. Evans and Donald, Introducing Posters of China's Cultural Revolution, p. 4.
36. Hall, Stuart (1980). "Race, Articulation, and Societies Structured in Dominance," in UNESCO (ed.), *Sociological Theories: Race and Colonialism*. Paris: UNESCO, p. 331.

37. Korangy, Alireza (2009). "A Literary and Historical Background of Martyrdom in Iran." *Comparative Studies of South Asia, Africa and the Middle East* 29(3): 528–41.
38. Wedeen, Lisa (1999). *Ambiguities of Domination: Politics, Rhetoric, and Symbols in Contemporary Syria*. Chicago: University of Chicago Press.
39. Sontag, Susan (2003). *Regarding the Pain of Others*. New York: Picador, p. 80.
40. Hobsbawm, Mass Producing Traditions.
41. Groys, *Art Power*.
42. Crane, Susan A. (2004). "Memory, Distortion, and History in the Museum," in Carbonell, Bettina Messias (ed.), *Museum Studies: An Anthology of Contexts*. Oxford: Blackwell, p. 323.
43. Groys, *Art Power*.
44. Donald, Stephanie (1999). "Children as Political Messengers: Art, Childhood, and Continuity," in Evans, Harriet and Stephanie Donald (eds.), *Picturing Power in the People's Republic of China: Posters of the Cultural Revolution*, pp. 79–100. Oxford: Rowman and Littlefield.
45. Sontag, *Regarding the Pain of Others*.
46. Sontag, *Regarding the Pain of Others*, p. 40.
47. Sontag, *Regarding the Pain of Others*, p. 87.
48. Sontag, *Regarding the Pain of Others*, p. 82.
49. Groys, *Art Power*.
50. Groys, *Art Power*, p. 25.
51. Kandiyoti, Deniz (1994). "Identity and its Discontents: Women and the Nation," in Williams, Patrick and Laura Chrisman (eds.), *Colonial Discourse and Post-colonial Theory: A Reader*, pp. 276–91. London: Harvester Wheatsheaf.
52. Shaery-Eisenlohr, Roschanack (2008). *Shi'ite Lebanon: Transnational Religion and the Making of National Identities*. New York: Columbia University Press.
53. MacLeod, Arlene Elowe (1992). "Hegemonic Relations and Gender Resistance: The new Veiling as Accommodating Protest in Cairo." *Signs* 17(3): 533–57.
54. Dabashi, Hamid (2011). *The Green Movement in Iran*, edited with an introduction by Navid Nikzadfar. New Brunswick, NJ: Transaction Publishers.
55. Motamedarya, Interview with the author.
56. McClintock, Anne (1997). "'No Longer in a Future Heaven': Gender, Race, and Nationalism," in McClintock, Anne, Aamer Mufti, and Ella Shohat (eds.), *Dangerous Liaisons: Gender, Nation, and Postcolonial Perspectives*. Minneapolis: University of Minnesota Press, p. 90.
57. Shaery-Eisenlohr, *Shi'ite Lebanon*.
58. Naji, Ahmadinejad; Hafezi, Parisa and Hashem Kalantari (2012). "Khamenei Allies Trounce Ahmadinejad in Iran Elections." *Reuters*, 4 March. Available: http://www.reuters.com/article/2012/03/04/us-iran-election-result-idUSTRE82306420120304.
59. Al-Shayji, Abdallah (2008). "Panorama interview." *Al-Arabiya*. Broadcast 15 March. Transcript available:http://www.alarabiya.net/programs/2008/03/17/47093.html.
60. Polletta, Francesca (1997). "Culture and Its Discontents: Recent Theorizing on the Cultural Dimensions of Protest." *Sociological Inquiry* 67(4): 431–450.
61. Sreberny, Annabelle and Gholam Khiabany (2010). *Blogistan: The Internet and Politics in Iran*. London: I.B.Tauris.
62. I refer the reader to Sreberny and Khiabany's excellent work *Blogistan* for a discussion of Iranian blogs.
63. Quoted in Keshmirshekan, Hamid (2011). "Contemporary or Specific: The Dichotomous Desires in the Art of Early Twenty-First Century Iran." *Middle East Journal of Culture and Communication* 4(1), p. 55.
64. Hanaei, Arash (2008). Interview with the author. Tehran, March.
65. Ibid.
66. Ghasemi, Amirali (2008). Interview with the author. Tehran, March.

67. Handler, Joel F. (1992). "Postmodernism, Protest, and the New Social Movements." *Law and Society Review* 26(4), p. 699.
68. Ghasemi, Interview with the author.
69. hooks, bell (1990). *Yearning: Race, Gender, and Cultural Politics*. Boston: South End Press.
70. Wedeen, *Ambiguities of Domination*.
71. Moakhar, Interview with the author.
72. Groys, *Art Power*, p. 9.
73. Moakhar, Mahmoud Bakhshi (2008). Interview with the author. Tehran, March.
74. Ghasemi, Interview with the author.
75. Polletta, Culture and Its Discontents, p. 434, emphasis added.
76. NPR (2009). Expert: "Iran Protests Full of Symbolism." *NPR* website. Broadcast on 18 June. Available: http://www.npr.org/templates/story/story.php?storyId=105620617.
77. Dabashi, *The Green Movement*, p. 62.
78. Diamond, Larry (2010). "Liberation Technology." *Journal of Democracy* 21(3): 69–83.
79. Sreberny and Khiabany, *Blogistan*.
80. Dabashi, *The Green Movement*.
81. Kraidy, Marwan and Sara Mourad (2010). "Hypermedia and Global Communication Studies: Lessons from the Middle East." *Global Media Journal* 8(16). Available: http://lass.calumet.purdue.edu/cca/gmj/sp10/gmj-sp10-article8-kraidy-mourad.htm.
82. Afshari, Ali and H. Graham Underwood (2009). "The Green Wave." *Journal of Democracy* 20(4): 6–10. It should be noted that there was initial confusion regarding Neda's identity, as the photograph of another smiling woman with a similar name, Neda Soltani, was widely used by protesters and the media in error at first (as seen in Figure 31), before Neda Agha-Soltan's photograph emerged.
83. Kraidy and Mourad, Hypermedia and Global Communication Studies.
84. Dabashi, *The Green Movement*, p. 40.
85. Dabashi, *The Green Movement*, p. 161.

4

1. Debord, Guy (1994). *The Society of the Spectacle*. Trans. Donald Nicholson-Smith. New York: Zone Books, p. 2.
2. DeLuca, Kevin Michael (1993). *Image Politics: The New Rhetoric of Environmental Activism*. New York: The Guilford Press, pp. 21–2.
3. Lamloum, Olfa (2011). "Al-i'lam al-ijtima'i wa thawrat al-jeel al-arabi al-jadid." *Al-Jazeera Research Center*. Available: http://www.aljazeera.net/NR/exeres/AC7A8E0B-9952–435F-9A6C-6D025279CC8E.htm.
4. Miladi Noureddine (2011). "Tunisia: A Media Led Revolution?" *Aljazeera.net*, 17 January. Available: http://english.aljazeera.net/indepth/opinion/2011/01/2011116142317498666.html
5. Ibid.
6. Lang, Sabine (2004). "Local Political Communication: Media and Local Politics in the Age of Globalization," in Esser, Frank and Barbara Pfetsch (eds.), *Comparing Political Communication: Theories, Cases, and Challenges*, pp. 151–83. Cambridge: Cambridge University Press.
7. Handler, Joel F. (1992). "Postmodernism, Protest, and the New Social Movements." *Law and Society Review* 26(4), p. 712.
8. Bayat, Asef (2010). *Life as Politics: How Ordinary People Change the Middle East*. Stanford, CA: Stanford University Press, p. 14.
9. Bayat, *Life as Politics*, pp. 19–20.
10. Bayat, *Life as Politics*, p. 20.
11. Reed, Thomas Vernon (2005*). The Art of Protest: Culture and Activism from the Civil Rights Movement to the Streets of Seattle*. Minneapolis: University of Minnesota Press, p. xvii.

12. Reed, *The Art of Protest*, pp. 299–300.
13. Sabry, Tarik (2010). *Cultural Encounters in the Arab World: On Media, the Modern and the Everyday*. London: I.B.Tauris, pp. 47–48.
14. Website of the People's Assembly Museum. Available: http://www.sis.gov.eg/En/EParl/PFilms/Hose/190201000000000001.htm.
15. Agamben, Giorgio (1998). *Homo Sacer: Sovereign Power and Bare Life*. Translated by Daniel Heller-Roazen. Stanford: Stanford University Press.
16. Agamben, *Homo Sacer*, p. 9.
17. Agamben, *Homo Sacer*, p. 7.
18. Agamben, *Homo Sacer*, p. 15.
19. Deleuze, Gilles and Félix Guattari (1987). *A Thousand Plateaus: Capitalism and Schizophrenia*. Minneapolis: University of Minnesota Press, p. 445.
20. Quoted in Agamben, *Homo Sacer*, p. 18.
21. Springborg, Robert (1989). *Mubarak's Egypt: Fragmentation of the Political Order*. Boulder, CO: Westview Press, p. 25.
22. Voltmer, Katrin (2006). "Conclusion: Political Communication between Democratization and the Trajectories of the Past," in Voltmer, Katrin (ed.), *Mass Media and Political Communication in New Democracies*. New York: Routledge, pp. 215–22.
23. Abdel Aziz, Sami (2008). Interview with the author. Cairo, March.
24. Meital, Yoram (2006). "The Struggle over Political Order in Egypt: The 2005 Elections." *Middle East Journal* 60(2), p. 270.
25. Younis, Nora (2008). Interview with the author. Cairo, March.
26. Collombier, Virginie (2007). "The Internal Stakes of the 2005 Elections: The Struggle for Influence in Egypt's National Democratic Party." *Middle East Journal* 61(1), p. 100.
27. Al-Shawbaky, Amr (2006). "Al-idarah al-hizbiyya lilintikhabat al-ri'asiyya wa al-tashri'iyya," in Rabi', Amr Hashem (ed.), *Nothom idarat al-intikhabat fi misr ma' moqarana bihalat bouldan okhra*, pp. 61–74. Cairo: Center for Political and Strategic Studies, p. 64.
28. Reed, *The Art of Protest*, p. xiv.
29. Howeidy, Amira (2005). "A Chronology of Dissent." *Al-Ahram Weekly*, 23–29 June, issue no. 748. Available: http://weekly.ahram.org.eg/2005/748/eg10.htm
30. Al-Malky, Rania (2007). "Blogging for Reform: The Case of Egypt." *Arab Media and Society*, issue 1, Spring, pp. 1–31. Available: http://www.arabmediasociety.com/articles/downloads/20070312143716_AMS1_Rania_Al_Malky.pdf.
31. Howeidy, A Chronology of Dissent.
32. Younis, Interview with the author.
33. http://misrdigital.blogspirit.com/.
34. Al-Malky, Blogging for Reform.
35. Younis, Interview with the author.
36. Radsch, Courtney (2008). "Core to Commonplace: The Evolution of Egypt's Blogosphere." *Arab Media and Society*, Fall 2008, issue 6. Available: http://www.arabmediasociety.com/articles/downloads/ 20080929140127_AMS6_Courtney_Radsch.pdf.
37. Gharbeia, Amr (2008). Interview with the author. Cairo, March.
38. Abbas, Wael (2008). Interview with the author. Cairo, March.
39. http://www.arabawy.org/.
40. http://www.flickr.com/photos/elhamalawy/.
41. Radsch, Core to Commonplace.
42. Gharbeia, Interview with the author.
43. Etling, Bruce et al. (2009). *Mapping the Arabic Blogosphere: Politics, Culture, and Dissent*: Internet & Democracy Case Study Series, Berkman Center Research Publication number 2009–06. Berkman Center for Internet & Society. Available: http://www.alhaqqsociety.org/research/MappingTheArabicBlogosphere.pdf, p. 15.
44. http://gharbeia.net/; http://ahmad.gharbeia.org/.

45. Barber, Benjamin R. (2003). "Which Technology and Which Democracy?" in Jenkins, Henry, David Thorburn and Brad Seawell (eds.), *Democracy and New Media*, pp. 33–48. Cambridge, MA: The MIT Press, p. 33.
46. Al-Malky, Blogging for Reform.
47. Radsch, Core to Commonplace.
48. Gharbeia, Interview with the author.
49. Dahlgren, Peter (2009). *Media and Political Engagement: Citizens, Communication, and Democracy*. Cambridge: Cambridge University Press.
50. Younis, Interview with the author.
51. Bayat, *Life as Politics*, p. 22.
52. For images of Mustafa Hussein's poster in the 5 September 2005 Kifaya demonstration, see http://misrdigital.blogspirit.com/files/coverage/yameen27sep05.htm.
53. http://mostafa.foolab.org/node/149.
54. *Alexandria, Again and Forever*, 1990.
55. For images of those posters and others, visit Tantawy's archive: http://tantawy.tk/.
56. Stanyer, James (2007). *Modern Political Communication: National Political Communication Systems in an Uncertain, Fragmented and Unequal Age*. Cambridge: Polity Press, p. 174, emphasis added.
57. Stanyer, *Modern Political Communication*, p. 175.
58. Auyero, Javier (2004). "When Everyday Life, Routine Politics, and Protest Meet." *Theory and Society* 33(3), p. 439.
59. http://baheyya.blogspot.com/2005/09/color-of-protest.html.
60. Etling et al., *Mapping the Arabic Blogosphere*, p. 10.
61. Ibid, emphasis added.
62. Tarzi, Fadl (2011). "Arab Media Influence Report 2011 – Social Media and the Arab Spring." *News Group International*. Available: http://newsgroup.ae/amir2011/amir-march-29.pdf.
63. http://ana-ikhwan.blogspot.com/2007/06/blog-post_30.html.
64. Ibid.
65. Ishani, Maryam (2011). "The Hopeful Network." *Foreign Policy*, February 7. Available: http://www.foreignpolicy.com/articles/2011/02/07/the_hopeful_network.
66. Rafael, Vicente L. (2003). "The Cell Phone and the Crowd: Messianic Politics in Recent Philippine History." *Public Culture* 15(3), p. 403.
67. Sherif, Ahmad (2008). Email interview with the author. April.
68. Faris, David (2008). "Revolutions Without Revolutionaries? Network Theory, Facebook, and the Egyptian Blogosphere." *Arab Media and Society*, Fall 2008, issue 6. Available: http://www.arabmediasociety.com/articles/downloads/20080929153219_AMS6_David_Faris.pdf, p. 9.
69. Handler, Postmodernism, Protest, and the New Social Movements, pp. 697–8.
70. Khamis, Sahar and Katherine Vaughn (2011). "Cyberactivism in the Egyptian Revolution: How Civic Engagement and Citizen Journalism Tilted the Balance." *Arab Media and Society*, issue 13, Summer. Available: http://www.arabmediasociety.com/?article=769.
71. Sultan Al Qassemi, quoted in Beaumont Peter (2011). "The Truth about Twitter, Facebook and the Uprisings in the Arab World." *The Guardian*, February 25. Available: www.guardian.co.uk/world/2011/feb/25/twitter-facebook-uprisings-arab-libya.
72. Samnani, Hina and Lolla Mohammed Nur (2011). "Crowdmapping the Arab Spring – Next Social Media Breakthrough?" *Voice of America News*, 28 June. Available: http://www.voanews.com/english/news/middle-east/Crowdmapping-Arab-Spring-Next-Social-Media-Breakthrough-124662649.html.
73. Axford, Barrie and Richard Huggins (2002). "Political Marketing and the Aestheticisation of Politics: Modern Politics and Postmodern Trends," in O'Shaughnesy, Nicholas J. and Stephan C. M. Henneberg (eds.), *The Idea of Political Marketing*. London: Praeger, pp. 198–208.

74. Strömbäck, Jesper (2008). "Four Phases of Mediatization: An Analysis of the Mediatization of Politics." *Press/Politics* 13(3), p. 243.
75. Gitlin, Todd (1980). *The Whole World is Watching*. Berkeley, CA: University of California Press.
76. Sontag, Susan (2003). *Regarding the Pain of Others*. New York: Picador, p. 26.
77. Al Qassemi, quoted in Beaumont, The Truth about Twitter, Facebook and the Uprisings in the Arab World.
78. Shahbander, Ghada (2011). Conversation with the author. Stanford, California, July.
79. Agamben, *Homo Sacer*.
80. Van Dijk, Jan A.G.M. (2005). *The Deepening Divide: Inequality in the Information Society*. Thousand Oaks, CA: Sage, p. 184.
81. Kreutz, Christian (2010). "Mobile Activism in Africa: Future Trends and Software Developments," in Ekine, Sokari (ed.), *SMS Uprising: Mobile Phone Activism in Africa*, pp. 17–31. Cape Town: Pambazuka Press.
82. Gergen, Kenneth J. (2002). "The Challenge of Absent Presence," in Katz, James E. and Mark A. Aakhus (eds.), *Perpetual Contact: Mobile Communication, Private Talk, Public Performance*. Cambridge: Cambridge University Press, p. 239.
83. Beaumont, The Truth about Twitter, Facebook and the Uprisings in the Arab World.
84. DeLuca, *Image Politics*, p. 1.
85. Dubai School of Government (2011). *Arab Social Media Report*, Volume 1 Issue 2. Available: http://www.dsg.ae/portals/0/ASMR2.pdf, p. 5.
86. Beaumont, The Truth about Twitter, Facebook and the Uprisings in the Arab World.
87. Khamis and Vaughn, Cyberactivism in the Egyptian Revolution.
88. De Certeau, Michel (1984). *The Practice of Everyday Life*. Berkeley: University of California Press, pp. 36–37, xix.
89. Khamis and Vaughn, Cyberactivism in the Egyptian Revolution.
90. Salah, Ahmed (2011). Presentation at "From Political Activism to Democratic Change" conference, Stanford University, 12 May.
91. Bredekamp, Horst (2011). *Theorie des Bildakts*: Über das Lebensrecht des Bildes, Frankfurt/M.: Suhrkamp Verlag.
92. Ibid.
93. Bredekamp, Horst (2010). *The Audience as Prisoner: Reflections on the Activity of the Object*. Lecture at Princeton University, 2 March. Video available: http://video.ias.edu/audience-as-prisoner.
94. Archard, David (2000). "Nationalism and Political Theory," in O'Sullivan, Noel (ed.), *Political Theory in Transition*, pp. 155–71. London: Routledge, p. 165.
95. Mills, Caroline (1993). "Myths and Meanings of Gentrification," in Duncan, James and David Ley (eds.), *Place/Culture/Representation*. London: Routledge, p. 150.
96. Dasgupta, Sudeep (2005). "Visual Culture and the Place of Modernity," in Abbas, Ackbar and John Nguyet Erni (eds.), *Internationalizing Cultural Studies*. Oxford: Blackwell, p. 435.
97. Jaworski, Adam and Crispin Thurlow (2010). "Introducing Semiotic Landscapes," in Jaworski, Adam and Crispin Thurlow (eds.), *Semiotic Landscapes*, pp. 1–40. London: Continuum.
98. Sörlin, Sverker (1999). "The Articulation of Territory: Landscape and the Constitution of Regional and National Identity." *Norwegian Journal of Geography* 53(2–3): 103–12.
99. Jaworski and Thurlow, Introducing Semiotic Landscapes, p. 6.
100. Jaworski and Thurlow, Introducing Semiotic Landscapes, p. 7.
101. De Certeau, *The Practice of Everyday Life*, p. 117.
102. Castells, Manuel (2005). "Grassrooting the Space of Flows," in Abbas, Ackbar and John Nguyet Erni (eds.), *Internationalizing Cultural Studies*. Oxford: Blackwell, p, 628.
103. Castells, Grassrooting the Space of Flows, p. 629.

104. Lefebvre, Henri (1971). *Everyday Life in the Modern World*. London: Allen Lane The Penguin Press, p. 36.
105. Ehrenreich, Barbara (2007). *Dancing in the Streets: A History of Collective Joy*. New York: Metropolitan, p. 259.
106. Shepard, Benjamin, L. M. Bogad, and Stephen Duncombe (2008). "Performing vs. the Insurmountable: Theatrics, Activism, and Social Movements." *Liminalities: A Journal of Performance Studies* 4(3), p. 13.
107. Castells, Manuel (1983). *The City and the Grassroots: A Cross-cultural Theory of Urban Social Movements*. London: Arnold.
108. Pile, Steve (1997). "Introduction: Opposition, Political Identities and Spaces of Resistance," in Pile, Steve and Michael Keith (eds.), *Geographies of Resistance*. London: Routledge, p. 16.
109. Featherstone, Mike (1991). *Consumer Culture and Postmodernism*. London: Sage, p. 66.
110. hooks, bell (1990). *Yearning: Race, Gender, and Cultural Politics*. Boston: South End Press.
111. Routledge, Paul (1997). "A Spatiality of Resistances: Theory and Practice in Nepal's Revolution of 1990," in Pile, Steve and Michael Keith (eds.), *Geographies of Resistance*. London: Routledge, p. 71.
112. De Certeau, *The Practice of Everyday Life*, p. 118.
113. For a collection of photographs of street art, see http://thembalewis.com/street-art#/i/0.
114. Handler, Postmodernism, Protest, and the New Social Movements, p. 723.
115. Jaworski and Thurlow, Introducing Semiotic Landscapes, p. 9
116. Banksy (2004). *Wall and Piece*. London: Arrow Books.
117. Jarman, Neil (2005). "Painting Landscapes: The Place of Murals in the Symbolic Construction of Urban Space," in Geisler, Michael (ed.), *National Symbols, Fractured Identities: Contesting the National Narrative*, pp. 172–92. Lebanon, NH: Middlebury College Press.
118. Wedeen, Lisa (1999). *Ambiguities of Domination: Politics, Rhetoric, and Symbols in Contemporary Syria*. Chicago: University of Chicago Press.
119. Jarman, Painting Landscapes.
120. Jaworski and Thurlow, Introducing Semiotic Landscapes.
121. The protest itself saw people carrying placards with a stencil of Field Marshal Tantawi behind red prison bars.
122. Lundby, Knut (2009). "Introduction: 'Mediatization' as Key," in Lundby, Knut (ed.), *Mediatization: Concept, Changes, Consequences*, pp. 1–18. New York: Peter Lang.
123. http://ganzeer.com/cairostreetart/index.html.
124. Jarman, Painting Landscapes.
125. Jaworski and Thurlow, Introducing Semiotic Landscapes, p. 8.
126. Jarman, Painting Landscapes.
127. Chow, Karen (2009). Aesthetics and Interactive Arts. In Bentkowska-Kafel, Anna, Trish Cashen, and Hazel Gardiner (eds.), *Digital Visual Culture: Theory and Practice*. Bristol: Intellect, pp. 15–22.
128. Cottle, Simon (2011). "Media and the Arab Spring." *Journalism* 12(5), p. 654.
129. Hjarvard, Stig (2008). "The Mediatization of Society: A Theory of the Media as Agents of Social and Cultural Change." *Nordicom Review* 8(2), p. 129.
130. Jansson, (2002). The Mediatization of Consumption: Towards an analytical framework of image culture. *Journal of Consumer Culture* 2(1), p. 15.
131. Marden, Peter (1997). "Geographies of Dissent: Globalization, Identity, and the Nation." *Political Geography* 16(1): 37–64.
132. Harb, Zahera (2011). "Arab Revolutions and the Social Media Effect." *M/C Journal* 14(2). Available: http://journal.media-culture.org.au/index.php/mcjournal/article/viewArticle/364.

133. Routledge Paul (1993). *Terrains of Resistance: Nonviolent Social Movements and the Contestation of Place in India*. Westport, CT: Praeger.
134. Anderson, Benedict (1983). *Imagined Communities: Reflections on the Origin and Spread of Nationalism*. London: Verso.
135. Abu Hilaleh, Yasser (2011). "Rasasa fi sad shab ash'alat al-thawra." *Al-Hayat*, 16 August. Available: http://www.ademocracynet.com/Arabic/index.php?page=articles& action=Detail&id=1757.
136. De Certeau, Michel (1997). *Culture in the Plural*. Minneapolis: University of Minnesota Press.
137. Erickson-Nepstad, Sharon (2002). "Creating Transnational Solidarity: The Use of Narrative in the U.S.-Central America Peace Movement," in Smith, Jackie and Hank Johnston (eds.), *Globalization and Resistance: Transnational Dimensions of Social Movements*. Oxford: Rowman and Littlefield, pp. 133–52.
138. http://www.aljazeera.net/NR/exeres/31750396-4E76-4A27-828C-533D62066E12. htm.
139. Libya.tv (2011). *Iftitah mathaf aslihat kataeb al-qathafi fi zawihat al-mahjoub bi misrata*, 23 June. Available: http://www.libya.tv/2011/06/افتتاح-متحف-أسلحة-كتائب-القذافي-في-ز او/.
140. Al-Jazeera (2011). "Mathaf yokhallid thikra al-thawra al-misriyya." *Al-Jazeera* website, 22 August. Available: http://www.aljazeera.net/NR/exeres/E6A95EA4–6707-4B24-AFA2-CB22474FDAB6.htm?GoogleStatID=9.
141. Kavanagh, Gaynor (2004). "Melodrama, Pantomime or Portrayal? Representing Ourselves and the British Past through Exhibitions in History Museums," in Carbonell, Bettina Messias (ed.), *Museum Studies: An Anthology of Contexts*, pp. 348–55. Oxford: Blackwell.
142. Archard, Nationalism and Political Theory, p. 165.
143. Chelkowski, Peter and Hamid Dabashi (2000). *Staging a Revolution: The Art of Persuasion in the Islamic Republic*. London: Booth-Clibborn Editions, p 305.
144. Routledge, Paul (1997). "Space, Mobility, and Collective Action: India's Naxalite Movement." *Environment and Planning* 29, p. 2167.
145. Livingstone, Sonia (2009). "On the Mediation of Everything." *Journal of Communication* 59, p. 9.
146. Mawari, Munir (2011). Presentation at "From Political Activism to Democratic Change" conference, Stanford University, 13 May.
147. Billig, Michael (1995). *Banal Nationalism*. London: Sage.
148. Meyrowitz, Joshua (1985). *No Sense of Place: The Impact of Electronic Media on Social Behaviour*. New York: Oxford University Press.
149. Featherstone, Mike (1995). *Undoing Culture: Globalization, Postmodernism and Identity*. London: Sage.
150. Thompson, John B. (1995). *The Media and Modernity: A Social Theory of the Media*. Cambridge: Polity.
151. Hjarvard, The Mediatization of Society, p. 127.
152. Bredekamp, *Theorie des Bildakts*.
153. Mitchell, William J. Thomas (2006). *What Do Pictures Want?* Interview by Asbjørn Grønstad and Øyvind Vågnes. *Image & Narrative*, November. Available: http://www.visual-studies.com/interviews/mitchell.html.

5

1. Lynch, Marc (2005). *Voices of the New Arab Public: Iraq, Al-Jazeera, and Middle East Politics Today*. New York: Columbia University Press; Pintak, Lawrence (2006). *Reflections in a Bloodshot Lens: America, Islam, and the War of Ideas*. London: Pluto Press; Sakr, Naomi (2007). *Arab Television Today*. London: I.B. Tauris; Zayani,

Mohamed and Sofiane Zahraoui (2007). *The Culture of Al Jazeera: Inside an Arab Media Giant*. London: McFarland & Company; Pintak, Lawrence (2008). "Satellite TV and Arab Democracy." *Journalism Practice* 2(1): 15–26.

2. This section is a modified version of work that appeared as Khatib, Lina (2009). "Satellite Television, the War on Terror, and Political Conflict in the Arab World," in Dodds, Klaus and Alan Ingram (eds.), *Spaces of Security and Insecurity: Geographies of the War on Terror*, pp. 205–20. Aldershot: Ashgate Publishing.

3. Zayani, Mohamed (2005). "Witnessing the Intifada: Al Jazeera's Coverage of the Palestinian-Israeli Conflict," in Zayani, Mohamed (ed.), *The Al Jazeera Phenomenon: Critical Perspectives on New Arab Media*. London: Pluto Press, pp. 171–182.

4. Zayani, Witnessing the Intifada, p. 174.

5. Ayish, Muhammad I. (2002). "Political Communication on Arab World Television: Evolving Patterns." *Political Communication*, 19(2), p. 149.

6. Baudrillard, Jean (2002). "L'Esprit du Terrorisme." *The South Atlantic Quarterly*, 101(2), p. 403.

7. Fandy, Mamoun (2007). *(Un)Civil War of Words: Media and Politics in the Arab World*. Westport, Connecticut: Praeger Security International.

8. Patiz, Norman (2004). "Radio Sawa and Alhurra TV: Opening Channels of Mass Communication in the Middle East," in Rugh, William (ed.), *Engaging the Arab and Islamic Worlds through Public Diplomacy: A Report and Action Recommendations*. Washington DC: Public Diplomacy Council, pp. 69–89.

9. El-Nawaway, Mohamed and Adel Iskandar (2003). *Al-Jazeera: The Story of the Network that is Rattling Governments and Redefining Modern Journalism*. Boulder, Colorado: Westview.

10. Weeden, Lisa (1999). *Ambiguities of Domination: Politics, Rhetoric and Symbols in Contemporary Syria*. Chicago: Chicago University Press, p. 158.

11. Al-Hail, Ali (2000). "The Age of New Media: The Role of Al-Jazeera Satellite TV in Developing Aspects of Civil Society in Qatar." *Transnational Broadcasting Studies*, issue 4, Spring. Available: http://www.tbsjournal.com/Archives/Spring00/Articles4/Ali/Al-Hail/al-hail.html.

12. Amin, Hussein (2000). "Satellite Broadcasting and Civil Society in the Middle East: The Role of Nilesat." *Transnational Broadcasting Studies*, issue 4, Spring. Available: http://www.tbsjournal.com/Archives/Spring00/Articles4/Ali/Amin/amin.html.

13. Lynch, *Voices of the New Arab Public*.

14. Alterman, Jon (1999). "Transnational Media and Social Change in the Arab World." *Transnational Broadcasting Studies*, issue 2 (Spring). Available: http://www.tbsjournal.com/Archives/Spring99/Articles/Alterman/alterman.html.

15. Lynch, Voices of the New Arab Public, p. 4.

16. Noureddine, Raya (2011). "Al-hay'a at-ta'dibiya bi'ssahafiyeen toqarrer waqf sahifat 'al-mossad' 6 ashhur." *Dostor Newspaper*, 22 June. Available: http://www.dostor.org/culture/news/11/june/22/45897.

17. Strömbäck, Jesper (2008). "Four Phases of Mediatization: An Analysis of the Mediatization of Politics." *Press/Politics* 13(3), p. 236.

18. Ghanem, Salma (1997). "Filling in the Tapestry: The Second Level of Agenda Setting," in McCombs, Maxwell, Donald L. Shaw and David Weaver (eds.), *Communication and Democracy: Exploring the Intellectual Frontiers in Agenda-setting Theory*. Mahwah, NJ: Lawrence Erlbaum Associates, pp. 3–14.

19. Cottle, Simon (2011). "Media and the Arab Spring." *Journalism* 12(5), p. 648.

20. Finnemann, Niels Ole (2011). "Mediatization Theory and Digital Media." *Communications: European Journal of Communication Research* 36(1): 67–89.

21. Harb, Zahera (2011). "Arab Revolutions and the Social Media Effect." *M/C Journal* 14(2). Available: http://journal.media-culture.org.au/index.php/mcjournal/article/viewArticle/364.

22. I thank Radwan Ziadeh for this point.
23. Lemert, James B. et al. (1977). "Journalists and Mobilizing Information." *Journalism Quarterly* 54: 721–26.
24. Voltmer, Katrin (2006). "The Mass Media and the Dynamics of Political Communication in Processes of Democratization: An Introduction," in Voltmer, Katrin (ed.), *Mass Media and Political Communication in New Democracies*. New York: Routledge, pp. 1–20.
25. Entman, Robert (1993). "Framing: Toward Clarification of a Fractured Paradigm." *Journal of Communication* 43(Autumn), p. 55.
26. This section draws on Khatib, Lina (2011). "How to Lose Friends and Alienate Your People." *Jadaliyya*, 26 March. Available: http://www.jadaliyya.com/pages/index/1014/how-to-lose-friends-and-alienate-your-people-.
27. Heydemann, Steve (2007). *Upgrading Authoritarianism in the Arab World*. Saban Center Analysis Paper Number 13, October. Washington, DC: Brookings Institution. Available: http://www.brookings.edu/~/media/Files/rc/papers/2007/10arabworld/10arabworld.pdf.
28. Quoted in Heydemann, *Upgrading Authoritarianism in the Arab World*, p. 1.
29. Schatz, Edward (2008). "Transnational Image Making and Soft Authoritarian Kazakhstan." *Slavic Review* 67(1), p. 51.
30. Schatz, Transnational Image Marking and Soft Authoritarian Kazakhstan, p. 52.
31. Tuchman, Gaye (1978). *Making News: A Study in the Construction of Reality*. New York: The Free Press.
32. Diamond, Larry (2006). "Authoritarian Learning: Lessons from the Colored Revolutions." *Brown Journal of World Affairs* XII(2): 215–22.
33. This author can testify to that as she was in Cairo on 25–26 January, comparing state television broadcasts with the happenings in Tahrir Square.
34. Gitlin, Todd (1980). *The Whole World is Watching*. Berkeley, CA: University of California Press, p. 7.
35. DeLuca, Kevin Michael (1993). *Image Politics: The New Rhetoric of Environmental Activism*. New York: The Guilford Press, p. 89.
36. Jervis, Robert (1970). *The Logic of Image in International Relations*. Princeton, NJ: Princeton University Press, p. 123.
37. Sennitt, Andrew (2011). "'Arab Spring' Breaks State Monopoly on Information." *Radio Netherlands Worldwide Media Network*, 16 June. Available: http://blogs.rnw.nl/medianetwork/arab-spring-breaks-state-monopoly-on-information.
38. Jervis, The Logic of Image in International Relations, p. 132.
39. Schatz, Transnational Image Marking and Soft Authoritarian Kazakhstan.
40. Kraidy, Marwan (2009). *Reality Television and Arab Politics: Contention in Public Life*. Cambridge: Cambridge University Press.
41. Silverstone, Roger (1994). *Television and Everyday Life*. London: Routledge, p. 110.

6

1. Lacoutre, Jean (1970). *The Demigods: Charismatic Leadership in the Third World*. New York: Alfred A. Knopf, p. 55.
2. Anderson, Lisa (1991). "Absolutism and the Resilience of Monarchy in the Middle East." *Political Science Quarterly* 106(1): 1–15.
3. Lacoutre, The Demigods, p. 31.
4. Weber, Max (1978). *Economy and Society*. Berkley, CA: University of California Press, pp. 241–2.
5. Quoted in Aburish, Said K. (2004). *Nasser: The Last Arab*. London: Duckworth, p. 54.

6. Harvey, Arlene (2001). "A Dramaturgical Analysis of Charismatic Leader Discourse." *Journal of Organizational Change Management* 14(3); 258.
7. Lacoutre, *The Demigods*.
8. Aburish, *Nasser*.
9. Ibid.
10. Ibid.
11. Ronen, Yehudit (2008). *Qaddafi's Libya in World Politics*. Boulder, CO: Lynne Reinner.
12. Ronen, *Qaddafi's Libya in World Politics*, p. 201.
13. Ibid.
14. Lacoutre, *The Demigods*, p. 33.
15. Ronen, *Qaddafi's Libya in World Politics*, p. 202.
16. Crystal, Jill (1994). "Authoritarianism and its Adversaries in the Arab World." *World Politics* 46(2), p. 271.
17. Aburish, Said K. (1998). *Arafat: From Defender to Dictator*. London: Bloomsbury.
18. Aburish, *Arafat*, p. 79.
19. Time (2011). "Gaddafi Fashion: The Emperor Has Some Crazy Clothes." *Time Magazine* Photo Essay. Available: http://www.time.com/time/photogallery/0,29307,2055860,00.html.
20. Hammond, J. (2011). "Omar Mukhtar, Icon of the Libyan Uprising." *The Arabist*, 24 February. Available: http://www.arabist.net/blog/2011/2/24/omar-mukhtar-icon-of-the-libyan-uprising.html.
21. Lacoutre, *The Demigods*.
22. Recall a similar image used by Hosni Mubarak.
23. Crystal, Authoritarianism and its Adversaries in the Arab World, p. 281.
24. Anderson, Absolutism and the Resilience of the Monarchy in the Middle East.
25. Crystal, Authoritarianism and its Adversaries in the Arab World.
26. Bensman, Joseph and Givant, Michael (1986). "Charisma and Modernity: The Use and Abuse of a Concept," in Glassman, Ronald M. and William H. Swatos, Jr. (eds.), *Charisma, History, and Social Structure*. New York: Greenwood Press, p. 30.
27. Fanon, Frantz (2004). *The Wretched of the Earth*. New York: Grove Press.
28. Lacoutre, *The Demigods*, p. 64.
29. Lacoutre, *The Demigods*.
30. Hammond, J. (2011). "Omar Mukhtar, Icon of the Libyan Uprising." *The Arabist*, 24 February. Available: http://www.arabist.net/blog/2011/2/24/omar-mukhtar-icon-of-the-libyan-uprising.html.
31. Barakat, Ibtisam (2011). "Qaddafi: 'Song of the Rain'." *Jadaliyya*, 22 February. Available: http://www.jadaliyya.com/pages/index/715/qaddafi_song-of-the-rain.
32. Fahim, Kareem and David D. Kirpatrick (2011). "Qaddafi's Grip on the Capital Tightens as Revolt Grows." *New York Times*, 22 February. Available: http://www.nytimes.com/2011/02/23/world/africa/23libya.html?pagewanted=1.
33. Mulholland, Rory (2011). "Libyan Street Art – In Pictures." *The Observer*, 5 June. Available: http://www.guardian.co.uk/world/gallery/2011/jun/05/libya-gaddafi-street-art?INTCMP=ILCNETTXT3487#/?picture=375309099&index=6.
34. Mulholland, Rory (2011a). "The Libyan Artists Driving Gaddafi to the Wall." *The Observer*, 5 June. Available: http://www.guardian.co.uk/world/2011/jun/05/gaddafi-rebels-art-graffiti-benghazi.
35. Hinnebusch, Raymond A. (1993). "State And Civil Society in Syria." *Middle East Journal* 47(2), p. 246.
36. Hinnebusch, Raymond A. (1976). "Local Politics in Syria: Organization And Mobilization in Four Village Cases." *Middle East Journal* 30(1), p. 1.
37. Wedeen, Lisa (1999). *Ambiguities of Domination: Politics, Rhetoric, and Symbols in Contemporary Syria*. Chicago: University of Chicago Press, p. 6.
38. Ibid.

39. Wedeen, *Ambiguities of Domination*, p. 2.
40. Ibid.
41. Lesch, David (2005). *The New Lion of Damascus: Bashar al-Asad and Modern Syria*. New Haven and London: Yale University Press, p. 3.
42. Ghadbian, Najib (2001). "The New Asad: Dynamics of Continuity and Change in Syria." *Middle East Journal* 55(4), p. 625.
43. Lesch, *The New Lion of Damascus*, p. 67.
44. Lesch, *The New Lion of Damascus*, p. 68.
45. Ghadbian, The New Asad.
46. Hinnebusch, Raymond (2001). *Syria: Revolution from Above*. London: Routledge, p. 165.
47. Ghadbian, The New Asad, p. 633.
48. Perthes, Volker (2004). *Syria under Bashar al-Assad: Modernisation and the Limits of Change*. Adelphi Paper 366. Oxford: IISS and Oxford University Press.
49. Muaddi Darraj, Susan (2005). *Bashar al-Assad*. Philadelphia: Chelsea House Publishers.
50. Quoted in Wedeen, *Ambiguities of Domination*, p. 76.
51. Havel, Václav (1985). *The Power of the Powerless: Citizens against the State in Central-Eastern Europe*. New York: Palach Press, p. 52.
52. Crystal, Authoritarianism and its Adversaries in the Arab World, p. 274.
53. Caldwell, Leah (2011). "The New Face of Asad on YouTube." *Arab Media and Society*, issue 13, Summer. Available: http://www.arabmediasociety.com/topics/index.php?t_article=326.
54. Hinnebusch, State And Civil Society in Syria, p. 243.
55. Hinnebusch, Syria: Revolution from Above, p. 166.
56. Steavenson, Wendell (2011). "Roads to Freedom." *The New Yorker*, 29 August, p. 29.
57. hooks, bell (1990). *Yearning: Race, Gender, and Cultural Politics*. Boston: South End Press.
58. Agamben, Giorgio (1998). *Homo Sacer: Sovereign Power and Bare Life*. Translated by Daniel Heller Roazen. Stanford: Stanford University Press.
59. Lacoutre, *The Demigods*, p. 42.
60. Schweitzer, Arthur (1984). *The Age of Charisma*. Chicago: Nelson-Hall.
61. Lacoutre, *The Demigods*.
62. Bensman and Givant, Charisma and Modernity, p. 29.
63. Crispin Miller, Mark (1988). *Boxed In: The Culture of TV*. Evanston, Illinois: Northwestern University Press, p. 331.

Bibliography

Aaker, David (1995). *Building Strong Brands*. New York: The Free Press.

Al-Abaya (2006). Dir. Reda Qashmar. Produced by and broadcast on Al-Manar.

Abbas, Wael (2008). Interview with the author. Cairo, March.

Abdel Aziz, Sami (2008). Interview with the author. Cairo, March.

Abu Hilaleh, Yasser (2011). "Rasasa fi sad shab ash'alat al-thawra." *Al-Hayat*, 16 August. Available: http://www.ademocracynet.com/Arabic/index.php?page=articles&action=Detail&id=1757.

Aburish, Said K. (1998). *Arafat: From Defender to Dictator*. London: Bloomsbury.

— (2004). *Nasser: The Last Arab*. London: Duckworth.

Afshari, Ali and H. Graham Underwood (2009). "The Green Wave." *Journal of Democracy* 20(4): 6–10.

Agamben, Giorgio (1998). *Homo Sacer: Sovereign Power and Bare Life*. Translated by Daniel Heller-Roazen. Stanford: Stanford University Press.

Al-Agha, Joseph Elie (2006). *The Shifts in Hizbullah's Ideology: Religious Ideology, Political Ideology, and Political Program*. Amsterdam: Amsterdam University Press.

Al-Intiqad (2011). "MP Moussawi Condemns Ugly Massacres Conducted by Qaddafi against the Libyan People." *Al-Intiqad* website, 23 February (Arabic). Available: http://www.alin-tiqad.com/essaydetails.php?eid=41095&cid=75&st=%E1%ED%C8%ED%C7.

Ajemian, Peter (2008). "Resistance Beyond Time and Space: Hezbollah's Media Campaigns." *Arab Media & Society*, issue 5, Spring, pp. 1–17. Available: http://www.arabmediasociety.com/articles/downloads/20080510192814_AMS5_Pete_Ajemian.pdf.

Alterman, Jon (1999). "Transnational Media and Social Change in the Arab World." *Transnational Broadcasting Studies*, issue 2, Spring. Available: http://www.tbsjournal.com/Archives/Spring99/Articles/Alterman/alterman.html.

Amin, Hussein (2000). "Satellite Broadcasting and Civil Society in the Middle East: The Role of Nilesat." *Transnational Broadcasting Studies*, issue 4, Spring. Available: http://www.tbsjournal.com/Archives/Spring00/Articles4/Ali/Amin/amin.html.

Amin, Hussein (2002). "Freedom as Value in Arab Media. Perceptions and Attitudes among Journalists." *Political Communication* 19(2): 125–35.

Al-Amin, Ibrahim (2008). "Speech on 15 May." *Al-Manar*. Available: http://www.almanar.com.lb/NewsSite/NewsDetails.aspx?id=43820&language=ar.

Anderson, Benedict (1983). *Imagined Communities: Reflections on the Origin and Spread of Nationalism*. London: Verso.

Anderson, Lisa (1991). "Absolutism and the Resilience of Monarchy in the Middle East." *Political Science Quarterly* 106(1): 1–15.

Ansari, Ali (2008). Iran under Ahmadinejad: Populism and its Malcontents. *International Affairs* 84(4): 683–700.

Archard, David (2000). "Nationalism and Political Theory." In O'Sullivan, Noel (ed.), *Political Theory in Transition*, pp. 155–71. London: Routledge.

Arkin, William M. (2007). "Divining Victory: Airpower in the 2006 Israel-Hezbollah War." *Strategic Studies Quarterly* 1(2): 98–141.

Arzheimer, Kai and Elisabeth Carter (2006). "Political Opportunity Structures and the Extreme Right." *European Journal of Political Research* 45(3): 419–43.

Atrissi, Talal (2010). "Matha yourid al-shia min dawlatihim?" *An-Nahar*, Wednesday 25 August. Available: http://www.annahar.com/content.php?priority=6&table=main&type=main&day=Wed.

Auyero, Javier (2004). "When Everyday Life, Routine Politics, and Protest Meet." *Theory and Society* 33(3): 417–41.

Axford, Barrie and Richard Huggins (2002). "Political Marketing and the Aestheticisation of Politics: Modern Politics and Postmodern Trends." In O'Shaughnesy, Nicholas J. and Stephan C. M. Henneberg (eds.), *The Idea of Political Marketing*, pp. 198–208. London: Praeger.

Ayish, Muhammad I. (2002). "Political Communication on Arab World Television: Evolving Patterns." *Political Communication*, 19(2): 137–54.

Banksy (2004). *Wall and Piece*. London: Arrow Books.

Barak, Oren (2007). "'Don't mention the war?': The Politics of Remembrance and Forgetfulness in Postwar Lebanon." *Middle East Journal* 61(1): 49–70.

Barakat, Ibtisam (2011). "Qaddafi: 'Song of the Rain'." *Jadaliyya*, 22 February. Available: http://www.jadaliyya.com/pages/index/715/qaddafi_song-of-the-rain.

Barber, Benjamin R. (2003). "Which Technology and Which Democracy?" In Jenkins, Henry, David Thorburn and Brad Seawell (eds.), *Democracy and New Media*, pp. 33–48. Cambridge, MA: The MIT Press.

Barthes, Roland (1977). *Image, Music, Text*. New York: Hill and Wang.

Baudrillard, Jean (1999). *Simulacra and Simulation*. Ann Arbor: The University of Michigan Press.

— (2002). "L'Esprit du Terrorisme." *The South Atlantic Quarterly* 101(2): 403–15.

Bayat, Asef (1997). *Street Politics: Poor People's Movements in Iran*. New York: Columbia University Press.

— (2010). *Life as Politics: How Ordinary People Change the Middle East*. Stanford, CA: Stanford University Press.

Baylouny, Anne Marie (2006). *Al-Manar and Alhurra: Competing Satellite Stations and Ideologies*. DTIC Document. Available: http://www.dtic.mil/cgi-bin/GetTRDoc?AD=ADA47 8865&Location=U2&doc=GetTRDoc.pdf.

BBC (2009). "Hezbollah Confirms Egypt Arrest." *BBC* website, 10 April. Available: http://news.bbc.co.uk/2/hi/7994304.stm.

Beaumont Peter (2011). "The Truth about Twitter, Facebook and the Uprisings in the Arab World." *The Guardian*, 25 February. Available: www.guardian.co.uk/world/2011/feb/25/twitter-facebook-uprisings-arab-libya.

Belt, David Douglas (2006). "Global Islamism: Understanding and Strategy." *Connections* 4: 41–63.

Benjamin, Walter (2008). *The Work of Art in the Age of Mechanical Reproduction*. London: Penguin.

Bennett, W. Lance (2003). "Lifestyle Politics and Citizen-Consumers: Identity, Communication and Political Action in Late Modern Society." In Corner, John and Dick Pels (eds.), *Media and the Restyling of Politics*, pp. 137–50. London: Sage.

Bensman, Joseph and Michael Givant (1986). "Charisma and Modernity: The Use and Abuse of a Concept." In Glassman, Ronald M. and William H. Swatos, Jr. (eds.), *Charisma, History, and Social Structure*, pp. 27–56. New York: Greenwood Press.

Bergmann, Knut and Wolfram Wickert (1999). "Selected Aspects of Communication in German Election Campaigns." In Newman, Bruce I. (ed.), *Handbook of Political Marketing*, pp. 455–84. London: Sage.

Betsky, Aaron et al. (1997). *Icons: Magnets of Meaning*. San Francisco: Chronicle Books.

Bhabha, Homi (1994). *The Location of Culture*. London: Routledge.

Billig, Michael (1995). *Banal Nationalism*. London: Sage.

Blumenthal, Sidney (1980). *The Permanent Campaign: Inside the World of Elite Political Operatives*. Boston: Beacon.

Blumler, Jay G. and Dennis Kavanagh (1999). "The Third Age of Political Communication: Influences and Features." *Political Communication* 16(3): 209–30.

Bredekamp, Horst (2010). *The Audience as Prisoner: Reflections on the Activity of the Object*. Lecture at Princeton University, 2 March. Video available: http://video.ias.edu/audience-as-prisoner.

— (2011). *Theorie des Bildakts*: Über das Lebensrecht des Bildes, Frankfurt/M.: Suhrkamp Verlag.

Burke, Edmund (1756). *A Philosophical Enquiry into the Origin of Our Ideas of the Sublime and Beautiful*. London: J. Dodsley.

Butler, Patrick and Neil Collins (1999). "A Conceptual Framework for Political Marketing." In Newman, Bruce I. (ed.), *Handbook of Political Marketing*, pp. 55–72. Thousand Oaks, CA: Sage.

Caldwell, Leah (2011). "The New Face of Asad on YouTube." *Arab Media and Society*, issue 13, Summer. Available: http://www.arabmediasociety.com/topics/index.php?t_article=326.

Castells, Manuel (1983*). The City and the Grassroots: A Cross-cultural Theory of Urban Social Movements*. London: Arnold.

— (2000). "Materials for an Exploratory Theory of the Network Society." *British Journal of Sociology* 51(1): 5–24.

— (2005). "Grassrooting the Space of Flows." In Abbas, Ackbar and John Nguyet Erni (eds.), *Internationalizing Cultural Studies*, pp. 627–36. Oxford: Blackwell.

Chelkowski, Peter (2002). "The Art of Revolution and War: The Role of the Graphic Arts in Iran." In Balaghi, Shiva and Lynn Gumpert (eds.), *Picturing Iran: Art, Society and Revolution*, pp. 127–41. London: I.B.Tauris.

Chelkowski, Peter and Hamid Dabashi (2000). *Staging a Revolution: The Art of Persuasion in the Islamic Republic*. London: Booth-Clibborn Editions.

Chow, Karen (2009). "Aesthetics and Interactive Arts." In Bentkowska-Kafel, Anna, Trish Cashen, and Hazel Gardiner (eds.), *Digital Visual Culture: Theory and Practice*, pp. 15–22. Bristol: Intellect.

Collombier, Virginie (2007). "The Internal Stakes of the 2005 Elections: The Struggle for Influence in Egypt's National Democratic Party." *Middle East Journal* 61(1): 95–111.

Comaroff, Jean and John Comaroff (1991). *Of Revelation and Revolution: Christianity, Colonialism, and Consciousness in South Africa*, volume 1. Chicago: University of Chicago Press.

Conway, Maura (2006). "Terrorism and the Internet. New Media – New Threat?" *Parliamentary Affairs* 59(2): 283–98.

Corner, John and Dick Pels (2003). "Introduction: The Re-styling of Politics." In Corner, John and Dick Pels (eds.), *Media and the Restyling of Politics*, pp. 1–18. London: Sage.

Cottle, Simon (2011). "Media and the Arab Spring." *Journalism* 12(5): 647–59.

Crane, Susan A. (2004). "Memory, Distortion, and History in the Museum." In Carbonell, Bettina Messias (ed.), *Museum Studies: An Anthology of Contexts*, pp. 318–34. Oxford: Blackwell.

Crispin Miller, Mark (1988). *Boxed In: The Culture of TV*. Evanston, IL: Northwestern University Press.

Crystal, Jill (1994). "Authoritarianism and Its Adversaries in the Arab World." *World Politics* 46(2): 262–89.

Dabashi, Hamid (2011). *The Green Movement in Iran*, edited with an introduction by Navid Nikzadfar. New Brunswick, NJ: Transaction Publishers.

Dahlgren, Peter (2009). *Media and Political Engagement: Citizens, Communication, and Democracy*. Cambridge: Cambridge University Press.

Dalacoura, Katerina (2001). "Islamist Movements as Non-state Actors and their Relevance to International Relations." In Josselin, Daphné and William Wallace (eds.), *Non-state Actors in World Politics*, pp. 235–50. Palgrave Macmillan, London.

Dasgupta, Sudeep (2005). "Visual Culture and the Place of Modernity." In Abbas, Ackbar and John Nguyet Erni (eds.), *Internationalizing Cultural Studies*, pp. 427–38. Oxford: Blackwell.

Debord, Guy (1994). *The Society of the Spectacle*. New York: Zone Books.

De Certeau, Michel (1984). *The Practice of Everyday Life*. Berkeley: University of California Press.

— (1997). *Culture in the Plural*. Minneapolis: University of Minnesota Press.

Deleuze, Gilles and Félix Guattari (1987). *A Thousand Plateaus: Capitalism and Schizophrenia*. Minneapolis: University of Minnesota Press.

DeLuca, Kevin Michael (1993). *Image Politics: The New Rhetoric of Environmental Activism*. New York: The Guilford Press.

Diamond, Larry (2006). "Authoritarian Learning: Lessons from the Colored Revolutions." *Brown Journal of World Affairs* XII(2): 215–22.

— (2010). "Liberation Technology." *Journal of Democracy* 21(3): 69–83.

Donald, Stephanie (1999). "Children as Political Messengers: Art, Childhood, and Continuity." In Evans, Harriet and Stephanie Donald (eds.), *Picturing Power in the People's Republic of China: Posters of the Cultural Revolution*, pp. 79–100. Oxford: Rowman and Littlefield.

Dubai School of Government (2011). *Arab Social Media Report*, Volume 1, Issue 2. Available: http://www.dsg.ae/portals/0/ASMR2.pdf.

Dutton, Jane E. and Janet M. Dukerich (1991). "Keeping an Eye on the Mirror: Image and Identity in Organizational Adaptation." *The Academy of Management Journal* 34(3): 517–54.

Ehrenreich, Barbara (2007). *Dancing in the Streets: A History of Collective Joy*. New York: Metropolitan.

Eiesenstein, Elizabeth (1991). "The Rise of the Reading Public." In Crowley, David and Paul Heyer (eds.), *Communication in History: Technology, Culture, and Society*, pp. 94–102. New York: Longman.

Entman, Robert (1993). "Framing: Toward Clarification of a Fractured Paradigm." *Journal of Communication* 43(Autumn): 51–55.

Erickson-Nepstad, Sharon (2002). "Creating Transnational Solidarity: The Use of Narrative in the U.S.-Central America Peace Movement." In Smith, Jackie and Hank Johnston (eds.), *Globalization and Resistance: Transnational Dimensions of Social Movements*, pp. 133–52. Oxford: Rowman and Littlefield.

Etling, Bruce et al. (2009). *Mapping the Arabic Blogosphere: Politics, Culture, and Dissent*: Internet & Democracy Case Study Series, Berkman Center Research Publication number 2009–06. Berkman Center for Internet & Society, pp. 1–62. Available: http://www.alhaqq-society.org/research/MappingTheArabicBlogosphere.pdf.

Evans, Harriet and Stephanie Donald (1999). "Introducing Posters of China's Cultural Revolution." In Evans, Harriet and Stephanie Donald (eds.), *Picturing Power in the People's Republic of China: Posters of the Cultural Revolution*, pp. 1–26. Oxford: Rowman and Littlefield.

Evans, Jessica (2005). "Celebrity, Media and History." In Evans, Jessica and David Hesmondhalgh (eds.), *Understanding Media: Inside Celebrity*, pp. 11–56. Maidenhead: Open University Press.

Falkowski, Andrzej and Wojciech Cwalina (1999). "Methodology of Constructing Effective Political Advertising: An Empirical Study of the Polish Presidential Election in 1995." In Newman, Bruce I. (ed.), *Handbook of Political Marketing*, pp. 283–304. Thousand Oaks, CA: Sage.

Fandy, Mamoun (2007). *(Un)Civil War of Words: Media and Politics in the Arab World*. Westport, CT: Praeger Security International.

Fanon, Frantz (2004). *The Wretched of the Earth*. New York: Grove Press.

Faris, David (2008). "Revolutions Without Revolutionaries? Network Theory, Facebook, and the Egyptian Blogosphere." *Arab Media and Society*, issue 6, Fall, pp. 1–11. Available: http://www.arabmediasociety.com/articles/downloads/20080929153219_AMS6_David_Faris.pdf.

Featherstone, Mike (1991). *Consumer Culture and Postmodernism*. London: Sage.

— (1995). *Undoing Culture: Globalization, Postmodernism and Identity*. London: Sage.

Finnemann, Niels Ole (2011). "Mediatization Theory and Digital Media." *Communications: European Journal of Communication Research* 36(1): 67–89.

Flaskerud, Ingvild (2010). *Visualizing Belief and Piety in Iranian Shiism*. London: Continuum.

Fluck, Winfried (2003). "Aesthetic Experience of the Image." In Haselstein, Ulla, Berndt Ostendorf, and Peter Schneck (eds.), *Iconographies of Power: The Politics and Poetics of Visual Representation*, pp. 11–41. Heidelberg: Winter.

Foucault, Michel (1980). *Power/Knowledge: Selected Interviews and Other Writings*. New York: Pantheon Books.

— (1995). *Discipline and Punish: The Birth of the Prison*. New York: Vintage Books.

Fuery, Patrick and Kelli Fuery (2003). *Visual Cultures and Critical Theory*. London: Arnold.

Gamson, William et al. (1992). "Media Images and the Social Construction of Reality." *Annual Review of Sociology* 18: 373–93.

Gergen, Kenneth J. (2002). "The Challenge of Absent Presence." In Katz, James E. and Mark A. Aakhus (eds.), *Perpetual Contact: Mobile Communication, Private Talk, Public Performance*, pp. 227–41. Cambridge: Cambridge University Press.

Gershoni, Israel and James Jankowski (2004). *Commemorating the Nation: Collective Memory, Public Commemoration, and National Identity in Twentieth-Century Egypt*. Chicago: Middle East Documentation Center.

Ghadbian, Najib (2001). "The New Asad: Dynamics of Continuity and Change in Syria." *Middle East Journal* 55(4): 624–41.

Ghaddar, Hanin (2012). "Adieu, Hezbollah." *Now Lebanon*, 19 March. Available: http://www.nowlebanon.com/NewsArticleDetails.aspx?ID=377701.

Ghanem, Salma (1997). "Filling in the Tapestry: The Second Level of Agenda Setting." In McCombs, Maxwell, Donald L. Shaw and David Weaver (eds.), *Communication and Democracy: Exploring the Intellectual Frontiers in Agenda-setting Theory*, pp. 3–14. Mahwah, NJ: Lawrence Erlbaum Associates.

Gharbeia, Amr (2008). Interview with the author. Cairo, March.

Ghasemi, Amirali (2008). Interview with the author. Tehran, March.

Gibbins, John R. and Bo Reimer (1999). *The Politics of Postmodernity: An Introduction to Contemporary Politics and Culture*. London: Sage.

Gitlin, Todd (1980). *The Whole World Is Watching*. Berkeley: University of California Press.

Glasser, Susan B. and Steve Coll (2005). "The Web as Weapon." *The Washington Post*, 9 August, p. A01.

Glassman, Ronald M. (1986). "Manufactured Charisma and Legitimacy." In Glassman, Ronald M. and William H. Swatos, Jr. (eds.), *Charisma, History, and Social Structure*, pp. 115–28. New York: Greenwood Press.

Glassman, Ronald M. and William H. Swatos, Jr. (1986). "Introduction." In Glassman, Ronald M. and William H. Swatos, Jr. (eds.), *Charisma, History, and Social Structure*, pp. 3–8. New York: Greenwood Press.

Grafe, Peter (1994). *Wahlkampf: Die Olympiade der Demokratie*. Frankfurt: Eichborn.

Groys, Boris (2008). *Art Power*. Cambridge, MA: The MIT Press.

Gruber, Christiane (2008). "The Message is on the Wall: Mural Arts in Post-Revolutionary Iran." *Persica* 22: 14–46.

Hacker, Kenneth L. (1995). "Introduction: The Importance of Candidate Images in Presidential Elections." In Hacker, Kenneth L. (ed.), *Candidate Images in Presidential Elections*, pp. xi–xix. London: Praeger.

Hackman, Michael Z. and Craig E. Johnson (2004). *Leadership: A Communication Perspective*. Long Grove, IL: Waveland Press.

Hafezi, Parisa and Hashem Kalantari (2012). "Khamenei Allies Trounce Ahmadinejad in Iran Elections." *Reuters*, 4 March. Available: http://www.reuters.com/article/2012/03/04/us-iran-election-result-idUSTRE82306420120304.

Al-Hail, Ali (2000). "The Age of New Media: The Role of Al-Jazeera Satellite TV in Developing Aspects of Civil Society in Qatar." *Transnational Broadcasting Studies*, issue 4, Spring. Available: http://www.tbsjournal.com/Archives/Spring00/Articles4/Ali/Al-Hail/al-hail.html.

Hall, Stuart (1980). "Race, Articulation, and Societies Structured in Dominance." In UNESCO (ed.), *Sociological Theories: Race and Colonialism*, pp. 305–45. Paris: UNESCO.

Hanaei, Arash (2008). Interview with the author. Tehran, March.

Handler, Joel F. (1992). "Postmodernism, Protest, and the New Social Movements." *Law and Society Review* 26(4): 697–732.

Hansen, Lene (2006). *Images, Identity and Security: Bringing Together International Politics and Media Research*. Nordicom conference paper. Available: http://www.nordicom.gu.se/common/publ_pdf/269_hansen.pdf.

Harb, Zahera (2011a). "Arab Revolutions and the Social Media Effect." *M/C Journal* 14(2). Available: http://journal.media-culture.org.au/index.php/mcjournal/article/viewArticle/364.

— (2011b). *Channels of Resistance in Lebanon: Liberation Propaganda, Hezbollah and the Media*. London: I.B.Tauris.

Harnden, Toby (2004). "Video Games Attract Young to Hizbollah." *The Telegraph*, 21 February.

Harvey, Arlene (2001). "A Dramaturgical Analysis of Charismatic Leader Discourse." *Journal of Organizational Change Management* 14(3): 253–65.

Haugbolle, Sune (2007). "Memory as Representation and Memory as Idiom." In Choueiri, Youssef (ed.), *Breaking the Cycle: Civil Wars in Lebanon*, pp. 121–33. London: Stacey International.

— (2010). *War and Memory in Lebanon*. Cambridge: Cambridge University Press.

Havel, Václav (1985). *The Power of the Powerless: Citizens against the State in Central-Eastern Europe*. New York: Palach Press.

Hegel, Georg Wilhelm Friedrich (1956). *The Philosophy of History*. New York: Dover.

Hemphill, David F. (2001). "Incorporating Postmodernist Perspectives into Adult Education." In Sheared, Peggy and Vanessa Sissel (eds.), *Making Space: Merging Theory and Practice in Adult Education*, pp. 15–28. Westport, CT: Greenwood.

Hepp, Andreas, Stig Hjarvard, and Knut Lundby (2010). "Mediatization, Empirical Perspectives: An Introduction to a Special Issue." *Communications* 35: 223–28.

Heydemann, Steve (2007). *Upgrading Authoritarianism in the Arab World*. Saban Center Analysis Paper Number 13, October. Washington, DC: Brookings Institution. Available: http://www.brookings.edu/~/media/Files/rc/papers/2007/10arabworld/10arabworld.pdf.

Hinnebusch, Raymond A. (1976). "Local Politics in Syria: Organization And Mobilization In Four Village Cases." *Middle East Journal* 30(1): 1–24.

— (1993). "State And Civil Society in Syria." *Middle East Journal* 47(2): 243–57.

— (2001). *Syria: Revolution from Above*. London: Routledge.

Hjarvard, Stig (2008). "The Mediatization of Society: A Theory of the Media as Agents of Social and Cultural Change." *Nordicom Review* 8(2): 105–34.

Hobsbawm, Eric (1993). "Mass Producing Traditions: Europe, 1870–1914." In Hobsbawm, Eric and Terence O. Ranger (eds.), *The Invention of Tradition*, pp. 263–308. Cambridge: Cambridge University Press.

hooks, bell (1990). *Yearning: Race, Gender, and Cultural Politics*. Boston: South End Press.

El Houri, Walid and Dima Saber (2010). "Filming Resistance: A Hezbollah Strategy." *Radical History Review* 106: 70–85.

Howeidy, Amira (2005). "A Chronology of Dissent." *Al-Ahram Weekly*, 23–29 June, issue no. 748. Available: http://weekly.ahram.org.eg/2005/748/eg10.htm.

Hunt, Sonja M. (1984). "The Role of Leadership in the Construction of Reality." In Kellerman, Barbara (ed.), *Leadership: Multidisciplinary Perspectives*, pp. 157–78. Englewood Cliffs, New Jersey: Prentice-Hall.

Ishani, Maryam (2011). "The Hopeful Network." *Foreign Policy*, 7 February. Available: http://www.foreignpolicy.com/articles/2011/02/07/the_hopeful_network.

Jain, Dipak and Suvit Maesincee (2002). *Marketing Moves: A New Approach to Profits, Growth and Renewal*. Boston: Harvard Business School Press.

Jansson, André (2002). "The Mediatization of Consumption: Towards an Analytical Framework of Image Culture." *Journal of Consumer Culture* 2(1): 5–31.

Jarman, Neil (2005). "Painting Landscapes: The Place of Murals in the Symbolic Construction of Urban Space." In Geisler, Michael (ed.), *National Symbols, Fractured Identities: Contesting the National Narrative*, pp. 172–92. Lebanon, NH: Middlebury College Press.

Jaworski, Adam and Crispin Thurlow (2010). "Introducing Semiotic Landscapes." In Jaworski, Adam and Crispin Thurlow (eds.), *Semiotic Landscapes*, pp. 1–40. London: Continuum.

Al-Jazeera (2011). "Mathaf yokhallid thikra al-thawra al-misriyya." *Al-Jazeera* website, 22 August. Available: http://www.aljazeera.net/NR/exeres/E6A95EA4-6707-4B24-AFA2-CB22474FDAB6.htm?GoogleStatID=9.

Jervis, Robert (1970). *The Logic of Image in International Relations*. Princeton, NJ: Princeton University Press.

Jorisch, Avi (2004). "Al-Manar: Hizbullah TV, 24/7." *Middle East Quarterly* XI(1): 17–31. Available: http://www.meforum.org/583/al-manar-hizbullah-tv-24-7.

Kaid, Linda Lee and Mike Chanslor (1995). "Changing Candidate Images: The Effects of Political Advertising." In Hacker, Kenneth L. (ed.), *Candidate Images in Presidential Elections*, pp. 83–97. Westport, CT: Praeger Publishers.

Kalb, Marvin and Carol Saivetz (2007). "The Israeli-Hezbollah War of 2006: The Media as a Weapon in Asymmetrical Conflict." *The Harvard International Journal of Press/Politics* 12(3): 43–66.

Kandiyoti, Deniz (1994). "Identity and its Discontents: Women and the Nation." In Williams, Patrick and Laura Chrisman (eds.), *Colonial Discourse and Post-colonial Theory: A Reader*, pp. 276–91. London: Harvester Wheatsheaf.

Kavanagh, Gaynor (2004). "Melodrama, Pantomime or Portrayal? Representing Ourselves and the British Past through Exhibitions in History Museums." In Carbonell, Bettina Messias (ed.), *Museum Studies: An Anthology of Contexts*, pp. 348–55. Oxford: Blackwell.

Kellerman, Barbara (1984). "Leadership as a Political Act." In Kellerman, Barbara (ed.), *Leadership: Multidisciplinary Perspectives*, pp. 63–90. Englewood Cliffs, NJ: Prentice-Hall.

Keshmirshekan, Hamid (2011). "Contemporary or Specific: The Dichotomous Desires in the Art of Early Twenty-First Century Iran." *Middle East Journal of Culture and Communication* 4(1): 44–71.

Khalaf, Samir (2006). *Heart of Beirut: Reclaiming the Burj*. London: Saqi Books.

Khalili, Laleh (2007). *Heroes and Martyrs of Palestine: The Politics of National Commemoration*. Cambridge: Cambridge University Press.

Khamis, Sahar and Katherine Vaughn (2011). "Cyberactivism in the Egyptian Revolution: How Civic Engagement and Citizen Journalism Tilted the Balance." *Arab Media and Society*, issue 13, Summer. Available: http://www.arabmediasociety.com/?article=769.

Khaniki, Hadi (2008). Interview with the author. Tehran, March.

Khatib, Lina (2007). "Television and Public Action in the Beirut Spring." In Sakr, Naomi (ed.), *Arab Media and Political Renewal: Community, Legitimacy and Public Life*, pp. 28–43. London: I.B.Tauris.

— (2010). "Hezbollah's Mobilization of Multitudes." *Foreign Policy Middle East Channel*, 29 October. Available: http://mideast.foreignpolicy.com/posts/2010/10/29/hizbullah_s_mobilization_of_the_multitudes?showcomments=yes.

— (2011). "Hizbullah's Political Strategy." *Survival: Global Politics and Strategy* 53(2): 61–76.

Khouri, Rami G. (2011). "Middle East Awakening." *The Cairo Review of Global Affairs* 1: 126–34.

King, Pu-Tsung (1997). "The Press, Candidate Images, and Voter Perceptions." In McCombs, Maxwell E., Donald L. Shaw, and David H. Weaver (eds.), *Communication and Democracy: Exploring the Intellectual Frontiers in Agenda-setting Theory*, pp. 29–40. Mahwah, NJ: Lawrence Erlbaum Associates.

Korangy, Alireza (2009). "A Literary and Historical Background of Martyrdom in Iran." *Comparative Studies of South Asia, Africa and the Middle East* 29(3): 528–41.

Kotler, Philip and Neil Kotler (1999). "Political Marketing: Generating Effective Candidates, Campaigns, and Causes." In Newman, Bruce I. (ed.), *Handbook of Political Marketing*, pp. 3–18. Thousand Oaks, CA: Sage.

Kraidy, Marwan (2007). "Saudi Arabia, Lebanon and the Changing Arab Information Order." *International Journal of Communication*. 1: 139–56.

— (2009). *Reality Television and Arab Politics: Contention in Public Life*. Cambridge: Cambridge University Press.

Kraidy, Marwan and Sara Mourad (2010). "Hypermedia and Global Communication Studies: Lessons from the Middle East." *Global Media Journal* 8(16). Available: http://lass.calumet.purdue.edu/cca/gmj/sp10/gmj-sp10-article8-kraidy-mourad.htm.

Kreutz, Christian (2010). "Mobile activism in Africa: Future Trends and Software Developments." In Ekine, Sokari (ed.), *SMS Uprising: Mobile Phone Activism in Africa*, pp. 17–31. Cape Town: Pambazuka Press.

Lacoutre, Jean (1970). *The Demigods: Charismatic Leadership in the Third World*. New York: Alfred A. Knopf.

Lamloum, Olfa (2011). "Al-i'lam al-ijtima'i wa thawrat al-jeel al-arabi al-jadid." *Al-Jazeera Research Center*. Available: http://www.aljazeera.net/NR/exeres/AC7A8E0B-9952-435F-9A6C-6D025279CC8E.htm.

Lang, Sabine (2004). "Local Political Communication: Media and Local Politics in the Age of Globalization." In Esser, Frank and Barbara Pfetsch (eds.), *Comparing Political Communication: Theories, Cases, and Challenges*, pp. 151–83. Cambridge: Cambridge University Press.

Lees-Marshmant, Jennifer (2001). *Political Marketing and British Political Parties: The Party's Just Begun*. Manchester: Manchester University Press.

Lefebvre, Henri (1971). *Everyday Life in the Modern World*. London: Allen Lane, The Penguin Press.

Lemert, James B. et al. (1977). "Journalists and Mobilizing Information." *Journalism Quarterly* 54: 721–26.

Leonard, Mark (2002). "Diplomacy by Other Means." *Foreign Policy* 132 (Sep.–Oct.): 48–56.

Lesch, David (2005). *The New Lion of Damascus: Bashar al-Asad and Modern Syria*. New Haven and London: Yale University Press.

Libya.tv (2011). *Iftitah mathaf aslihat kataeb al-qathafi fi zawihat al-mahjoub bi misrata*, 23 June. Available: http://www.libya.tv/2011/06//.

Livingstone, Sonia (2009). "On the Mediation of Everything." *Journal of Communication* 59: 1–18.

Lundby, Knut (2009). "Introduction: 'Mediatization' as Key." In Lundby, Knut (ed.), *Mediatization: Concept, Changes, Consequences*, pp. 1–18. New York: Peter Lang.

Lynch, Marc (2006a). "Al-Qaeda's Media Strategies." *The National Interest* 83: 50–56.

— (2006b). *Voices of the New Arab Public: Iraq, Al-Jazeera, and Middle East Politics Today*. New York: Columbia University Press.

Maasri, Zeina (2009). *Off the Wall: Political Posters of the Lebanese Civil War*. London: I.B.Tauris.

MacLeod, Arlene Elowe (1992). "Hegemonic Relations and Gender Resistance: The New Veiling as Accommodating Protest in Cairo." *Signs* 17(3): 533–57.

Majed, Ziad (2012). "The Hizbullah Regime." *Ziad Majed blog*, 28 February (Arabic). Available: www.ziadmajed.net.

Al-Malky, Rania (2007). "Blogging for Reform: The Case of Egypt." *Arab Media and Society*, issue 1, Spring, pp. 1–31. Available: http://www.arabmediasociety.com/articles/downloads/20070312143716_AMS1_Rania_Al_Malky.pdf.

Manheim, Jarol B. (1994). *Strategic Public Diplomacy and American Foreign Policy: The Evolution of Influence*. Oxford: Oxford University Press.

Marden, Peter (1997). "Geographies of Dissent: Globalization, Identity, and the Nation." *Political Geography* 16(1): 37–64.

Matar, Dina (2008). "The Power of Conviction: Nassrallah's Rhetoric and Mediated Charisma in the Context of the 2006 July War." *Middle East Journal of Culture and Communication* 1(2): 122–37.

Mawari, Munir (2011). Presentation at "From Political Activism to Democratic Change" conference, Stanford University, 13 May.

Mazzoleni, Gianpietro and Winfried Schulz (1999). "'Mediatization' of Politics: A Challenge for Democracy?" *Political Communication* 16(3): 247–61.

McClintock, Anne (1997). "'No Longer in a Future Heaven': Gender, Race, and Nationalism." In McClintock, Anne, Aamer Mufti, and Ella Shohat (eds.), *Dangerous Liaisons: Gender, Nation, and Postcolonial Perspectives*, pp. 89–112. Minneapolis: University of Minnesota Press.

McCloud, Scott (1993). *Understanding Comics: The Invisible Art*. New York: Harper Paperbacks.

McLaughlin, W. Sean (2003). "The Use of the Internet for Political Action by Non-state Dissident Actors in the Middle East." *First Monday* 8(11, 3 November). Available: http://firstmonday.org/htbin/cgiwrap/bin/ojs/index.php/fm/article/view/1096/1016.

Meital, Yoram (2006). "The Struggle over Political Order in Egypt: The 2005 Elections." *Middle East Journal* 60(2): 257–79.

Meyrowitz, Joshua (1985). *No Sense of Place: The Impact of Electronic Media on Social Behaviour*. New York: Oxford University Press.

Miladi, Noureddine (2011). "Tunisia: A Media Led Revolution?" *Aljazeera.net*, 17 January. Available: http://english.aljazeera.net/indepth/opinion/2011/01/2011116142317498666.html.

Milani, Abbas (2005). "U.S. Foreign Policy and the Future of Democracy in Iran." *The Washington Quarterly* 28(3): 41–56.

Miller, Mark M., Julie L. Andsager, and Bonnie P. Reichert (1998). "Framing the Candidates in Presidential Primaries: Issues and Images in Press Releases and News Coverage." *Journalism and Mass Communication Quarterly* 75(2): 312–24.

Mills, Caroline (1993). "Myths and Meanings of Gentrification." In Duncan, James and David Ley (eds.), *Place/Culture/Representation*, pp. 149–70. London: Routledge.

Mitchell, William J. Thomas (2006). What Do Pictures Want? Interview by Asbjørn Grønstad and Øyvind Vågnes. *Image & Narrative*, November. Available: http://www.visual-studies.com/interviews/mitchell.html.

Moakhar, Mahmoud Bakhshi (2008). Interview with the author. Tehran, March.

Morgan, David (2005). *The Sacred Gaze: Religious Visual Culture in Theory and Practice*. Berkeley: University of California Press.

Motamedarya, Simin (2008). Interview with the author. Tehran, March.

Mowlana, Hamid (1997). *Global Information and World Communication*. London: Sage.

Muaddi Darraj, Susan (2005). *Bashar al-Assad*. Philadelphia: Chelsea House Publishers.

Mulholland, Rory (2011a). "The Libyan Artists Driving Gaddafi to the Wall." *The Observer*, 5 June. Available: http://www.guardian.co.uk/world/2011/jun/05/gaddafi-rebels-art-graffiti-benghazi.

Mueller, Claus (1973). *The Politics of Communication: A Study in the Political Sociology of Language, Socialization, and Legitimation*. New York: Oxford University Press.

Mulholland, Rory (2011b). "Libyan Street Art – In Pictures." *The Observer*, 5 June. Available: http://www.guardian.co.uk/world/gallery/2011/jun/05/libya-gaddafi-street-art?INTCMP=ILCNETTXT3487#/?picture=375309099&index=6.

Naji, Kasra (2008). *Ahmadinejad: The Secret History of Iran's Radical Leader*. London: I.B. Tauris.

Nasr, Assem (2010). "Imagining Identities: Television Advertising and the Reconciliation of the Lebanese Conflict." *Arab Media and Society*, issue 10, Spring, pp. 1–30.

Nasrallah, Hassan (1997). "Speech about the martyrdom of Hadi Nasrallah." *Al-Manar*, 13 September. Available: http://www.youtube.com/watch?v=I3AOlwDL_M0.

— (2000a). "Speech about the liberation of South Lebanon." *Al-Manar*, 25 May: Available: http://www.youtube.com/watch?v=oeIBWvE5vNA&feature=related.

— (2000b). "Speech about the liberation of South Lebanon." *Al-Manar*, 25 May. Available: http://www.youtube.com/watch?v=V_EAmIzqtu8.

— (2010). "Speech accusing Israel of assassinating Rafic Hariri." Press TV, 9 August. Available: http://www.youtube.com/watch?v=5odeTwU2zjw.

— (2011). "Speech on the lesson of the Tunisia Revolution." *Orange TV*, 16 January. Available: http://mrzine.monthlyreview.org/2011/nasrallah170111.html.

El-Nawaway, Mohamed and Adel Iskandar (2003). *Al-Jazeera: The Story of the Network that is Rattling Governments and Redefining Modern Journalism*. Boulder, CO: Westview.

Negrine, Ralph and Stylianos Papathanassopoulos (1996). "The 'Americanization' of Political Communication: A Critique." *Press/Politics* 1(2): 45–62.

Newman, Bruce I. (1994). *The Marketing of the President: Political Marketing as Campaign Strategy*. London: Sage.

— (1999). "A Predictive Model of Voter Behavior: The Repositioning of Bill Clinton." In Newman, Bruce I. (ed.), *Handbook of Political Marketing*, pp. 259–82. Thousand Oaks, CA: Sage.

Nimmo, Dan and Robert L. Savage (1976). *Candidates and their Images: Concepts, Methods, and Findings*. Santa Monica, CA: Goodyear.

Norton, Augustus Richard (2000). "Hizballah and the Israeli Withdrawal from Southern Lebanon." *Journal of Palestine Studies* 30(1): 22–35.

— (2006). *Lebanon: Securing a Lasting Cease-Fire.* Opening statement (updated) of testimony for a hearing of the US Senate Foreign Relations Committee 13. Available: http://www.globalsecurity.org/military/library/congress/2006_hr/060913-norton.pdf.

— (2009). *Hezbollah: A Short History.* Princeton, NJ: Princeton University Press.

Noureddine, Raya (2011). "Al-hay'a at-ta'dibiya bi'ssahafiyeen toqarrer waqf sahifat 'al-mossad' 6 ashhur." *Dostor Newspaper,* 22 June. Available: http://www.dostor.org/culture/news/11/june/22/45897.

NPR (2009). "Expert: Iran Protests Full of Symbolism." *NPR* website. Broadcast on 18 June. Available: http://www.npr.org/templates/story/story.php?storyId=105620617.

Parry-Giles, Shawn J. and Trevor Parry-Giles (1999). "Meta-Imaging, *The War Room*, and the Hyperreality of U.S. Politics." *Journal of Communication* 49(1): 28–45.

— (2007). "The Man from Hope: Hyperreal Intimacy and the Invention of Bill Clinton." In Negrine, Ralph and James Stanyer (eds.), *The Political Communication Reader,* pp. 250–55. London: Routledge.

Patiz, Norman (2004). "Radio Sawa and Alhurra TV: Opening Channels of Mass Communication in the Middle East." In Rugh, William (ed.), *Engaging the Arab and Islamic Worlds through Public Diplomacy: A Report and Action Recommendations,* pp. 69–89. Washington DC: Public Diplomacy Council.

Pels, Dick (2003). "Aesthetic Representation and Political Style: Re-balancing Identity and Difference in Media Democracy." In Corner, John and Dick Pels (eds.), *Media and the Restyling of Politics,* pp. 41–66. London: Sage.

Peraino, Kevin (2006). "Winning Hearts and Minds." *Newsweek,* 2 October. Available: http://www.newsweek.com/2006/10/01/winning-hearts-and-minds.html.

Perloff, Richard M. (1999). "Elite, Popular, and Merchandised Politics: Historical Origins of Presidential Campaign Marketing." In Newman, Bruce I. (ed.), *Handbook of Political Marketing,* pp. 19–40. Thousand Oaks, CA: Sage.

Perthes, Volker (2004). *Syria under Bashar al-Assad: Modernisation and the Limits of Change.* Adelphi Paper 366. Oxford: IISS and Oxford University Press.

Pile, Steve (1997). "Introduction: Opposition, Political Identities and Spaces of Resistance." In Pile, Steve and Michael Keith (eds.), *Geographies of Resistance,* pp. 1–32. London: Routledge.

Pintak, Lawrence (2006). *Reflections in a Bloodshot Lens: America, Islam, and the War of Ideas.* London: Pluto Press.

— (2008a). *The Role of the Media as Watch-dogs, Agenda-setters and Gate- Keepers in Arab States.* Paper 5.3, The Role of the News Media in the Governance Reform Agenda. World Bank/Harvard Kennedy School.

— (2008b). "Satellite TV and Arab Democracy." *Journalism Practice* 2(1): 15–26.

Plasser, Fritz with Gunda Plasser (2002). *Global Political Campaigning: A Worldwide Analysis of Campaign Professionals and Their Practices.* London: Praeger.

— (2007). "Global Political Campaigning: A Worldwide Analysis of Campaigning Professionals and Their Practices." In Negrine, Ralph and James Stanyer (eds.), *The Political Communication Reader,* pp. 138–44. London: Routledge.

Polletta, Francesca (1997). Culture and Its Discontents: Recent Theorizing on the Cultural Dimensions of Protest. *Sociological Inquiry* 67(4): 431–50.

Poulson, Stephen C. (2009). "Nested Institutions, Political Opportunity and the Decline of the Iranian Reform Movement Post 9/11." *American Behavioral Scientist* 53(1): 27–43.

Press TV (2011). "Hezbollah Hails Egypt Revolution, 11 February." *Press TV* website. Available: http://www.presstv.ir/detail/164799.html.

Quilty, Jim and Lysanda Ohrstrom (2007). "The Second Time as Farce: Stories of Another Lebanese Reconstruction." *Middle East Report* 243: 31–48.

Qin, Jialun (2007). "Analyzing Terror Campaigns on the Internet: Technical Sophistication, Content Richness, and Web Interactivity." *Human-Computer Studies* 65: 71–84.

Radsch, Courtney (2008). "Core to Commonplace: The Evolution of Egypt's Blogosphere." *Arab Media and Society*, issue 6, Fall. Available: http://www.arabmediasociety.com/articles/downloads/20080929140127_AMS6_Courtney_Radsch.pdf.

Radunski Peter (1980). *Wahlkämpfe: Moderne wahlkampfführung als politische Kommunikation.* Munich: Olzog.

Rafael, Vicente L. (2003). "The Cell Phone and the Crowd: Messianic Politics in Recent Philippine History." *Public Culture* 15(3): 399–425.

Rajaee, Farhang (1993). *The Iran-Iraq War: The Politics of Aggression.* Gainesville: University Press of Florida.

Ram, Haggai (2002). "Multiple Iconographies: Political Posters in the Iranian Revolution." In Balaghi, Shiva and Lynn Gumpert (eds.), *Picturing Iran: Art, Society and Revolution*, pp. 89–102. London: I.B.Tauris.

Reed, Thomas Vernon (2005). *The Art of Protest: Culture and Activism from the Civil Rights Movement to the Streets of Seattle.* Minneapolis: University of Minnesota Press.

Roka, Jolan (1999). "Do the Media Reflect or Shape Public Opinion?" In Newman, Bruce I. (ed.), *Handbook of Political Marketing*, pp. 505–18. Thousand Oaks, CA: Sage.

Ronen, Yehudit (2008). *Qaddafi's Libya in World Politics.* Boulder, CO: Lynne Reinner.

Rosen, David M. (1984). "Leadership in World Cultures." In Kellerman, Barbara (ed.), *Leadership: Multidisciplinary Perspectives*, pp. 39–62. Englewood Cliffs, New Jersey: Prentice-Hall.

Routledge Paul (1993). *Terrains of Resistance: Nonviolent Social Movements and the Contestation of Place in India.* Westport, CT: Praeger.

— (1997a). "A Spatiality of Resistances: Theory and Practice in Nepal's Revolution of 1990." In Pile, Steve and Michael Keith (eds.), *Geographies of Resistance*, pp. 68–86. London: Routledge.

— (1997b). "Space, Mobility, and Collective Action: India's Naxalite Movement." *Environment and Planning* 29: 2165–89.

Saad-Ghorayeb, Amal (2002). *Hizbu'llah: Politics and Religion.* London: Pluto Press.

Sabry, Tarik (2010). *Cultural Encounters in the Arab World: On Media, the Modern and the Everyday.* London: I.B.Tauris.

Safa, Osama (2006). "Lebanon Springs Forward." *Journal of Democracy* 17(1): 22–37.

Sakr, Naomi (2007). *Arab Television Today.* London: I.B.Tauris.

Salah, Ahmed (2011). Presentation at "From Political Activism to Democratic Change" conference, Stanford University, 12 May.

Saleh, Naziha (2011). "Will Syria be the Key of the 'New Middle East' Map?" *Moqawama.org*, 28 June. Available: http://www.english.moqawama.org/essaydetails.php?eid=14367&cid=269.

Samnani, Hina and Lolla Mohammed Nur (2011). "Crowdmapping the Arab Spring – Next Social Media Breakthrough?" *Voice of America News*, 28 June. Available: http://www.voanews.com/english/news/middle-east/Crowdmapping-Arab-Spring-Next-Social-Media-Breakthrough-124662649.html.

Scammell, Margaret (1995). *Designer Politics: How Elections are Won.* New York: St. Martin's Press.

— (1999). "Political Marketing: Issues for Political Science." *Political Studies*, XLVII: 718–39.

Schatz, Edward (2008). "Transnational Image Making and Soft Authoritarian Kazakhstan." *Slavic Review* 67(1): 50–62.

Schickel, Richard (2000). *Intimate Strangers: The Culture of Celebrity in America.* Chicago: Ivan R. Dee.

Schweiger, Günter and Gertraud Schrattenecker (1995). *Werbung.* Stuttgart: Gustav Fischer Verlag.

Schweitzer, Arthur (1984). *The Age of Charisma.* Chicago: Nelson-Hall.

Scott, James (1990). *Domination and the Arts of Resistance: Hidden Transcripts.* New Haven: Yale University Press.

Sennitt, Andrew (2011). "'Arab Spring' Breaks State Monopoly on Information." *Radio Netherlands Worldwide Media Network*, 16 June. Available: http://blogs.rnw.nl/medianetwork/arab-spring-breaks-state-monopoly-on-information.

Shadid, Anthony (2006). "Israel, Hizbollah Vow Wider War." *The Washington Post*, Saturday 15 July, p. A01. Available: http://www.washingtonpost.com/wp-dyn/content/article/2006/07/14/AR2006071400385.html.

Shaery-Eisenlohr, Roschanack (2008). *Shi'ite Lebanon: Transnational Religion and the Making of National Identities*. New York: Columbia University Press.

Shaw, Michael (2006). "Cracking The Cedar: How Hezbollah Re-Envisioned The Democracy Movement (And The West Hardly Noticed)." *Bag News*, 16 December. Available: http://www.bagnewsnotes.com/2006/12/cracking-the-cedar-how-hezbollah-re-envisioned-the-democracy-movement-and-the-west-hardly-noticed/.

Al-Shawbaky, Amr (2006). "Al-idarah al-hizbiyya lilintikhabat al-ri'asiyya wa al-tashri'iyya." In Rabi', Amr Hashem (ed.), *Nothom idarat al-intikhabat fi misr ma' moqarana bihalat bouldan okhra*, pp. 61–74. Cairo: Center for Political and Strategic Studies.

Al-Shayji, Abdallah (2008). "Panorama interview." *Al-Arabiya*. Broadcast 15 March. Transcript available:http://www.alarabiya.net/programs/2008/03/17/47093.html.

Shepard, Benjamin, L. M. Bogad, and Stephen Duncombe (2008). "Performing vs. the Insurmountable: Theatrics, Activism, and Social Movements." *Liminalities: A Journal of Performance Studies* 4(3): 1–30.

Sherif, Ahmad (2008). Email interview with the author. April.

Shyles, Leonard (1984). "Defining 'Images' of Presidential Candidates from Televised Political Spot Advertisements." *Political Behavior* 6(2): 171–81.

Silverstone, Roger (1994). *Television and Everyday Life*. London: Routledge.

— (2005). "The Sociology of Mediation and Communication." In Craig J. Calhoun, Chris Rojek, and Bryan S. Turner (eds.), *The Handbook of Sociology*, pp. 188–207. London: Sage.

Solanas, Fernando and Octavio Getino (1970). "Towards a Third Cinema." *Cineaste* IV(3): 1–10.

Sontag, Susan (2003). *Regarding the Pain of Others*. New York: Picador.

Sörlin, Sverker (1999). "The Articulation of Territory: Landscape and the Constitution of Regional and National Identity." *Norwegian Journal of Geography* 53(2–3): 103–12.

Springborg, Robert (1989). *Mubarak's Egypt: Fragmentation of the Political Order*. Boulder, CO: Westview Press.

Sreberny, Annabelle and Gholam Khiabany (2010). *Blogistan: The Internet and Politics in Iran*. London: I.B. Tauris.

Stack, Megan (2005). *Lebanon Finally Facing Its War*. Los Angeles Times, 14 April.

Stanyer, James (2007). *Modern Political Communications: National Political Communication Systems in an Uncertain, Fragmented and Unequal Age*. Cambridge: Polity Press.

Staten, Cliff (2008). "From Terrorism to Legitimacy: Political Opportunity Structures and the Case of Hezbollah." *The Online Journal of Peace and Conflict Resolution* 8(1): 32–49.

Steavenson, Wendell (2011). "Roads to Freedom." *The New Yorker*, 29 August, pp. 26–32.

Street, John (1997). *Politics and Popular Culture*. Philadelphia: Temple University Press.

Strömbäck, Jesper (2008). "Four Phases of Mediatization: An Analysis of the Mediatization of Politics." *Press/Politics* 13(3): 228–46.

Suchman, Mark C. (1995). "Managing Legitimacy: Strategic and Institutional Approaches." *The Academy of Management Review* 20(3): 571–610.

Sussman, Gerald (2005). *Global Electioneering: Campaign Consulting, Communications, and Corporate Financing*. Oxford: Rowman and Littlefield.

Tarzi, Fadl (2011). "Arab Media Influence Report 2011 – Social Media and the Arab Spring." *News Group International*. Available: http://newsgroup.ae/amir2011/amir-march-29.pdf.

Tayyar.org (2007). "Hezbollah Launches Another Anti-Israel Computer Game." *Free Patriotic Movement* website, 15 August. Available: http://www.tayyar.org/tayyar/articles.php?type=news&article_id=32018.

Thompson, John B. (1995). *The Media and Modernity: A Social Theory of the Media*. Cambridge: Polity.

Time (2011). "Gaddafi Fashion: The Emperor Has Some Crazy Clothes." *Time Magazine* Photo Essay. Available: http://www.time.com/time/photogallery/0,29307,2055860,00.html.

Tuchman, Gaye (1978). *Making News: A Study in the Construction of Reality*. New York: The Free Press.

Van Bakel, Martin, Renée Hagesteijn and Pieter van de Velde (1986). "Introduction." In Van Bakel, Martin, Renée Hagesteijn and Pieter van de Velde (eds.), *Private Politics: A Multi-Disciplinary Approach to "Big Man" Systems*, pp. 1–10. Leiden: Brill.

van Dijk, Jan A.G.M. (2005). *The Deepening Divide: Inequality in the Information Society*. Thousand Oaks, CA: Sage.

van Ham, Peter (2001). "The Rise of the Brand State: The Postmodern Politics of Image and Reputation." *Foreign Affairs*, 10 October.

Voltmer, Katrin (2006a). "Conclusion: Political Communication between Democratization and the Trajectories of the Past." In Voltmer, Katrin (ed.), *Mass Media and Political Communication in New Democracies*, pp. 215–22. New York: Routledge.

— (2006b). "The Mass Media and the Dynamics of Political Communication in Processes of Democratization: An Introduction." In Voltmer, Katrin (ed.), *Mass Media and Political Communication in New Democracies*, pp. 1–20. New York: Routledge.

Weber, Max (1978). *Economy and Society*. Berkeley: University of California Press.

Wedeen, Lisa (1999). *Ambiguities of Domination: Politics, Rhetoric, and Symbols in Contemporary Syria*. Chicago: University of Chicago Press.

Weimann, Gabriel (2008a). "Hezbollah Dot Com: Hezbollah's Online Campaign." In Caspi, Dan and Tal Samuel-Azran (eds.), *New Media and Innovative Technologies*, pp. 17–38. Beer-Sheva, Israel: Ben-Gurion University Press.

— (2008b). "The Psychology of Mass Mediated Terrorism." *American Behavioral Scientist* 52(1): 69–86.

Welsh, Madeline B. (2011). "Oriental Hall, etc." *The Cairo Review of Global Affairs* 1: 9.

White, Hayden (1980). "The Value of Narrativity in the Representation of Reality." *Critical Inquiry* 7(1, Autumn): 5–27.

Younis, Nora (2008). Interview with the author. Cairo, March.

Zayani, Mohamed (2005). "Witnessing the Intifada: Al Jazeera's Coverage of the Palestinian-Israeli Conflict." In Zayani, Mohamed (ed.), *The Al Jazeera Phenomenon: Critical Perspectives on New Arab Media*, pp. 171–82. London: Pluto Press.

Zayani, Mohamed and Sofiane Zahraoui (2007). *The Culture of Al Jazeera: Inside an Arab Media Giant*. London: McFarland & Company.

Index